# Tim Burgess

# The Listening Party

ARTISTS, BANDS AND FANS REFLECT ON
100 FAVOURITE ALBUMS

**Project Editor** Pamela Afram
**Project Art Editor** Stefan Georgiou
**Picture Research** Sumedha Chopra, Martin Copeland, Vagisha Pushp
**Production Editor** Siu Yin Chan
**Senior Production Controller** Mary Slater
**Managing Editor** Sarah Harland
**Managing Art Editor** Victoria Short
**Publishing Director** Mark Searle

Packaged for DK by Emma Bastow and Eoghan O'Brien
**Editor** Emma Bastow
**Designer** Eoghan O' Brien
**Curated by** Paul Stokes
**Image research** Matt Turner

DK would like to thank Simon McEwen for proofreading and Helen Peters for indexing.

First American Edition, 2021
Published in the United States by DK Publishing
1450 Broadway, Suite 801, New York, NY 10018

A catalog record for this book is available from the Library of Congress.
ISBN 978-0-2415-1489-4

DK books are available at special discounts when purchased in bulk for sales promotions, premiums, fund-raising, or educational use. For details, contact: DK Publishing Special Markets, 1450 Broadway, Suite 801, New York, NY 10018
SpecialSales@dk.com

Fourth: Country Boy
Listening Party life hosted from rural Norfolk
Printed and bound in China

**For the curious**
**www.dk.com**

This book is dedicated to each and every artist and album that made the Listening Parties into what they have become—to all the people who joined in from around the world and to those amazing frontline workers who kept the world turning while we listened to records.

A huge thanks to Andrew Brindle, Mat Broughton, and Matt Sephton.

This book was made with Forest Stewardship Council ™ certified paper–one small step in DK's commitment to a sustainable future. For more information go to www.dk.com/our-green-pledge.

The publisher would like to thank the following for their kind permission to reproduce their photographs:

(Key: a-above; b-below/bottom; c-centre; f-far; l-left; r-right; t-top)

18 Getty Images: Hulton Archive / Martyn Goodacre (b). 20 Camera Press: Steve Double (tl). 21 Getty Images: Hulton Archive / Martyn Goodacre (cl, cr). 25 Getty Images: Redferns / Mick Hutson. 26 Getty Images: Hulton Archive / Martyn Goodacre (bl). 27 Getty Images: Kevin Cummins (cr); Hulton Archive / Koh Hasebe / Shinko Music (cl). 28 Getty Images: Redferns / Ian Dickson (b). 29 Camera Press: Ed Sirrs (t). 31 Avalon: Retna Pictures / A.Monfourny (bl). 37 Getty Images: Kevin Cummins (t). 38 Getty Images: Hulton Archive / Koh Hasebe / Shinko Music (bl). 40 Getty Images: Redferns / David Corio (b). 44 Camera Press: Steve Double (b). 47 Camera Press: Steve Double (b). 48 Getty Images: Hulton Archive / Gie Knaeps (bl). 49 Getty Images: Contour / David Goldman (t). 51 Avalon: Paul Slattery (t). 57 Avalon: Andrew Catlin (t). 58 Getty Images: Kevin Cummins (br). 59 Getty Images: Hulton Archive / Dave Tonge (bl). 61 Camera Press: Ed Sirrs. 62 Avalon: Roger Sargent (b). 63 Getty Images: Redferns / Patrick Ford (bl). 64 Avalon: Retna UK / © Patricia Brown (br). 65 Avalon: Retna UK / © Patricia Brown (b); © Nick Stevens (t). 66 Getty Images: Hulton Archive / Steve Rapport. 67 Getty Images: Redferns / Mike Prior. 68 Getty Images: Hulton Archive / Steve Rapport (tl); Redferns / Clare Muller (tr). 69 Getty Images: Hulton Archive / Steve Rapport. 76 Shutterstock.com: ITV (br). 77 Avalon: London Features (t). 78 Alamy Stock Photo: dpa picture alliance (t); Pictorial Press Ltd (bl). 80 Getty Images: Hulton Archive / Martyn Goodacre (br). 81 Getty Images:

Hulton Archive / Martyn Goodacre (bl). 83 Avalon: Ian Hooton (bl). 84 Getty Images: Redferns / Barney Britton (tl). 88 Getty Images: Redferns / Peter Pakvis (t). 90 Getty Images: Redferns / Mick Hutson (br). 91 Camera Press: Darren Filkins (bl). 92 Getty Images: Redferns / David Wolff - Patrick (b). 95 Getty Images: Hulton Archive / Martyn Goodacre (b). 100 Alamy Stock Photo: Andrew Hasson (br). 101 Alamy Stock Photo: Andrew Hasson (bl). 102 Getty Images: Scott Barbour. 104 Getty Images: FilmMagic, Inc / Jeff Kravitz (br). 107 Avalon: Tim Paton (b). 108 Getty Images: Hulton Archive / Photoshot / Nickie Divine (br). 111 Getty Images: Redferns / Ebet Roberts (t). 115 Getty Images: Debbie Hickey (tl). 116 Alamy Stock Photo: Graham Smillie (b). 117 Getty Images: Redferns / Rafael Macia (bl). 119 Alamy Stock Photo: Roger Garfield (b). 120 Alamy Stock Photo: dpa picture alliance (br). 123 Getty Images: Redferns / Lex van Rossen / MAI (t). 124 Getty Images: Redferns / Stuart Mostyn (tr). 125 Getty Images: Redferns / Hayley Madden. 126 Getty Images: Hulton Archive / Martyn Goodacre (b). 131 Getty Images: Redferns / Andy Willsher (tl). 133 Shutterstock.com: Sheila Rock (bl). 134 Shutterstock.com: Sheila Rock (bl). 135 Shutterstock.com: Sunshine International. 136 Getty Images: Hulton Archive / Brian Rasic (b). 141 Getty Images: Scott Dudelson (bl). 143 Getty Images: WireImage / Shirlaine Forrest (bl). 144 Alamy Stock Photo: Pictorial Press Ltd (br). 147 Alamy Stock Photo: AF archive (b). 149 Camera Press: Guy Bell (c). 150 Getty Images: Hulton Archive / Gie Knaeps (b). 151 Camera Press: Steve Double (bl). 152 Avalon: Svd / Scanpix / Retna Ltd. / © Stefan Bladh (br). 161 Alamy Stock Photo: TNT Magazine Pixate Ltd (t). 162 Getty Images: Redferns / David Corio (bl). 168 Getty Images: Redferns / Jana Legler (tl). 170 Alamy Stock Photo: Martyn Goddard (br). 171

Getty Images: Redferns / Virginia Turbett (bl). 172 Alamy Stock Photo: dpa picture alliance (b). 175 Getty Images: Archive Photos / Paul Natkin (tr); Mirrorpix / Alan Olley (tl). 175 Getty Images: Redferns / Wendy Redfern (t). 177 Avalon: Michael Malfer (bl). 181 Avalon: Marc Larkin. 189 Getty Images: Redferns / Nicky J. Sims (b). 192 Getty Images: WireImage / Kevin. Mazur (t). 193 Getty Images: Hulton Archive / Michael Putland (bl). 194 Getty Images: Michael Ochs Archives (bl, br). 195 Getty Images: Michael Ochs Archives (t). 197 Avalon: Retna / Justin Ng (bl). 198 Avalon: James Berry (b). 202 Getty Images: Redferns / Virginia Turbett (br). 205 Getty Images: WireImage / David Becker (t). 206 Getty Images: Redferns / Paul Bergen (br). 207 Bridgeman Images: Picture Alliance / © Fryderyk Gabowicz (bl). 210 Getty Images: Redferns / Lucy Johnston (br). 211 Getty Images: Claire R Greenway (bl). 213 Getty Images: Kevin Cummins (b). 214 Getty Images: Kevin Cummins. 217 Alamy Stock Photo: United Archives GmbH / kpa (cla). 221 Getty Images: Redferns / Wendy Redfern (b). 228 Getty Images: Hulton Archive / Bob Berg (b). 232 Getty Images: Mirrorpix (br). 237 Getty Images: Michael Hickey (bl). 238 Getty Images: WireImage / Paul Morigi (b). 240 Getty Images: Hulton Archive / Gie Knaeps (b).

243 Getty Images: Scott Legato (b). 244 Getty Images: Redferns / Anthony Pidgeon (bl). 245 Getty Images: Universal Images Group / PYMCA (bl). 247 Getty Images: Redferns / Lorne Thomson (b). 251 Getty Images: Corbis Entertainment / Sergione Infuso (b). 253 Alamy Stock Photo: WENN Rights Ltd (b). 254 Alamy Stock Photo: Pictorial Press Ltd (br). 255 Shutterstock.com: Andre Csillag (t). 256 Getty Images: Redferns / Pete Still (tl, tr, bl, br). 264 Getty Images: Redferns / Andy Willsher (bl). 269 Getty Images: Redferns / David Corio (bl). 269 eyevine: BIRRAUX / Dalle (b).

271 Getty Images: Future / Prog Magazine / Carsten Windhorst (b). 272 Getty Images: Future / Prog Magazine / Carsten Windhorst. 274 Getty Images: Redferns / Fin Costello (b). 277 Getty Images: Hulton Archive / Dave Tonge (tl). 280 Getty Images: Redferns / David Redfern. 287 Getty Images: Hulton Archive / Michael Putland (bl). 289 Getty Images: ullstein bild Premium / snapshot-photography / D.Vorndran (t). 299 Getty Images: Hulton Archive / Martyn Goodacre (bl). 300 Getty Images: Redferns / Mick Hutson

Tim Emoji: Pete Fowler. Back cover: Nik Void. 3 Rega (tl), Takekiyo (tr), Ben the Illustrator (c), Flare Audio (br), Takekiyo and Pete Fowler (bl). 7 Anthony Harrison. 15 Courtesy of Greene & Heaton Ltd. 70-73 Pictures by Dan Carey/Speedy Wunderland. 114 Bus pictures, courtesy of Christine Franz, thanks Claire Ormiston. Posed shot by Roger Sargent, courtesy of Rough Trade Records. Thanks Ben Ayres (b). 167 Anna Meredith, thanks to Rachel McWhinney. 183 Live photography Jake Green, courtesy of Warner Music. Thanks Jennifer Ivory and Andy Prevezer. 200-201 David Wrench, thanks to Charlotte Maher. 230 Enda Bowe, courtesy of Domino Recording Company. Thanks Colleen Maloney (b). 234 Tonje Thilesen, courtesy of Domino Recording Company. Thanks Colleen Maloney (c). 258 Picture courtesy of Ben Ayres (bl). 278-279 John Swannell. Courtesy of Rough Trade Records. Thanks Ben Ayres (b). 282-285 Main photo Simon Emmett for Kylie Minogue. Other images courtesy of BMG. Thanks to Anna Derbyshire. 290-291 Pictures courtesy of Tanita Tikaram, thanks to Sarah Pearson (b). 293 Emma Dudlyke, thanks to Sean Mayo at PIAS. 296 Mary McCartney/MPL Communications. Thanks to Stuart Bell.

19 Tim Burgess (l). 20 Tim Burgess (bl). 22 Bob Hardy (bl). 24 Bob Hardy (b). 32 Brian Cannon. 33-37 Bonehead. 36 Brian Cannon. 41 Tim Burgess. 42 Brix Smith. 52 Steve Mason (l). 52 John Maclean (c & r). 54 Nick Banks. 55 Nick Banks (l). 74 Mark Ronson. 76 Lloyd Cole (l). 78 Lloyd Cole (br). 79 Lloyd Cole (br). 88 Billy Bragg (b). 89 Billy Bragg. 94 Tom Rowland. 96 Tom Rowland. 97 Errol K. 97 Tom Rowland (bl). 98 Neil Barnes. 103 The Avalanches. 108 The Breeders. 109 Tim Smith. 110 Sarah Martin (bl). 112 Stuart Murdoch (b). 113 Sarah Martin (l). 113 Shared by @adrianday. 127 Miki Berenyi. 129-130 Martin Rossiter. 131 Martin Rossiter (bl). 138-139 Faris Badwan. 145 Steve Levine. 154 Cameron Murray. 155 Shared by @WeirdoMusic4evr. 156-158 Tim Burgess. 163 Dave Haslam (b). 173 Gary Kemp. 178 Damon Gough (l), (r). 178 Andy Votel (c). 180 Damon Gough (tr). 180 Andy Votel (b), (bl). 182 Bonehead. 184 Tim Burgess. 186 Cameron Murray. 190 Kate Nash (l). 190 Shared by @TheMassiveHeid (l). 196 Nadine Shah. 200 Marika Hackman (tl). 208 Shabazz Palaces. 212 Peter Hook (bl). 212 Reynard Toombs (b). 212 Andy Chislehurst (Birmingham_81). 218-219 Matt Johnson. 222-225 Al Doyle. 227 Gillian Gilbert. 229 Stephen Morris (l). 237 Cate Le Bon (b). 249 Andy Chislehurst (Birmingham_81). 260-261 Roisin Murphy (r). 262 Bráulio Amado (t,l). 262 Roisin Murphy (r). 267 Lol Tolhurst. 268 Lol Tolhurst (t,l). 269 Lol Tolhurst (t). 294 Paul McCartney. 296 Paul McCartney. 298 Tim Burgess.

All other images © Dorling Kindersley, unless stated otherwise on the page featured.

For further information see: www.dkimages.com

@Tim_Burgess

So here it is! The @RegaResearch #TimsTwitterListeningParty 🎧 turntable with plinth artwork by @BenIllustrator

@Tim_Burgess

This has just made my week/year! A brilliant @LISTENING_PARTY retro arcade game demo. Massive thanks to @takekiyo666

@Tim_Burgess

Imagine* if @Twitter got in touch and said they loved the listening parties and could they make us an emoji that appeared when anyone used #TimsTwitterListeningParty 🎧
*Reader, no need to imagine. That happened today.

@Tim_Burgess

First up is a collab with @flareaudio – these ace @LISTENING_PARTY earphones will be available to pre-order on Friday March 26th. Raising funds for the @musicvenuetrust

# Contents

# Strange Days

*Well, the music is your special friend,*
*Dance on fire as it intends,*
*Music is your only friend,*
*Until the end.*

Jim Morrison sang these words on a song called "When the Music's Over" on the album *Strange Days* in 1967. Fast forward 53 years and I'm sat in my studio in the middle of a global pandemic. Strange days, but the music's not over.

In February 2020 I had just finished a European tour with Liam Gallagher, playing to thousands of people each night in arenas from Scandinavia right down to Italy and back up again, ending in Paris at the end of the month. COVID-19 was following behind us throughout Europe, I think it really hit Italy just after we left and the country went into a full lockdown, and by the time we landed in the UK cases were on the rise here too. Then we went into lockdown in mid-March, which saw shops close, venues close, workplaces close, and schools close.

Around the 20th of March, Tim Burgess texted me to say that he was doing some listening parties on Twitter. I'd seen he'd done a few Charlatans ones a couple of years earlier, I'd listened in at the time, pressed play and followed the tweets as we listened back in real time. Now we were in the middle of a full UK lockdown and he asked would I do a listening party for Definitely Maybe, he'd already done one with Franz Ferdinand and I think the next one was with Dave Rowntree for Blur.

We set a date for the *Definitely Maybe* listening party sometime towards the end of March, and I had no idea how it would go. Thousands of people joined in on the night, and it was the first time I had listened to the album in full from start to finish since probably 1995. The reaction was mind blowing. I was listening back to the album with thousands of fans in real time, memories of recording the album came back, which I tweeted, people replied, people cried, people danced, people laughed.

Tim texted me next day and we were talking about the reaction to the night before, he was asking who else might be up for doing one. I suggested Ian Broudie from The Lightning Seeds; I texted Ian and he was up for it. I'm not sure if Tim expected the listening parties to last more than a couple of weeks, but over a year later they are still going strong and the list of bands and artists is unbelievable. Sir Paul McCartney, David Bowie, New Order, Love, The Communards, Sleaford Mods, Liam Gallagher, The Charlatans, Adam and the Ants, Tears for Fears, the list goes on and on and on.

I did listening parties for *Morning Glory*, *Be Here Now* and *The Masterplan*. I found 20 rolls of film I'd taken on tour somewhere in America in the mid '90s and shared some of those unseen pictures as we listened along. I think Liam was going to join in for *Be Here Now*, he texted me the day after and asked "what time is the listening party starting tonight?".

Too late Liam, you missed it.

At the back end of 2019 I joined Liam on stage in Hull for an MTV Unplugged concert at the City Hall, which was then released as a full album. We decided to do a listening party for the album release on the 12 June – loads of panicked phone calls half an hour before the start. Thousands joined in again, I think I was up until 3am still replying to people on Twitter. That's the power of music. I know from replies on the night of the parties, tweets from strangers, people on their own, telling us how much this had helped them through.

Music can do this: it can make you laugh, it can make you cry, it can make you dance, it can make you drive your car too fast. It brings people together. The listening parties made me laugh and cry, and I would never have thought 23 years ago that *Magic Pie* would have been trending at number one in the UK food and drink charts in 2020 – that made me laugh out loud. I've joined in with parties for other artists too, pressed play and rediscovered albums from bands I used to love, as well as new music from bands I'd never have listened to otherwise.

Live music was pulled from under all our feet in March 2020 – fans, artists and crew alike – but these parties have helped us all. One day soon we'll be back up on stage and you'll be out front, dancing, laughing, singing, partying together. Here's to Tim and all the bands involved and all the fans who have joined in every night. *Dance on fire as it intends, Music is your only friend. Until the end.*

*Bonehead*

Paul "Bonehead" Arthurs

# Introduction

As overnight sensations go, Tim's Twitter Listening Party was a slow and steady nine years, followed by a week where everything changed and it became "an internet phenomenon" according to the TV shows, radio stations and magazines that featured stories about the parties and sent things into an even crazier trajectory.

It all started when I was watching TV at The Charlatans' recording studio, not far from Northwich in Cheshire. I was occasionally glancing at Twitter on my phone – this was 2011, and it was quite a different world back then. Twitter was a new platform for me and I loved it's brevity and simplicity, but its potential had yet to be revealed to me. But it was just about to be...

I settled down to watch a film I'd seen many times before. It was late and I wanted to watch something that was familiar and that I knew I would enjoy. It was a world before Netflix and so I headed to Film4. It was a simpler time back then, we only had 462 channels – it wasn't like it is now. At 10pm on 4 September 2011 *Four Lions* started and two screens, the television and my phone, were jostling for attention. And in a moment the two worlds collided.

A few months previously I'd seen Riz Ahmed in his guise as a brilliant MC/rapper and so I'd followed him on Twitter, then here he was starring in the film. As the film started, Riz started tweeting, like a director's commentary on a DVD but without encroaching on the actual film at all. It was a sideline event but one that made watching the film more enjoyable, especially as I had seen it a couple of times before.

It hit me like a bolt of lightning – Channel 4 was doing all the heavy lifting involved in showing the film, while Riz only needed to tweet to add a 3D element for anyone watching. Imagine doing it with an album, where there was nothing to watch anyway. It seemed to be the perfect use of this platform that I'd not really figured out yet.

So within five days our first Listening Party was planned and a small audience was gathered. It worked as well as we had hoped and everyone seemed to enjoy it, plus there was no tidying up to do afterwards. And so that was that for nine years. In that time I released four solo albums, The Charlatans released two studio albums and, like the passing of the seasons, once a year we would all get together and listen to them again and share our memories and stories.

Then we got to the 25th anniversary of *Some Friendly* on 8 October 2015. We thought we'd do something special, but we didn't know what. We found us an interactive map online and asked everyone listening to the album to mark themselves on there, wherever they were in the world. For closer to home, we found a bar with decent Wi-Fi and invited people to come along and take part. It was mostly everybody staring at their screens, but with snacks and drinks provided. It was a bit like a premonition of going out in 2020.

The markers on our map came in thick and fast in the first couple of hours; 100 in the UK, followed by 78 in the US, 14 in Germany, 9 in France, 11 in Australia. After a day or two we had a couple of thousand RSVPs, and we noticed something – human beings on six of the world's seven continents were going to be listening to the exact same album at the exact same time, but nobody in Antarctica was bothering? We got that it was cold, but it just seemed like they needed a nudge. I tweeted that Antarcticans were needed to complete our map. We were guessing that it would be the first time that a record would be playing at the same time on every continent.

For a week or two, nobody was forthcoming. Then, like a person emerging from a blizzard, Dan got in touch. Known on Twitter as @dantarctic, he was part of the team working at The British Antarctic Survey – a brilliant project with teams working on ecological and scientific studies. And they had Wi-Fi sent directly to the base via a satellite. And what's more, Dan was a Charlatans fan. When we announced this, newspapers and radio stations around the world picked up the story and the Listening Parties became a little more well known.

Fast forward to March 2020. Lockdown loomed and, as with everyone around the world, plans were cancelled. I thought it was maybe the right time to do a run of The Charlatans' Listening Parties, so we announced the first. Right back to the start, nearing its 30th anniversary this time, *Some Friendly* was the chosen album for 23 March. With fewer options open to people, we had a bigger audience than before. Nobody was sure what to do – bands couldn't be in the same room as each other, people just had to stay home. So, putting an album on and listening to it all the way through seemed as good an option as any. It was looking like a long stretch ahead of us, so my thoughts were that we could do one album a week and that would be enough

We started the *Some Friendly* Listening Party and a tweet appeared from Alex Kapranos (lead singer from Franz Ferdinand). He'd got the album for his 17th birthday and it had left quite an impression on him. After the Listening Party I ended up in a conversation with Alex and as there was little or no light at the end of the lockdown tunnel, I asked if he would like to host one. He said yes, and that was maybe the big bang moment for the Listening Party universe that we know and love today.

I dashed for my little black book of numbers and started asking friends if they were up for the idea. I'd realised that the real hook wasn't that the artists could talk about their songs – as enjoyable as that is. It was the fact that time would be set aside and the album would be listened to, in full, all the tracks, no skipping, no shuffle. All attention, for better or for worse, was focused on the featured long player.

Alex revealed that he had not listened to Franz Ferdinand's eponymous debut since it was mastered. Which meant, incredibly, that up until 24 March 2020, if you had listened to that record in full, then you had heard it more recently than the singer had. Bonehead was the next person I messaged, a founding member of Oasis whose voice is often drowned out by the sideshow elements to the band. He was up for the idea and said he had some unseen pictures and stories to share. What had we started? Dave Rowntree from Blur was next. He had quite a collection of *Parklife* goodies that nobody had ever seen. Stephen Street, the album's producer, joined in and Graham Coxon added some info too. And everyone around the world watched, with the songs playing in, I'm guessing, six of the seven continents.

Whenever we announced a new Listening Party, the Twitter world flipped its lid a little more. And with no sport and no events at all, each night the bands' name and our hashtag would trend. So much so that within a few days Twitter themselves got in touch – they had seen the tremors that we'd caused and so many of their staff had taken part in the listening parties. They told us about emojis that they could make appear when people used certain hashtags, and so our Timoji was born from an original design that Pete Fowler had done for Tim Peaks. You know about Tim Peaks, right? If not, that's for another day!

The Charlatans had done a couple of legendary shows with Ride back in 1992, known as the Daytripper gigs. They had just got back together after a lengthy break, so I gave them a shout. They were up for it, too. We asked Wendy Smith from Prefab Sprout if she'd like to do a Listening Party for *Steve McQueen*, one of my favourite albums ever. Martin McAloon, their bass player and Neil Conti, the band's drummer joined in. Paddy McAloon himself sent a message to say hello and that he loved that everyone was playing the record.

We were enjoying some classic albums that people had developed a connection with over anything from 10 to 30 years, and it felt rewarding being the person who was bringing it all together. But we didn't want to just spend time looking backwards. We were living through a time when the world was on pause for so many people and it was a chance to introduce our ever-growing Twitter listening party people to bands and artists they might not have come across and records that were only just released. Pom Poko were a new band to many people and they ended their Listening Party with hundreds more fans, so now there were no limits to who we could invite.

The Chemical Brothers became masters of the art with many of their guest vocalists joining – they could hardly not ask me, now, could they? The Flaming Lips, Orange Juice, Cocteau Twins, Leftfield, Roisin Murphy, The Orielles, The Libertines and The Lovely Eggs. Our list just got longer and longer. A message from Liam Gallagher asking about doing his forthcoming live album? Sure, we got organised.

I put together a step-by-step guide for potential hosts and two Twitter followers, Matt and Mat, who didn't know each other, suggested that they could sort out a scheduling document, which was a lifesaver. Then that turned into a website. Jools Holland's show *Later* got in touch and ran a feature. Granada Reports and Channel 4 News were next. The *NME*, *Q* and *Rolling Stone* all published stories and Radios 4, 5 and 6 invited me on to talk through what was now routinely termed our "internet phenomenon". And still more artists confirmed. We were doing three parties a night and up to six on a weekend day.

British Sea Power, The Specials, Belle & Sebastian, Joan As Policewoman, MGMT, Sleeper, ABC, Anna Meredith, Super Furry Animals, Julia Holter – some of my favourite artists and albums of all time, and more and more people around the world joined in. The BPI (British Phonographic Institute) mentioned us in a report that saw vinyl sales surge to over 5 million in 2020.

Then I got a message on Twitter from @andrewb1970 who had casually spent a few weeks writing the software that meant anyone could replay the listening parties and see the tweets in real time as the album played. More countries were checked off on our map, until we reached 190 – there aren't many places across the globe left where at sometime, someone wasn't joining us for the shared experience of listening to a record. I cheekily tweeted that we'd find a spot for Paul McCartney if he fancied doing McCartney III, and a few weeks later a thumbs up emoji from the man himself sealed the deal.

And that pretty much brings us up to date, I didn't mention the message from DK Books saying they'd love to publish a title in glorious hardback, documenting our adventures, and that's exactly what you are reading right now.

# The Listening Party Fanzine

*To Tim,*

*This is for you. It's a combined effort to show our love and appreciation of your continued efforts to host the now-renowned Listening Parties on Twitter.*

Listening Party fans,
December 2020

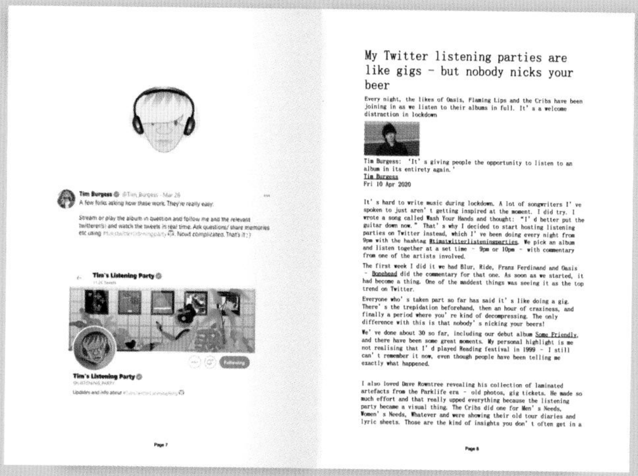

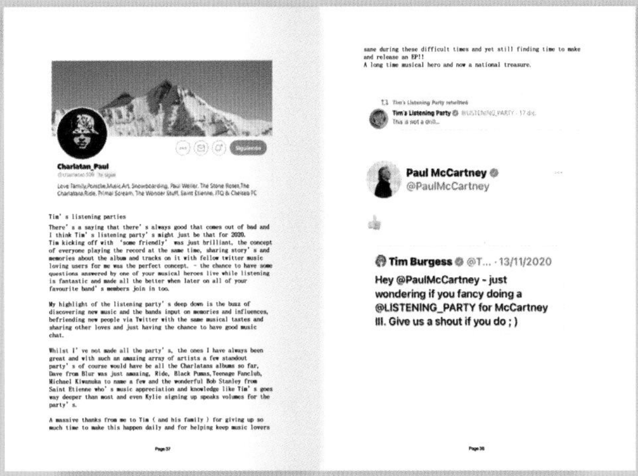

---

## My Twitter listening parties are like gigs – but nobody nicks your beer

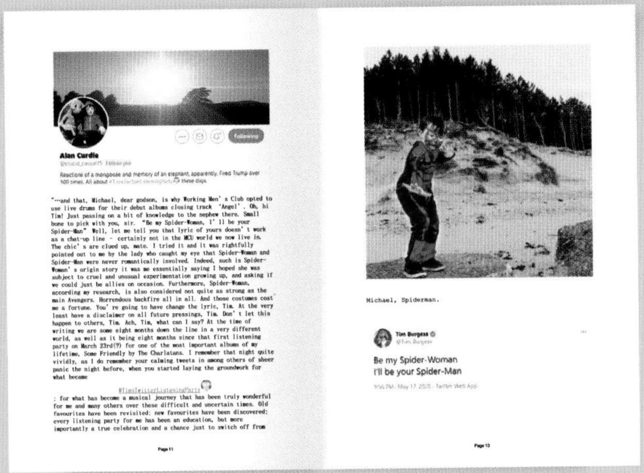

Every night, the likes of Oasis, Flaming Lips and the Cribs have been joining in as we listen to their albums in full. It's a welcome distraction in lockdown

Tim Burgess: 'It's giving people the opportunity to listen to an album in its entirety again.'
Tim Burgess
Fri 10 Apr 2020

It's hard to write music during lockdown. A lot of songwriters I've spoken to just aren't getting inspired at the moment. I did try. I wrote a song called Hush Your Heads and thought: "I'd better put the guitar down now." That's why I decided to start hosting listening parties on Twitter instead, which I've been doing every night from 9pm with the hashtag #timstwitterlisteningparties. We pick an album and listen together at a set time – 9pm or 10pm – with commentary from one of the artists involved.

The first week I did it we had Blur, Ride, Franz Ferdinand and Oasis. Doorhead did the commentary for that one. As soon as we started, it had become a thing. One of the maddest things was seeing it as the top trend on Twitter.

Everyone who's taken part so far has said it's like doing a gig. There's the trepidation beforehand, then an hour of craziness, and finally a period where you're kind of decompressing. The only difference with this is that nobody's nicking your beers!

We've done about 30 so far, including our debut album Some Friendly, and there have been some great moments. My personal highlight is me not realising that I'd played Reading festival in 1999 – I still can't remember it now, even though people have been telling me exactly what happened.

I also loved Dave Rowntree revealing his collection of laminated artefacts from the Parklife era – old photos, gig tickets. He made so much effort and that really upped everything because the listening party became a visual thing. The Cribs did one for Men's Needs, Women's Needs, Whatever and were showing their old tour diaries and lyric sheets. Those are the kind of insights you don't often get in a

---

**Alan Curdie**
@CrazyCurdie01 · Follows you

Reactions of a mongoose and memory of an elephant, apparently. Feed Trump over 140 times. All about #TimsTwitterListeningParty & these days

Michael, Spiderman.

**Tim Burgess** 
@Tim_Burgess

Be my Spider-Woman
I'll be your Spider-Man

"—and that, Michael, dear godson, is why Working Men's Club opted to use live drums for their debut album closing track 'Angel'. Oh, hi Tim! Just passing on a bit of knowledge to the nephew there. Small home to pick with you, tho. "Be my Spider-Woman, I'll be your Spider-Man". Well, let me tell you that lyric of yours doesn't work as a chat-up line – certainly not in the MCU world we now live in. The chic's are clued up, mate. I tried it and it was rightfully pointed out to me by the lady who caught my eye that Spider-Woman and Spider-Man were never romantically involved. Indeed, such is Spider-Woman's origin story it was an essentially saying I hoped she was subject to cruel and unusual experimentation growing up, and asking if we could just be allies on occasion. Furthermore, Spider-Woman, according my research, is also considered not quite as strong as the main Avengers. Horrendous backfire all in all. And these costumes cost me a fortune. You're going to have change the lyric, Tim. At the very least have a disclaimer on all future pressings, Tim. Don't let this happen to others, Tim. Ach, Tim, what can I say? At the time of writing we are some eight months down the line in a very different world, as well as it being eight months since that first listening party on March 23rd(?) for one of the most important albums of my lifetime, Some Friendly by The Charlatans. I remember that night quite vividly, as I do remember your calming tweets in among others of sheer panic the night before, when you started laying the groundwork for what became

#TimsTwitterListeningParties

; for what has become a musical journey that has been truly wonderful for me and many others over these difficult and uncertain times. Old favourites have been revisited, new favourites have been discovered; every listening party for me has been an education, but more importantly a true celebration and a chance just to switch off from

---

same during these difficult times and yet still finding time to make and release an EP!!
A long time musical hero and now a national treasure.

Tim's Listening Party retweeted
**Tim's Listening Party** @LISTENING_PARTY · 17.46
This is not a drill...

**Paul McCartney** 
@PaulMcCartney

**Tim Burgess** @T... · 13/11/2020
Hey @PaulMcCartney - just wondering if you fancy doing a @LISTENING_PARTY for McCartney III. Give us a shout if you do ; )

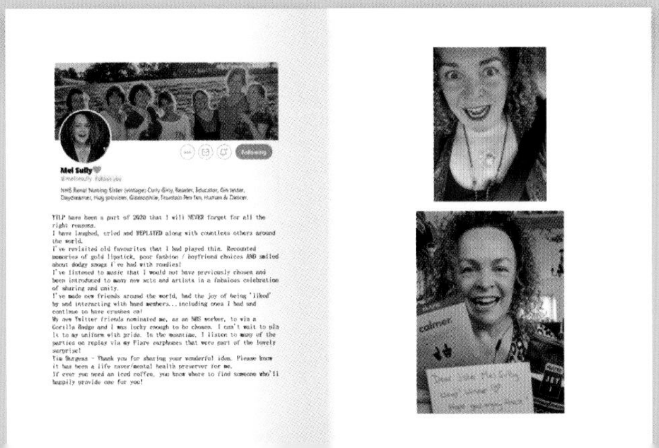

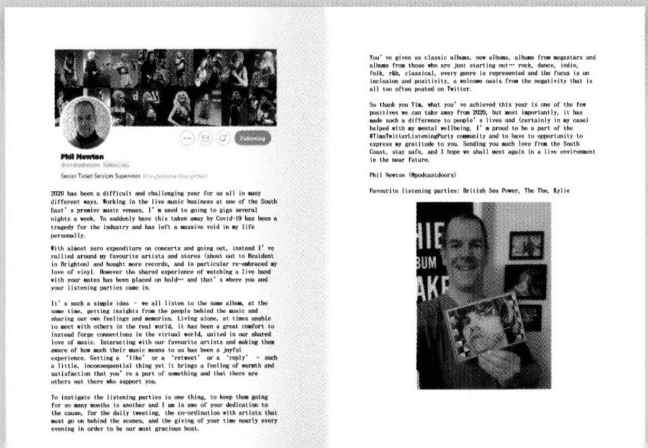

**Charlatan_Paul**
@charlatan339 · Follows you

Love family,Porsche,Music,Art,Snowboarding,Paul Weller,The Stone Roses,The Charlatans,Ride, Primal Scream, Saint Etienne, FIG & Chelsea FC

## Tim's listening parties

There's a saying that there's always good that comes out of bad and I think Tim's listening party's might just be that for 2020. Tim kicking off with 'some friendly' was just brilliant, the concept of everyone playing the record at the same time, sharing story's and memories about the album and tracks in it with fellow twitter music loving users for me was the perfect concept. – the chance to have some questions answered by one of your musical heroes live while listening in fantastic and made all the better when later on all of your favourite band's members join in too.

My highlight of the listening party's deep down is the buzz of discovering new music and the bands input on memories and influences, befriending new people via Twitter with the same musical tastes and sharing other loves and just having the chance to have good music chat.

Whilst I've not made all the party's, the ones I have always been great and with such an amazing array of artists a few standout party's of course would have be all the Charlatans albums so far, Dave from Blur was just amazing, Ride, Black Pumas, Teenage Fanclub, Michael Kiwanuka to name a few and the wonderful Bob Stanley from Saint Etienne who's music appreciation and knowledge like Tim's goes way deeper than most and even Kylie signing up speaks volumes for the party's.

A massive thanks from me to Tim ( and his family ) for giving up so much time to make this happen daily and for helping keep music lovers

---

**Mel Duffy**
@meltiessity · Follows you

NHS Renal Nursing Sister (vintage) Curly Girly, Reader, Educator, Gin lover, Daydreamer, Hug provider, Gloucestrian, Tountain Pen fan, Human & Dancer

TIM? have been a part of 2020 that I will NEVER forget for all the right reasons.
I have laughed, cried and REPLAYED along with countless others around the world.
I've revisited old favourites that I had played thin. Recounted memories of gold lipstick, pour fanbase / boyfriend choices AND smiled about dodgy songs I've had with roadies!
I've listened to music that I would not have previously chosen and been introduced to many new acts and artists in a fabulous celebration of sharing and unity.
I've made new friends around the world, had the joy of being 'liked' by and interacting with band members... including ones I had and continue to have crushes on!
My own Twitter friends nominated me, as an NHS worker, to win a Gorilla Badge and I was lucky enough to be chosen. I can't wait to win it to go outline with pride. In the meantime, I listen to many of the parties on replay via my Flare earphones that were part of the lonely surprise!
Tim Burgess - Thank you for sharing your wonderful idea. Please know it has been a life saver/mental health preserver for me.
If ever you need an iced coffee, you know where to find someone who'll happily provide one for you!

---

You've given us classic albums, new albums, albums from megastars and albums from those who are just starting out— rock, dance, indie, folk, r&b, classical, every genre is represented and the focus is on inclusion and positivity, a welcome oasis from the negativity that is all too often posted on Twitter.

So thank you Tim, what you've achieved this year is one of the few positives we can take away from 2020, but most importantly, it has made such a difference to people's lives and (certainly in my case) helped with my mental wellbeing. I'm proud to be a part of the #TimsTwitterListeningParty community and to have to opportunity to express my gratitude to you. Sending you much love from the South Coast, stay safe, and I hope we shall meet again in a live environment in the near future.

Phil Newton (@podcastdoors)

Favourite listening parties: British Sea Power, The The, Kylie

**Phil Newton**
@podcastdoors · Follows you

Senior Ticket Services Supervisor #burgessknow #burgettown

2020 has been a difficult and challenging year for us all in many different ways. Working in the live music business at one of the South East's premier music venues, I'm used to being busy several nights a week. To suddenly have this taken away by Covid-19 has been a tragedy for the industry and has left a massive void in my life personally.

With almost zero expenditure on concerts and going out, instead I've rallied around my favourite artists and stores (shout out to Resident in Brighton) and bought more records, and in particular re-embraced my love of vinyl. However the shared experience of watching a live band with your mates has been placed on hold— and that's where you and your listening parties come in.

It's such a simple idea – we all listen to the same album, at the same time, posting insights from the people behind the music and sharing our own feelings and memories. Living alone, at times unable to meet with others in the real world, it has been a great comfort to instead forge connections in the virtual world, united in our shared love of music. Interacting with our favourite artists and making them aware of how much their music means to us has been a joyful experience. Getting a 'like' or a 'retweet' or a 'reply' – such a little, inconsequential thing yet it brings a feeling of warmth and satisfaction that you're part of something, and that there are others out there who support you.

To instigate the listening parties is one thing, to keep them going for so many months is another and I am in awe of your dedication to the cause, for the daily tweeting, the co-ordination with artists that must go on behind the scenes, and the giving of your time nearly every evening in order to be our most gracious host.

# A Note From Pete Paphides

"OK. Drop the needle on the record/press play/start streaming. We're going in…"
Tim Burgess's opening tweet, *Some Friendly* Listening Party, 10pm, 23 March 2020

It was pretty clear from the outset that this was going to fly. It was a
fan's dream scenario. To have a favourite musician take you by the
hand and walk you through every single song on one of their classic
albums – as if that album were a series of rooms – and point to all the
pictures on the walls, the ephemera gathered on tables, the records,
books or films that ended up shaping what you're hearing. Here they
are telling you how all this stuff was alchemised into the songs you're
hearing. Songs that might have landed in your life at the precise point
you really needed them. Songs that might have even saved your life.

Taking us through *Some Friendly*, the debut album by his group The Charlatans,
Tim Burgess remembered how Opportunity emerged from his head just as effortlessly
as he emerged from the escalator at Warren Street on the day of the poll tax riots – the
song a reflexive manifestation of the crackling energy around him. Showing us a copy
of the letter he sent to Robert De Niro in order to secure his hero's blessing for the
Angel Heart sample in 109 Pt.2: "De Niro doing that made me vow to help bands
whenever I could. He really didn't have to help us."

   And on it went. One album into the next. One party into another. Blur's Dave
Rowntree shared a torn-out ad in a 1993 newspaper for a housing development which
boasted the headline "Parklife". For a generation of pop fans, that was like seeing the
*Daily Mail* story that prompted John Lennon to sing about four thousand holes in
Blackburn, Lancashire. Tweeting about New Order's 1983 masterpiece *Power
Corruption & Lies* Stephen Morris revealed that the drums from Age Of Consent
were lifted wholesale from a (never released) version of Joy Division's Love Will Tear
Us Apart! Minds blown!

For those of us who never found a gang that might, over time, become a band, that – with the right combination of chemistry, timing, skill, graft and luck – actually finds an audience and gets to make records, the Listening Parties were a peek into a process we never got to experience at first hand. We're often told about the importance of preserving mystique; that by learning too much about how great art is created, we run the risk of killing the magic. But the Listening Parties frequently proved that magic eludes even the most detailed reveals. Magic is made of much stronger stuff.

Let's look at it another way. When I was in my teens, studying for a philosophy A-level, we were taught about epiphenomenalism: the idea that the soul is an epiphenomenon – a metaphysical byproduct – of the human body. No amount of knowledge of the workings of the human body can get you any closer to understanding the nature of the soul. And even though the soul can't exist without the body, no corporeal investigation, no matter how thorough, can demystify it. And that's how it is with our favourite records. That's how it was during the Listening Party hosted by Paul McCartney on 21 December 2020 for the newly-released *McCartney III*. Talking about (what for me is) the album's stand-out track Slidin', McCartney talked about working up the song from a series of soundchecks and getting inspiration for the title by watching the Winter Olympics – but none of these explanations could account for the demonic energy of a song which evinces all the depth, darkness and sweetness of a vat of molasses.

The more prosaic the explanation of a song's creation was, the more it somehow seemed to illuminate that intangible extra stuff – the epiphenomenal magic – that turns it into art. That happened time and time again at the Listening Parties. Sometimes, that disjuncture was more obvious than with others. How to square Scritti Politti frontman Green's description of their song Small Talk ("a foundationless structure of exquisitely assembled discrete events circling unsupported in time... It's like prestidigitation – or, if you prefer, legerdemain") to the mercury surge of well-being that rises up inside you as those loved-up synth stabs dance around Green's yearning vocal? If even Green's vocabulary couldn't quite do justice to what was happening, what hope was there for the rest of us?!

Throughout 2020 and into 2021, these get-togethers began to feel like an important part of our pop-cultural life. With no gigs to attend; no pubs in which to gather; schedules obliterated, the Listening Parties extended an invitation to anyone with an internet connection. Artists need to commune with their audiences as much as their audiences need to check in with them. One unexpected delight was getting to see, in real time, artists who hadn't heard their records for several years, finally hear them as they sounded to their fans. Even Action Man's eyes would have struggled to stay dry during the Listening Party for Dexys Midnight Runners' *Searching For The Young Soul Rebels*, as Kevin Rowland expressed his joy at the sound of longtime fan fave Tell Me When My Light Turns Green: "I'm hearing this one in a different light," he boggled, between loving tweets from colleagues with whom, in some cases, he hadn't spoken for years.

Some parties you'd make a beeline for because you knew the records; but then there were others that afforded you the chance to discover something that had hitherto eluded you. It didn't matter if the artist had enjoyed globe-straddling success or was still finding their audience – one thing common to almost all artists hosting their first listening parties was the intensity of the experience. One musician friend who hosted a listening party texted me at 2am – fours hours after his event ended – with the words, "I'm wired as though I've just done a gig. Is this normal?". Having hosted one myself – a playlist based on my book *Broken Greek* – I was able to confirm to him that yes, this is exactly how it feels to host a Listening Party. It's like commentating on a televised football match whilst also playing in it.

Not all brilliant bands get to be Coldplay-huge or Iron Maiden-mega. And, for me, some of the best Listening Parties were the ones in which less well-known musicians got to witness the immediate response that their music elicited in the Listening Party hardcore who would just as regularly show up for the stuff they didn't know. With a suitably attentive guide, certain records were effectively portals into worlds that couldn't have been more of a contrast to the groundhog days of our locked-down lives. Sarathy Korwar's *More Arriving* – a kaleidoscopic, synaesthetic cavalcade of rhyme and rhythm – was a dramatic case in point: songs both birthed and inspired by the nascent rap scenes of Mumbai and New Delhi, then dramatically animated by Sarathy's electrifying drumming and his shifting coterie of collaborators. And here was Sarathy, pointing at details of particular interest, propelling you to the very moments that spawned entire songs: "Jallaad means executioner, but in this context… of someone killing the tune! This was a recording I found on my handheld microphone from 2016. Sitting with a bunch of young rappers and b-boys, smoking a bong, on a balcony in Dharavi (India's largest slum). We were listening to Sex Machine and this 13 yr-old dude called James Brown a jallaad!"

Oh to have been on a balcony in Dharavi! Oh, to have been anywhere! But for a moment, we kind of were. This, as much as anything, explains why, in this most peculiar of years, the Listening Parties felt like a musical equivalent of Enid Blyton's *Faraway Tree*. Remove the album from its sleeve. Flick the switch. As the turntable rotates, so do your surroundings. From the Scottish new town romance of Aztec Camera's *High Land Hard Rain* to the magisterial future disco of Hercules & The Love Affair's self-titled 2008 opus; from Art Brut's guilelessly life-affirming debut *Bang Bang Rock & Roll* to the imperious soul power of *We Are King* by Los Angeles R&B vocal trio King.

The bottom line? There's just something about roughly a dozen songs, lovingly sequenced by their creator, all further unified by a title and artwork, that just works. It worked 50 years ago when the prohibitive cost of albums would lead people to gather in the bedrooms of friends who happened to own one. And it still worked when vinyl – the software for which the album was invented – looked like it was about to become obsolete. It worked so well that, in the end, we didn't allow it to become obsolete. In the age of streaming, there's nothing to stop an album being five hours long. But, like I said, there's just something about a dozen or so songs. An album that you can listen to alone. Or together with kindred souls. Or, in the case of Tim's Twitter Listening Parties, both at the same time. It works, and it'll keep on working in another 50 years. So drop the needle on the record. Press play. Start streaming. We're going in.

Pete Paphides

# Some Friendly
## The Charlatans
Beggars Banquet, 1990

PHOTOGRAPHY:
Derek Philip

⚑ We all have to start somewhere, and The Charlatans' debut album is a first big step forward for a lot of reasons. Released at the beginning of the '90s, *Some Friendly* was not only the band's opening statement, an introduction to what the Northwich group were all about, but it also represented an opening of the road for British music. Influenced by The Stone Roses and Happy Mondays, The Charlatans had a big foot in the Madchester scene of the late '80s, but with their West Midlands roots, Jon Baker (guitars), Rob Collins (keys), Martin Blunt (bass) Jon Brookes (drums) and a chap called Tim Burgess (vocals, hi! – **@Tim_Burgess**) extended the burgeoning guitar-driven renaissance to acts without M1 postcodes. It is why The Charlatans have been called peers of the Roses and the Mondays and Britpop "stalwarts", yet remain one of the most forward-thinking rock bands around today.

With its deep organ grooves, meditative vocals and shuffling beats, *Some Friendly* gave The Charlatans the foundations "to be themselves", a lesson not lost on many who followed their lead.

Also, in terms of starts, *Some Friendly* was also the very first ever Listening Party.

The Party was the first to take place just after lockdown restrictions were imposed in the spring of 2020, but back in 2011, when the idea of everyone listening to a record at the same time and sharing that experience on Twitter was first tried, *Some Friendly* was the record on the turntable.

So this really is an album of firsts, both in terms of its music and influence. *Some Friendly* has repeatedly brought people together and created some very special things.

The very first issue of The Charlatans' official fanzine published in February 1990. Publishers, the Transworld Consortium, took their name from a codename in Ian Fleming's James Bond novel, while the title comes from the band's song Polar Bear. **@Tim_Burgess**: "Life's a bag of revels, I am looking for the orange one was something me and my mate Cheddar came up with on a walk around Northwich." (Shared during the Listening Party by **@Nick_Gtx**.)

Tim Burgess back in the "Early days indeed" (shared during the Listening Party by **@marcusbella**).

## 1. YOU'RE NOT VERY WELL

**@Tim_Burgess**

About leaving home. I moved away from Northwich to the Isle Of Dogs – this song is about the fear and wonder of the big city. London was like a real life Monopoly board. Taking me back already. We couldn't believe it when we got the chance to go in and record the songs we'd written. We didn't really demo YNVW it was a late one to arrive we just recorded it after practicing and playing it live.

## 2. WHITE SHIRT

**@Tim_Burgess**

I was listening to Velocity Girl by Primal Scream – I wanted a song with that kind of feel to it. In the town where I lived, there was a dress code if you wanted to get in to any pubs/clubs. A white shirt and shoes were compulsory. It's about doing what you can to get where you need to be. We couldn't believe when we started going to The Hacienda and you could wear anything. But I can't be arsed to change xx

Very Friendly. The Charlatans backstage at Legends in Warrington on 26 January 1990.

### 3. THE ONLY ONE I KNOW

@Tim_Burgess

This one didn't make it onto the original copies of the album but it'd be rude to miss it out. Think we thought the 12-inch [single] stood up as a piece of work on its own. Don't think we realised its cultural impact – don't think it occurred to us that that's why most were buying the album. The police arriving and breaking up the video shoot [for the single] is real. They made it even better.

### 4. OPPORTUNITY

@Tim_Burgess

I walked out of Warren Street tube station on the day of the poll tax riots and ended up right in the middle of it all. I felt it was a time of real change, optimistic and youthful. I was 22 and at the start of my adventure. When I wrote this song 6 minutes (live it was 10) 3 chords, 6 verses, no solos just a power chord when the singing stopped – such an amazing song. Jon Brookes and Rob Collins in full effect. Rob is so understated and majestic on this. Jon's beat is like a mantra. Jon wanted the beat to be like Talk Talk's Life's What You Make It.

### 5. THEN

@Tim_Burgess

I still love that opening line ["I wanna bomb your submarines"]. It's about searching, I could see my friends settling down but I felt I had to get out there and find something that would give my life some meaning. Martin Blunt is a bass god. I always said that Rob [on BVs for this track] was the best singer in The Charlatans.

(Below) Setlist from The Charlatans' gig at Stoke Wheatsheaf on 10 January 1990. @Tim_Burgess: New song was Opportunity and Who Killed Your Lover was an early version of Believe You Me. Some Friendly AKA You're Not Very Well.

(Below right) A bootleg tape of the same gig shared by @iangatley27.

## 6. 109 PT.2

✓ **@Tim_Burgess**
We had an instrumental 109 that we began our live set with (from the very beginning). This was an update - a chance to remix and recreate. I played the synth and worked the night shift with [producer] Chris Nagle after everyone had gone to bed. The voice you can hear is Robert De Niro – playing the devil in Angel Heart. We wrote to him to ask his permission to use it. We were knocked out when he said yes. De Niro doing that made me vow to help bands whenever I could. He really didn't have to help us.

## 7. POLAR BEAR

✓ **@Tim_Burgess**
A live favourite. A clarinet played by our engineer at The Windings: Pee Wee C. Walking home after a club (a change of scene is all I need to breathe again) the world was changing it felt like opportunities in life were coming my way. It's about everything. Love, losing out, the new scene, endless possibilities, youth. Lots of amazing things happened. Got a dancefloor thang going on. Even better than I remember. I might even be dancing.

## 8. BELIEVE YOU ME

✓ **@Tim_Burgess**
It's about being a Gemini

I. There's someone else inside of me

II. Open it up and take it out (removing the other part of me)

Rob Collins – incredibly double tracked all the Hammond on this track – he was beyond brilliant. There was nobody like him. A genius.

NEW SONG
WHITE SHIRT
THEN
YOU CAN TALK TO ME
INDIAN ROPE
WHO KILLED YOUR LOVER
SONIC
THE ONLY ONE I KNOW
POLAR BEAR
SOME FRIENDLY
SPROSTON GREEN

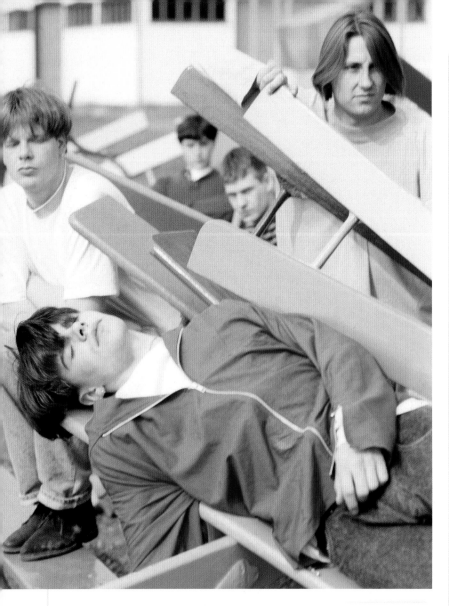

## 9. FLOWER

🔵 **@Tim_Burgess**

Pixies 'inspired' bass line. One of the first songs we wrote when the five of us came to be The Charlatans. We rehearsed in Walsall. [The Charlatans guitarist] Jon Baker introduced to me to a psych/mod club (Martin was there too), Spacemen 3/Syd Barrett/Small Faces as well as Stone Roses and Inspiral Carpets. Good times

## 10. SONIC

🔵 **@Tim_Burgess**

I wrote the lyrics while I worked in an ICI office in Runcorn. I wanted the band to be the answer to our dreams ; ) I never imagined it would last so long, or that we would go through so much. It's alright saying that's what you're going to do. Not sure even I thought it would really happen but we were posters on teenage walls, slabs of vinyl on kid's record players, badges on school bags, playing on Top Of The Pops and on the cover of magazines. It meant so much to us.

## 11. SPROSTON GREEN

🔵 **@Tim_Burgess**

Origins me singing in a biscuit Tin trying to create a vocal sound like The Beatles' Tomorrow Never Knows. Martin nicked the bass line from a local (Midlands) heavy rock group. [Deep Purple] We were super tight knit. Just the five band members a manager and our tech/photographer Derek Phillip and a van. We were mobile and tough, escaping reality living the dream. Chris Nagle was added to the personnel early on. Factory Records in house engineer, [New Order and Joy Division producer] Martin Hannett's right hand man. He had the chops but like us he was looking for his own personal identity. Together we created something lasting. They were positive times. We made it our time.

Village green preservation society: revisiting the most influential village in Cheshire.

The Charlatans in 1990. Images from this shoot later become the cover for *Some Friendly's* US release where the band were styled Charlatans UK due to a clash with a 1960s psych group.

(Clockwise from below)
Onstage in 1990;
Poster for the *Some
Friendly* tour; Looking
for the orange one –
an advert for a secret
gig; Celebrating with
fans after the show.

# the charlatans

**some friendly
on tour 1990**

| | | | |
|---|---|---|---|
| Oct 21 | Birmingham Hummingbird | Nov 2 | Blackburn, King George's Hall |
| Oct 22 | Cambridge Corn Exchange | Nov 3 | Sheffield Octagon Centre |
| Oct 25 | Manchester Academy | Nov 5 | Brighton The Event |
| Oct 26 | Leeds University | Nov 7&8 | Kilburn National Ballroom |
| Oct 27 | Liverpool Royal Court | Nov 10 | Exeter University |
| Oct 29 | Newcastle Mayfair | Nov 11 | Cardiff University |
| Oct 30 | Glasgow Barrowlands | Nov 12 | Nottingham Rock City |
| Oct 31 | Edinburgh Network | Nov 13 | Hanley Victoria Halls |

dead
dead
good

Secret GiG..!

soMewHeRE in THE

noRtH-wEst

"enD augUst"

Send 5-50 to UsuaL AddREss

# *Franz Ferdinand*
## Franz Ferdinand
Domino, 2004

Naming your band after the archduke whose assassination triggered the World War I could be considered a bit *square*, but it is this exact quality that makes Franz Ferdinand so cutting edge: they just do things their own way. This spirit has subsequently led them to form a supergroup with US duo Sparks (brilliantly called FFS) and get a rare remix from French dance pioneers Daft Punk, but it is with their self-titled debut album that it all began. While drawing on the art school and art-rock traditions of their hometown Glasgow, plus a European outlook derived from the band members' Greek and German heritage, Alex Kapranos (vocals/guitar – **@alkapranos**), Paul Thomson (drums), Bob Hardy (bass – **@B0bHardy**), and then guitarist Nick McCarthy, created a debut record that truly went its own way. A work full of snappy songs that would prove equally at home in an art gallery installation as the pop charts.

Stormy recording sessions in Malmo, Sweden; Hardy learning how to play the bass from scratch while writing the songs; and internet cadged from art school were just a few of the revelations that Franz' listening party threw up – as was the need for you to move your feet. "Here we go. Needle on the record. Islands in the streaming. Girls, get ready to Dance," declared Kapranos as things kicked off. Even in book form, those same rules apply.

**@B0bHardy**
Here's a photo from the sessions in Malmo.

## 1. JACQUELINE

● @alkapranos

Like on a few of the songs on the record, Jacqueline was/is a real character. Jacqueline Cameron [now an SNP councilor for Johnstone South and Elderslie] is one of the funniest people I know. The intro is a true story she told me about when she worked at the poetry library. She was actually 27, not 17 at the time, but that didn't rhyme. I seem to remember ripping my voice so I sounded rougher when I sang the choruses. I wanted a contrast between them and the verses. The chorus lyric was very much a mantra by which I lived my life: avoid a career at all costs. Only work when you need money.

## 2. TELL HER TONIGHT

● @alkapranos

Nick wrote the lyric for this one. He sang the verse and we both sang the chorus. I think it is also based on a true story, or maybe even a series of them. The guitar riff was me trying to play Funky Town by Lipps Inc and getting it woefully wrong, and using it here instead. Verse, bassline and intro was an attempt to write one of those big elastic band sounding riffs like Walk On The Wild Side or Cannonball. The verse was my attempt at early [Paul] McCartney. There are a few nods to pre-psychedelic Beatles on the record. I loved the way those early Beatles records had the vocals mixed so high. Tore [Johansson], our producer, said it was old fashioned. Funny, as most pop music now is essentially just vocal with a bit of beat & bass.

## 3. TAKE ME OUT

● @Tim_Burgess

What a game changer Take Me Out was. What was the moment you realised this song was going to be so huuuuuge?

● @BObHardy

First time we managed to play it all the way through in a practice room, haha.

## 4. THE DARK OF THE MATINÉE

● @BObHardy

Alex and I wrote the chorus lyrics for this via email, I was sitting in the library at the Glasgow School of Art as that was my only internet access.

● @alkapranos

I wrote the verses as a recollection of the walk home from school when I was in my early teens, with a girl called Natasha Arnold, who was a year older than me. I had an unbearable unrequited crush on her. She wasn't interested in me romantically at all. She was cool. I remember her literally undoing the top and bottom buttons of my blazer, untucking my shirt a little and dishevelling my tie, so I looked cooler. We would have long philosophical talks, she the optimist, me the cynic.

## 5. AUF ACHSE

● @alkapranos

Nick wrote the keyboard line for this, and it's how the song started. It's a great melody. He thought he was playing the theme from a German soap opera about the adventures of a truck driver. It's where the title comes from it means On The Axle. Like On The Road, but German.

## 6. CHEATING ON YOU

● @alkapranos

This was my attempt to subvert that early Beatles pop stuff I love. Those songs were often about the naivity and innocence of first love. Here we're singing in that upbeat celebratory style, but about the miserable end of a relationship. Glib Optimism Vs Grim Reality.

## 7. THIS FIRE

● @BObHardy

We didn't finish This Fire until much later, after the Malmo sessions. I remember we were on tour, Alex and I were sharing a Travelodge room. One night he woke up with a start and said "IT NEEDS TO GO HIGH" and that was the solution to the middle.

● @alkapranos

Amazing. I don't remember that. I was thinking about the songs every waking minute. Every sleeping minute too, it seems.

## 8. DARTS OF PLEASURE

● @alkapranos

Oh I like Darts of pleasure. One of the first songs we played together. This started off as a slow introspective acoustic song. There's a B-side called Words So Leisured that gives you an idea of what

**@BObHardy**
We rehearsed 40' in our courtroom practice room at the jail. This photo was taken around then.

**@alkapranos**
I seem to remember being pleased with myself at the time [I wrote Cheating On You] about some smart arse thing that the bassline does against the chords from a musical theory perspective, but I can't remember what it is. It's quite catchy.

it was like. We recorded this before the main session, around about May 2003 in a studio on the outskirts of London somewhere by a graveyard, along with Van Tango and Shopping for Blood.

## 9. MICHAEL

**@alkapranos**
Another true story with real characters. Am I allowed to tell it yet? We wrote it the day after a particularly good night out. Knocked it out in as long as it took to play it more or less. Michael is actually in the video. Starring as himself. He really does look beautiful in the video too. Fuck. I'm really wired on this one. We really wanted to make the guitars clean, but aggressive. The breakdown bit is mean. I like it. My favourite bit of the song. We were trying to play techno with guitars.

**@BObHardy**
This is me and Alex Kapranos on Renfrew Street outside the art school around the time we we're getting ready to go to record the album.

## 10. COME ON HOME

**@alkapranos**
Ah, this song makes me a little sad when I hear it. I was deeply in love, but there was disintegration beginning when I wrote this. Damn. She was a huge inspiration. Indescribable.

## 11. 40'

**@alkapranos**
This is my favourite song on the LP. The guitar line is very Greek. It shows my love of Rembetika [Greek music genre]. Well, at least to me it does. That bell sound is the sound of the gate to the studio being struck. The words in the chorus are my favourite on the LP. I remember overdubbing this keyboard solo. Really smashing the keys. A lot of fun.

**@BObHardy**
I vividly remember recording 40' in Malmo one evening, lights dimmed, whisky poured. It gave me goosebumps at the time and I'm getting them now too.

# *Parklife*
## Blur
Food Records, 1994

Things Dave Rowntree has done successfully include: animating cartoons, working as a solicitor, getting his pilot's licence, lobbying the European Parliament about music copyright, standing as a Labour councillor… oh, and being the drummer in '90s Britpop band Blur. There's one extra accomplishment Dave can now add to that expanding list: being a Listening Party host extraordinaire.

Blur's man behind the kit not only took us through the band's third album *Parklife* – the inadvertent blueprint for Britpop – with stories, photos and throwbacks from the band's early days, but he brought some friends along too as the album's main producer Stephen Street and his (slightly tardy) bandmate Graham Coxon also joined in.

"*Parklife* was the moment every band dreams of," frontman Damon Albarn once said of the record. "It feels like you've made a universal connection with your audience. You can't go wrong." And Dave (drums – **@DaveRowntree**), Graham (guitar – **@GrahamCoxon**) and Stephen (producer – **@StreetStephen**) certainly captured that feeling in their tweets. So here's a Listening Party that revealed the band members' love of astronomy, what Lot 105 is all about, and the significance of a cowbell…

**PHOTOGRAPHY:**
Bob Thomas

Trouble In The Message Centre. Damon Albarn and Alex James at the 1994 Mercury Prize ceremony. Despite being the favourites, Parklife was unexpectedly beaten by M People on the night.

### 1. GIRLS & BOYS

☑ **@DaveRowntree**

It's a song about sex. Luckily no one knew that or it wouldn't have got in the charts. Kevin Godley of the band Godley and Cream directed the video. We wanted it to look like a cheap video from the 1980s. It's amazing how expensive it was to make a cheap looking video. Alex once said if he had all the money we'd spent on videos he'd spend it on videos. I'd spend it on toilet paper and hand sanitiser. But you can't go back.

### 2. TRACY JACKS

☑ **@Tim_Burgess**

My favourite on the album switches between this, End Of A Century and To The End.

☑ **@DaveRowntree**

Not my favourite song on the album, but as far as I know the only Blur track where I play cowbell. Not much call for 'More Cowbell' in the 1990s.

### 3. END OF A CENTURY

☑ **@DaveRowntree**

I love playing this live because of the big anthemic brass section chorus. And it talks about ants – probably the least rock n roll of all the insects.

↑
International teachers of Britpop. Blur photographed in Tokyo (left) and Los Angeles (right) following the release of Parklife.

### 4. PARKLIFE

☑ **@DaveRowntree**

The smashing sound at the beginning of the track is me sitting in the studio smashing the plate I'd just eaten my dinner on. I did it in one take. I'm a professional.

London Loves. Damon and Graham onstage at Shepherd's Bush Empire a month after *Parklife's* release.

### 5. BANK HOLIDAY

✔ **@DaveRowntree**
Every album has got to have a punk song. Bank Holidays are public holidays in the UK, and people generally spend the day drinking.

### 6. BADHEAD

✔ **@DaveRowntree**
This is one of my all-time favourite Blur songs. I love the huge chorus and the brass, and the melancholic feel. Our lives changed after Parklife. We got in the charts – unheard of for an indie band, and even got gold discs.

### 7. THE DEBT COLLECTOR

✔ **@DaveRowntree**
This one features Damon's cheesy organ that he'd bought in an auction. It was Lot 105, which became a very important number for Blur. Lovely brass arrangement, and Kate St John on oboe, I think.

### 8. FAR OUT

✔ **@DaveRowntree**
Alex's [James, bassist] song about moons in the solar system. Alex and I are both keen astronomers, and were involved in the brilliant but ill-fated Beagle II Mars lander.

### 9. TO THE END

✔ **@DaveRowntree**
I'm crying. I love this tune! This was Recorded at RAK studios with Steven Hague producing. He would touch a fader on the desk with one finger, rock steady, while bopping around to the music. I think this is Stephen Hague, but I'm happy to be corrected. I can't find him on twitter or I'd link him. Maybe that's why he's not on twitter. We used to only use producers called Stephen. Now we only use producers called Stephen Street.

✔ **@GrahamCoxon**
Mike Thorne!

✔ **@DaveRowntree**
You're right!

### 10. LONDON LOVES

✔ **@DaveRowntree**
Fine work from Graham on this one. Hard to duplicate the vibe live, though we've tried many times!

### 11. TROUBLE IN THE MESSAGE CENTRE

✔ **@DaveRowntree**
Some of the lyrics were taken from the writing on a hotel telephone in the USA. The song is a great one to play live. Mind you, they're all great to play live. I love playing live.

All the people…
Damon meets
the crowd during
Blur's Wolverhampton
Civic Hall gig on
11 May 1994.

● **@StreetStephen**

Got our Magazine vibe on for this one! Was great to see the band play it on the last dates they played!

## 12. CLOVER OVER DOVER

● **@DaveRowntree**

Another beautiful melancholy song. Damon writes these so well. Strangely meaningful again now we've left the EU.

## 13. MAGIC AMERICA

● **@DaveRowntree**

We spent a lot of time touring America and grew to love it after a few false starts. The song is more about Walt Disney's fake America than the real thing.

## 14. JUBILEE

● **@DaveRowntree**

This is one of my favourite songs to play live on the rare occasions we do play it these days. It's another track which features the Kick Horns. I remember playing it at Mile End stadium show [in 1995] which was the biggest show we'd ever played by far – it was one of the most wonderful days of my life. We felt these overpowering waves of love from the audience.

## 15. THIS IS A LOW

● **@DaveRowntree**

All the strange phrases are names of the shipping regions around the UK. We used to listen to the shipping forecast on tour – it was very nostalgic and made us miss home. Alex came back from holiday and found a handkerchief with all the shipping forecasts regions on and Damon pinned it on the studio wall.

● **@GrahamCoxon**

I wanted to get a solo like the solo (Jeff Beck and Jimmy Page at the same time!!) section in "Stroll On" from *Blow Up* but slowed right down.

## 16. LOT 105

● **@DaveRowntree**

Named after the organ… I think I mentioned that we pinned things on the studio wall during the Parklife sessions. Well not saying that's where the album title came from or anything…

# Going Blank Again
## Ride
Creation, 1992

The humble guitar pedal has been responsible for some amazing sounds, but so far it has only inspired the name of one genre. Emerging in the early 1990s, *shoegaze* saw bands taking the jangle and volume of classic British rock like The Who and The Kinks and diving inside those tunes, mutating them into huge sonic clouds driven by undulating melodies and vocals that sometimes led or sometimes just sat as part of the over all ambience. To achieve this effect guitars not only had to be turned up loud, but the players relied on an array of effects pedals and spent a large amount of time staring at the floor, or 'shoegazing', in anticipation of which box to hit next. Oxford's Ride had the best shoes and pedals, with their second album *Going Blank Again* adding a sculpted, riff-driven swagger to their shoegaze blueprint. Andy Bell (guitars – **@Andybebop**), Loz Colbert (drums – **@doctorloz**), Steve Queralt (bass – **@SteveQueralt**) and frontman Mark Gardener's (**@MarkGardener**) sound certainly struck a (reverb-drenched) chord.

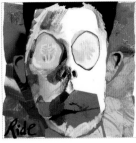

ARTWORK:
Christopher Gunson

LISTENING PARTY
**26 MARCH 2020**

### 1. LEAVE THEM ALL BEHIND

**@Andybebop (Andy Bell)**
We were in Amsterdam (or was it Rotterdam) and after a day in town had this spaced out soundcheck where we did this jam that for ages we called B song. There was no sequencer just the chords. I think we got it recorded on a Walkman otherwise we wouldn't have remembered how it went. We got into the studio and Mark had written pages and pages of lyrics during an acid trip. We sat down together and pulled out the best lines, and that was the lyrics.

### 2. TWISTERELLA

**@doctorloz (Loz Colbert)**
Guess it's kinda twee, but Motown influenced this song... from a long way away perhaps!

**@Andybebop**
Twisterella is the name of a song written by the character Billy Liar in the 60s film of the same name. It's a top film if you haven't seen it. The video was based on a Who appearance on Ready Steady Go. I was channelling Townsend but with Daltreys wraparound shades on.

### 3. NOT FAZED

**@Andybebop**
We'd only been out of school a couple of years and this is my anti school song. I'd always liked The Headmaster Ritual by the Smiths and wanted to write my own version. Musically I was ripping off the early Kinks riffs, and Mark's guitar gives it a Television's feel. We were all really into Television Marquee Moon album. Oooh, even a bit of cowbell!

**@doctorloz**
100% prime Andy Bell riff. Some jingle bells in there left over from 'I Wanna Be Your Dog'.

### 4. CHROME WAVES

**@Andybebop**
The intro guitar riff is kind of similar to Vapour Trail, 4 similar chord shapes around an E chord, but this time in a minor key. We wanted it to sound like Unfinished Sympathy by Massive Attack and that's why it's got the strings and bells. There was a Solina string synth at the studio – we couldn't afford real strings but I prefer fake ones anyway.

**@Tim_Burgess**
The Mary Whitehouse Experience did a sketch with two of them being me and Mark G. We knew we'd made it when people were doing impressions of us on the telly. Not sure it's happened since though…

✅ **@MarkGardener**
I remember Andy playing the chords on the American tour bus, and I was thinking, 'God, that is just so beautiful.'

### 5. MOUSE TRAP

✅ **@doctorloz**
Took a while to learn this one and get it right. Luckily we got to play a lot of these songs live while we were still recording them, if that makes sense. I was listening to a lot of Led Zeppelin for the first time – for the drums! I couldn't stand Plant at first but grew to like the sound of the whole band… but of course it was Mr Bonham that drew me in and I was learning from.

✅ **@Andybebop**
The riff for this was me trying to be Pete Townshend and Mark wrote a song around it. This was always an absolute belter live. Blur influence on the guitars via Graham Coxon.

### 6. TIME OF HER TIME

✅ **@Andybebop**
The title comes from a Norman Mailer short story I think, but that has nothing to do with the song. It was just a title I liked. The lead guitar is ripped off Terry Bickers (of The House of Love) I wanted to do something similar to his sound. That's why I used all the modulation, it's Terrys signature sound. Another one that's great live. One of Loz's favourite Ride tunes I think?

✅ **@doctorloz**
Yep, a favourite live as well… It's a straight out emotional song.

### 7. COOL YOUR BOOTS

✅ **@Andybebop**
The last 3 minutes of this is my favourite musical part of the album. We did this thing with the time signatures and going to double speed… Someone was holding up a sign for Loz that said "fast!" at random times, and there was also a weird length to every other line of chords. It just takes you by surprise when you're listening, always wrong-foots you, I like that. The title comes from the film *Withnail And I*, which all of the band loved. We all knew it off by heart. There are two spoken samples from the film in there too. "Even a stopped clock gives the right time twice a day" (spoken by "I") & "Cool your boots, man" (spoken by Danny the dealer).

### 8. MAKING JUDY SMILE

✅ **@SteveQueralt**
I bought a Steinberger bass – it's something you would never let anyone see you play in public, it was a headless bass. You could imagine Mark King from Level 42 playing one. It was a really nasty looking instrument, but it sounded really good.

### 9. TIME MACHINE

✅ **@Andybebop**
The last two songs on the album actually are 5 songs edited together. At one stage we wanted to do an *Abbey Road* style medley on side two. Time Machine has two songs in it. The start is part of a song called King Bullshit made by Steve and Loz. I think the title is from *Taxi Driver*, it's one of Steve's titles. Then you get the song Time Machine, a song I really love, which Mark wrote. My contribution was just the very hard tremolo guitar.

### 10. OX4

✅ **@doctorloz**
This bit we 're-amped' by playing a section of music through a leslie into another room, and recording the sound of that new room… something like that… makes it sound very atmospheric… Alvin Lucier would be proud. Anything emerging from/borne of noise is just great innit?

# *Definitely Maybe*
## Oasis
Creation, 1994

⚓ Is it my imagination or have we finally found something worth living for? Few albums have defined their own impact as succinctly or as accurately as the lyrics of *Definitely Maybe* did. A light blue touch-paper moment in British music, Oasis' debut album not only breathed energy back into rock'n'roll in the '90s, but its youthful anger and optimism, tied to anthemic melodies, pulse-racing drums and swaggering guitars imbued the album with a timeless quality that has kept the record sounding permanently fresh. Always one of the characters within the band who managed to shine out despite the Gallagher brothers' gravitational pull, founding member and guitarist Paul Arthurs (**@BoneheadsPage**), AKA Bonehead, not only added personality to one of the UK's greatest groups, but since leaving Oasis in 1999 has become a Twitter star in his own right with his offbeat opinions and observations. Having stood shoulder to shoulder with Liam and Noel for the making of the album, he led the way – with help from Oasis sleeve designer Brian Cannon (**@MicrodotCreativ**) and iconic Manchester photographer Kevin Cummins (**@KCMANC**) who has documented much of the band's career – through a truly special Listening Party. And that's not our opinion, it is Paul's. "[This is] More nerve wracking than Knebworth," Bonehead tweeted as *Definitely Maybe* started playing. "Fingers are all over the place!" See you down the front.

PHOTOGRAPHY:
Michael Spencer Jones

SLEEVE DESIGN:
Brian Cannon

**@MicrodotCreativ**
(Below left) The first thing I did for the band was the logo – inspired by the Decca Records logo seen on a Rolling Stones album. Here's the prototype. (Bottom left) Original running sheet for Live Forever mapping out all the tracks on the recording. (Below right) The original artwork in my handwriting used for the text on the sleeve.

| ARTIST OASIS | Reel No. | Band |
|---|---|---|
| TITLE LIVE FOREVER | | try varispeed ↓ |
| | Reel 2 #1 | |
| 1 Hat | | 0 – Count |
| 2 Kick | | 11 – verse 1 |
| 3 Snare. | | 33 – chorus 1 |
| 4 Tom 1 | | 58 – verse 2 |
| 5 Tom 2. | | 120 – chorus 2 |
| 6 tambourine. | | 144 – solo. |
| 7 ↑ cymbals L | | (206) |

↗

**@BoneheadsPage**
From the same shoot with Tom Sheehan [in New York, see page 36]. Worst hangover EVER for me. Ninety degrees I nearly died. Straight in the Irish pub on 7th Ave after it.

### 1. ROCK 'N' ROLL STAR

✓ **@BoneheadsPage**
What an album opener? Doesn't need an introduction, still gets crowds bouncing now, 26 years later on stage with Liam. When I think of my guitar sound it's always this track I look to.

✓ **@MicrodotCreativ (Brian Cannon)**
And we're off! Before we had settled on the idea of shooting the sleeve in Bonehead's house, Liam's 'concept' for the artwork was a knife in a lump of butter – true story!

### 2. SHAKERMAKER

✓ **@BoneheadsPage**
12 bar blues innit. Melody stolen from the Coca Cola advert. I've still got the clock from the back cover of the single designed by Brian Cannon. This was our 2nd single off the album, charted at number 11. originally had the words I'd like to buy the world a coke to keep it company, but we had to take them off or else, said Coca Cola. Whatever.

### 3. LIVE FOREVER

✓ **@BoneheadsPage**
3rd single off the album, and our first top 10 it's turned into an anthem down the years. Play the drum intro and say name that tune to anyone? Nice one Tony. X Only Tony could have drummed this album fact. Top solo. Took him 28 takes don't let Noel tell you otherwise.

@BoneheadsPage
Selfie before selfies were a thing.

@BoneheadsPage
Us and some mates and @MicrodotCreativ setting up the album cover at my house from my unseen film.

@BoneheadsPage
Here's a pic from the film I developed just about to go onstage at Glastonbury 1994.

### 4. UP IN THE SKY

@BoneheadsPage
I came up with the guitar hook in rehearsal, trying to do a Taxman type of thing. Noel took it home and came in next day with the finished song.

@MicrodotCreativ
The first thing I did for the band was the logo – inspired by the Decca Records logo seen on a Rolling Stones album - here's the prototype in which I used an approximation of the Adidas font – before changing it. The finished thing is Helvetica Black Oblique.

### 5. COLUMBIA

@BoneheadsPage
My favourite Oasis song to listen to/play, even now onstage with Liam. He dropped it from the set on a couple of gigs in Europe. I nearly went home ha ha. 3 chords all the way. Who needs a middle 8 and minor chords?. I've always said it's a dance track, it's a groover

### 6. SUPERSONIC

@BoneheadsPage
1st single, charted at number 31. I was at home listening to the charts on the radio. If it all ended then I'd have been happy. A record in the top 40? Recorded in the Pink Museum studio in Liverpool

with Dave Scott. We were in there to record Bring it on Down but it wasn't working. Noel wrote the words and music to supersonic on the day and we went in and did it.

@KCMANC (Kevin Cummins)
Then we went on tour with them to do their first NME cover feature: the glamour of Portmouth & Newport (Gwent). It was chaos and not just because of the band's behaviour, although Liam wearing his Man City shirt on stage didn't help. When we got back to Pompey hotel, the pool was next to the bar. Liam chucked all the furniture in the pool. "You daft bastard, where are we going to sit. Get it out." He had to fish it all out so as we could sit down and have a drink. A lot of pointing went on then there was a, erm, sibling scuffle – then everything went back to normal. The hotel barman realised this was out of his remit so he called last orders. Noel was at the bar. There were 26 of us. "I'll have 6 double gin & tonics. He'll have 6 points of Guinness and 6 whisky chasers, he'll have 6…" The barman decided to stay but he needed a piss. He asked us to keep an eye on the bar. When he got back there wasn't a single drink left on his optics nor a single bottle of beer. "Fuck knows what happened mate. I think East 17 came down and robbed it. We weren't looking. It wasn't us. It was East 17 mate."

@BoneheadsPage
Last year I developed some film I took on the road. Never seen before. I'll post a few up. Here's me and Noel busking in San Fran.

(Top)
Hey you… Oasis on stage in Portsmouth, 2 May 1994.

(Bottom)
@BoneheadsPage
Liam in Central Park taken by me. We were doing a shoot with [photographer] Tom Sheehan.

## 7. BRING IT ON DOWN

**@BoneheadsPage**
Punk rock, what a vocal. Enough said.

**@MicrodotCreativ**
The front cover of Def Maybe was inspired by the back of the Beatles album 'Oldies But Goldies' I just loved the fly on the wall feel to the shot.

## 8. CIGARETTES & ALCOHOL

**@BoneheadsPage**
4th single, charted at number 7. Another of my favourites to play live and still gets the crowd going mental. Another top Liam vocal, but aren't they all? You gotta make it happen wooo!

## 9. DIGSY'S DINNER

**@BoneheadsPage**
One fingered piano solo from me took me about 10 takes, bonkers song I always thought with bonkers lyrics. Love it. What a solo. Ha, ha, ha.

## 10. SLIDE AWAY

**@BoneheadsPage**
Only song that survived the original sessions from Monnow Valley studios and the best ever vocal take from Liam in my opinion. When he sings "oh let me be the one" I'd let him be the one.

## 11. MARRIED WITH CHILDREN

**@BoneheadsPage**
This was recorded in the bedroom at Mark Coyle's [producer] house (rented off Mani) and kept as it was for the album. I love the guitar sound on this, it was an unplugged electric of Coyley's, miked up in the bedroom. Another great vocal from Liam too.

@MicrodotCreativ
Noel would hand write out the lyrics to every song so I could develop the concepts for the sleeve artwork – even album tracks.

Bring it on down

① WHAT WAS THAT SOUND RINGING AROUND YOUR BRAIN
TODAY WAS JUST A BLUR, YOU'VE GOT A HEAD LIKE A GHOST TRAIN
WHAT WAS THAT SOUND RINGING AROUND YOUR BRAIN
YOU'RE HERE ON YOUR OWN WHO YOU GONNA FIND TO BLAME

② YOU'RE THE OUTCAST, YOU'RE THE UNDERCLASS

# *Rio*
## Duran Duran
EMI, 1982

With their slick guitar lines, pounding productions, fast fashion and lyrics that seemed to have been scribbled out on Concorde, Duran Duran were an impossibly brilliant collision of glamour and pop. With yachts and far-flung locations filling their videos, Simon Le Bon (lead vocals – **@SimonJCLeBON**), Nick Rhodes (keyboards), John Taylor (bass), Andy Taylor (guitar) and Roger Taylor (drums) appeared to be the epitome of deluxe 1980s living. Yet Duran Duran were much deeper than their – admittedly luxurious – surface suggested. Following a musical line that descended from David Bowie's golden glam rock, and active participants in the New Romantic cultural explosion that emerged out of influential club nights in London and their native Birmingham, the warm songs on *Rio* not only made an immediate impression that have – despite boasting the trapping of its age – truly stood the test of time. Guiding us through Duran Duran's second album with a Listening Party, Le Bon offered us an overdue insight into *Rio's* musical creation, plus some suitably racy revelations about the record's reproductive qualities. Well, it is a pop classic for a reason…

**ARTWORK:**
Patrick Nagel

Pop world. Duran Duran photographed in Tokyo in April 1982 as Rio became a global hit.

## 1. RIO

### ⊘ @SimonJCLeBON

It all begins with a blow to the naked strings of the Steinway grand in Air studio 1, played backwards. If memory serves me, it was Nick dropping one of his pixie boots from a considerable height that worked best. What a bass line, check that out, that's John Taylor on fire.

## 2. MY OWN WAY

### ⊘ @SimonJCLeBON

"Saw you at the air race yesterday…" I had this sort of science fiction movie playing on a loop in my head that summer. I might have thought I had my own way, but there was only one place we were ever going – 45 between 6th and Broadway it's the address of the old Peppermint Lounge in NYC.

## 3. LONELY IN YOUR NIGHTMARE

### ⊘ @SimonJCLeBON

Definitely a song written by a lonely guy desperate to hook up with… somebody… ANYBODY! We recorded at Air Studios, 247 Oxford Street. It was above a big Burton Tailoring shop. You had to take a lift to get up to the top floor, no. 7 I think. Paul McCartney was working in studio 2, & at around 6pm most days, he'd pop his head round the door & wish us good night & good luck with the music. We'd usually be there until well past midnight.

## 4. HUNGRY LIKE THE WOLF

### ⊘ @SimonJCLeBON

Nick's girlfriend Cheryl starts the track giggling while he was doing something rude to her. Sounds like da lonely guy is beginning to get desperate…

## 5. HOLD BACK THE RAIN

### ⊘ @SimonJCLeBON

I was really worried about John he was staying up all night and completely missing days in the studio, I remember writing out the lyric by hand and sliding it under the door of his apartment. This song is about what it's like to be in a band, what it's like to look after each other.

## 6. NEW RELIGION

### ⊘ @SimonJCLeBON

This is my favourite track on the album. I'd heard about this thing called rap, and I wanted to try it out. It's such a white boy rap.

## 7. LAST CHANCE ON THE STAIRWAY

### ⊘ @SimonJCLeBON

The band were so impressed when I referred to Voltaire [in the lyrics]. [Producer] Colin Thurston had ordered two enormous trunks full of percussion instruments, and I spent hours trying out all sorts – cabasas, shakers, washboards, swanee whistles etc. There was also a vibraphone and a marimba which I play in the middle of this song.

## 8. SAVE A PRAYER

### ⊘ @SimonJCLeBON

I'd been away for a couple of day and the guys had come up with a chorus for a song and at first I'd felt a bit threatened, but then I came up with the melody and it was the most amazing piece of music. That synth Nick played is probably the most sampled Duran Duran thing ever. And the one thing I've heard about this song more than anything else, it's either the song that somebody lost their virginity to, or the song that they were conceived to. Big statement.

## 9. THE CHAUFFEUR

### ⊘ @SimonJCLeBON

I was out on Kibbutz it was '79, at the end of one hot long day I watched a couple of Israeli soldier girls cooling off by driving a tractor at full speed across the flat desert. The girl at the back was standing cruciform with her hair streaming out horizontal behind her, and the words "out on the tar plains" came to me.

# *The Wonderful And Frightening World Of...*
## The Fall
Beggars Banquet, 1984

Based on some of the stories of Mark E Smith's "human resources" approach towards his bandmates, *The Wonderful And Frightening World Of...* could well be a description of life in the band. And of course "Smithy" knew that. After all, he did once quip of his musical backing, "If it's me and your granny on bongos, it's The Fall." Remarkably, despite this possible in-joke, *The Wonderful And Frightening World Of...* is one of the Manchester band's most accessible and – dare we say – poppy records. Full of shuffling skiffle rhythms, rockabilly melodies and hooky choruses, there is a golden haze around Mark E Smith's vocals on this record, although the late singer's lyrics remain suitably surreal. It is also remarkable that while The Fall line-up who made this record – Karl Burns (drums), Paul Hanley (drums – **@hanleyPa**), Steve Hanley (bass – **@Stephenhanley6**), Craig Scanlon (guitars) and Brix Smith (guitars – **@Brixsmithstart**) – all eventually left the band in varying degrees of acrimony (the recently married Brix Smith, for example, would divorce the singer just five years later), their fondness for the band and this record saw three of them convene to stage this Listening Party.

**ARTWORK:**
Claus Castenskiold

Wonderful and frightening. Mark E Smith on stage at the Lyceum in London. Whatever the line-up, the world of The Fall revolved around the creative and caustic frontman for 42 years.

Mark E Smith mural in Prestwich by street artist Akse P19.

## 1. LAY OF THE LAND

**@hanleyPa**

That chant's from 'The Quartermass Conclusion' starring John Mills as Quatermass. I think it was repeated just before we recorded the album. Karl [Burns] played tambourine for most of this song. The most aggressive tambourine player ever. He hit it so hard he bent it in half. The thing about this song is that it's got two fantastic bass lines. Steve's playing the main one of course and then Karl's solo at the end which is phenomenal.

**@Brixsmithstart**

Lay Of The Land was inspired by a television series Mark and I were watching called Quatermass, in which a group of people chant Lay Lay Lay. It was set in the near future, which is of course now the past. It was also about Lay Lines and me and Mark were fascinated by them and studied ancient maps of Britain to understand where they were and how to harness their power. I was heavily into rockabilly at the time when I wrote it, hence the lopsided swaggery groove of my guitar. I was also trying to write a Fiery Jack type feel to Keep it The Fall-esque. Paul and Karl duelling skippy beats, amazing, and Steve's Grouch bass solo at the end is one of my favourite moments ever ever EVER!!!

**@Stephenhanley6**

New label Beggars Banquet. Famous producer John Leckie. I played a bass guitar through an amplifier.

FEAR IS SOMETHING I TRY NOT TO ABSORB

CHIPS@

#PAF2018

↑
@Brixsmithstart: Me, Mark and a Monkey. Taken around the same time as we recorded *The Wonderful And Frightening World Of The Fall*.

## 2. 2 × 4

**@Brixsmithstart**
It's called 2X4 is because I grew up watching cartoons & in America we call a plank of wood a 2X4. I remember Wiley Coyote and Roadrunner whacking each other with a 2X4. So I said to Mark, I want to say "Hit him on the head with a 2 x 4" and Mark wrote his lyrics.

**@hanleyPa**
The verse is in 4/4 but the chorus is in 5/4 – to make matters even stranger Steve plays the chorus over the verse at a couple of points. Jason Brown out of the Extricated was the one who pointed out how weird that was. Never occured to us.

**@Stephenhanley6**
Check out the audience on The Tube TV programme trying to dance to it.

## 3. COPPED IT

**@Brixsmithstart**
Mark loved the Virgin Prunes. At home he had a 7" called Sandpaper Lullaby. I become obsessed with it. I suggested Mark ask Gavin Friday to come and duet. Gavin said yes! "It ain't whatcha you do, it's the way that you do it"

**@hanleyPa**
This features Gavin Friday from the Virgin Prunes – we played with them a few times. They stayed at our house and mum and dad were delighted when they found out they were from Dublin. They bought her some flowers too. I play keyboards on this. I didn't have much faith in my ability but John Leckie was really encouraging. The lyrics for Copped It were dead old – it was one of the Falls earliest songs, though the music was different. It's about nicking song ideas off other people, which is ironic given the next track!

## 4. ELVES

**@Brixsmithstart**
Oh dear I know what Paul Hanley is going to say! Listening to it now it gets really Doorsy in the middle. "The fantastic is in league against me" brilliant! "Not never no never no more will I trust the elves of Dunsimore"

**@hanleyPa**
Why do I always get the blame for mentioning you-know-what? I never did!!! In [Fall biography] *The Big Midweek* Steve says I asked Brix about the riff's similarity to [Iggy Pop's] *I Wanna Be Your Dog*. But I don't think anyone did.

## 5. SLANG KING

**@Brixsmithstart**
This was my attempt and trying to funk it up. I like the keyboard but can't remember who played it. When Mark says Whickwire he is referring to a character in Rod Stirling's Twilight Zone. We were obsessed with that show. Mark thought Rod Stirling was a genius poet. Once when Mark and I were at our local corner shop, these too little girls really didn't have enough for a Curly Wurly and had to put it back!

#### @hanleyPa

Karl's drumming on this is tremendous. The intro especially. Slang King Mark showed me a rough approximation of the chorus riff on kazoo. The verse bit was in A – I insisted the chorus had to be in C as that was the only key where I could play the riff cos that made it all white notes. So really I wrote the chorus! John Leckie had worked with everyone – The Beatles, Syd Barrett, Mott The Hoople, Pink Floyd, T.Rex – but being The Fall we never asked him about any of that, we mainly spent the time taking the piss out of his purple trousers

## 6. BUG DAY

#### @hanleyPa

Apart from Mark I don't think anyone had much enthusiasm for this one. Mark told me to do some drums that were completely random. After I'd done it he said they were too random – so I had to overdub a more regular pattern. And that's life in The Fall in a nutshell.

#### @Brixsmithstart

I seem to remember this was improvised live. Again Leckie just gets the most amazing sound layers here. He is a sound sculpted. "Facing up to the sea is a very hard thing."

## 7. STEPHEN SONG

#### @hanleyPa

This really is Stephen's song, he showed it me and I put some guitar to it.  But like C.R.E.E.P, which was also nominally a co-write between me and Steve, the bass line's pretty much the whole song. It's Mark at his most poetic, I think. 'Floating grey abundance against my palace of conscience' Blimey. Another one featuring Gavin Friday. His vocal's brilliant. Me and Karl both play drums. Karl's doing that military thing you can hear at the end. I overdubbed a guitar bit on this. Brix had this Marshall stack set up in its own room and when you really cranked it up it sounded phenomenal.  I think everyone except Craig ended up playing through it at one point or another.

#### @Brixsmithstart

I love this song so much! Steve the bass line!!! And the lyrics are so absolutely genius. In a backing vocal Mark says "Adult Net, Net of Mesh"

this is where the name of my solo band came from The Adult Net. The Lyrics to Stephen Song are fucking SUBLIME.

## 8. CRAIGNESS

#### @Brixsmithstart

Craig brought in the riff as I recall. Mark and I live on Recory lane in Prestwich. Below us we had these creepy neighbours. A couple. The guy has one eye. His wife had blonde curly hair. She set the chip pan alight and caused a fire. When Mark says  "Ooo-ar ", he is making fun of the neighbour downstairs with one eye, like making out he was a pirate whose eye was put out. "It's grandpappy with Satan's eyes". I adore this song. I am playing the single note melodic hook. To go with Craig's soundscape melody.  It gets so so, SO psychedelic at the end! It's John Leckie at his sublime mindblowing best!!! "Mind moving slow is Sane. Mind moving fast is mad". What lyrics. What brilliance.

#### @hanleyPa

'Craigness' Craig's tune, unsurprisingly. The riff that me and Brix are playing originally had an extra note which changed the time signature, but none of us could get it right. We had to leave it out. It was always a shame when we couldn't accommodate Craig's wayward timing.

## 9. DISNEY'S DREAM DEBASED

#### @hanleyPa

'D D D' What a great title. Everyone except Mark plays guitar on this I think.

#### @Brixsmithstart

The story of the day Mark and I went to Disneyland and a woman was killed on the Matterhorn ride. It was extremely surreal and upsetting. It's actually word for word what happened that day. The whole story. It was like my childhood ended that day.

# *Heaven Or Las Vegas*
## Cocteau Twins
4AD, 1990

**PHOTOGRAPHY:**
Andy Rumball

**SLEEVE DESIGN:**
Paul West

⚓ There was already something mysterious about Elizabeth Fraser's vocals in the Cocteau Twins, long before the singer largely stepped back from releasing music. Against a glacial backdrop of synths, guitars and beats, her voice mesmerisingly soared with a pure beauty. Often fans were not sure exactly what she was singing, but they understood the emotion, pathos and meaning of every note. While something of a high water mark for the band creatively, 1990's *Heaven Or Las Vegas* was not one personally for the band. Despite Fraser and bandmate Robin Guthrie just having had a child together, their relationship was already in terminal decline, while bassist Simon Raymonde lost his father during the sessions. Yet despite these darkening, choppy waters, an album of bright beauty emerged from the trio's emotional seas. Now the man behind the influential record label Bella Union, Raymonde (**@mrsimonraymonde**) undertook to bring us an emotional look back at this special creative moment for Cocteau Twins.

BANDSTAND presents

COCTEAU
TWINS

plus Support

BARROWLANDS
244 GALLOWGATE,
GLASGOW
THU 25TH OCT/90
7.30PM

£7.50 Advance
000031

(Far left) Heavenly.
A ticket stub for the
band's Glasgow
Barrowland gig in
October 1990 shared
during the Listening
Party by @brianlforbes.

(Left) Les Enfants
Terribles. Cocteau
Twins' Robin Guthrie,
Simon Raymonde and
Elizabeth Fraser in
August 1990.

## 1. CHERRY-COLOURED FUNK

**@mrsimonraymonde**

I think the minute Robin and I finished the music for this piece, we KNEW it was special. We kinda improvised our music out of nothing, and if nothing was happening, we would go bowling…but thankfully not so often during this record.

## 2. PITCH THE BABY

**@mrsimonraymonde**

Beats baby… hip hop… One that was fairly obviously inspired by the birth of [Fraser's daughter] Lucy Belle. Robin should take all the credit for the musical part of this song. I actually didn't like it that much at the time, but grew to realise the error of this thinking

## 3. ICEBLINK LUCK

**@Tim_Burgess**

Stone cold classic. The first time I heard it it Just felt like a hit – I saw the video everywhere, Chart Show, Top of the Pops. Just gorgeous beyond belief.

## 4. FIFTY-FIFTY CLOWN

**@mrsimonraymonde**

Prince sampled this… like THE Prince! Love… thy will be done. He wrote it for Martika and it's just about audible in that version but while this remained in his vault till his death his own version was later released and it's much more obvious.

## 5. HEAVEN OR LAS VEGAS

**@mrsimonraymonde**

The title song was CLASSIC Elizabeth wasn't it. Her backing vocals are SOO UNDERRATED.

## 6. I WEAR YOUR RING

**@mrsimonraymonde**

Wrote the music for this one, and Frou-Frou Foxes in the days following my father's death. But Robin's drums, guitar additions and of course Liz's singing make it so emotional.

## 7. FOTZEPOLITIC

**@mrsimonraymonde**

For a song title that literally translates to 'Cunt politics' it sure is a jaunty little piece of music.

## 8. WOLF IN THE BREAST

**@mrsimonraymonde**

Raymonde and Guthrie in classic bass and guitar combo. I like the ones where I play two bass lines like this. This kinda song writes itself. And Fraser at her ecstatic best looking back on the birth of her first daughter. "Laughing on our bed, pretending us newly wed, especially when our angel unleashed that head-I feel perpetual". AMAZING, amazing. Still can't believe we did some of this stuff…

## 9. ROAD, RIVER AND RAIL

**@mrsimonraymonde**

This one is melancholy and again the classic bass and guitar writing combo. After Liz recorded her amazing vocals, we referred to it as Rod, river and reel. 'Through Paris, Brixton.' These little gems Elizabeth left us are all there. Even if you aren't sure what all the words are you still sing along and have a journey of expression and interaction that is so beautiful.

## 10. FROU-FROU FOXES IN MIDSUMMER FIRES

**@mrsimonraymonde**

The first day back to studio after my Dad's funeral, I was the only one there for a bit, and sat playing the piano. After an hour or so, I had something that I was keeping returning to. Robin walked in and listened quietly. "Don't stop" he said walking straight to the Akai MPC60 and getting his magic beats working. After laying the piano and drums down, we added his lovely textured guitars. Hard to listen to now (he says with tears streaming down the face) but very proud of us for doing it.

# *The Soft Bulletin*
## The Flaming Lips
Warner Bros, 1999

From inviting audience members to dance onstage in fancy-dress costumes, via rolling over the mosh-pit in an inflatable human-sized hamster ball, to showering their crowds repeatedly with balloons and confetti, live The Flaming Lips have become the masters of staging the ultimate sense-dazzling party. Yet, it is just the appropriate accompaniment for the Oklahoma trio's kaleidoscopic music. A musical rainbow of prog sounds, falsetto vocal, heartbreakingly beautiful melodies and sing-a-long sci-fi surreal lyrics (!), frontman Wayne Coyne (**@waynecoyne**), Michael Ivins (bass) and Steven Drozd's (guitars/keyboard – **@stevendrozd**) music is a swirl of the instinctual and the intricate.

PHOTOGRAPHY:
Lawrence Schiller

Unsurprisingly then the band's Listening Party for *The Soft Bulletin* proved to be both chaotic, precise and a proper party. The 1999 record has been released with several different tracklists depending on format and the country it is out in, so there was some confusion as to which order the band would run us through. Drozd opted for the US edition while Coyne seemed to be playing a different edition at his own speed.

Despite running order questions, this Listening Party proved to be rich in detail and even came with its own introductory remarks before pressing play. "The title The Soft Bullet was, initially – like say 2 years before the album came out – meant to 'abstractly' say The Soft Bullet In," wrote Coyne, also revealing the cover image came from a Life magazine book showing people taking LSD. "Luckily, in time, it seemed simpler and cooler just being the word Bulletin but, I knew I liked the title for a future album so I put the title on a cassette (back in maybe 1996) compilation that we listened to a lot in our van. And I knew Steven liked the title and we were starting to think about what kind of songs would be on an album called *The Soft Bulletin*…" The answer is on the following pages.

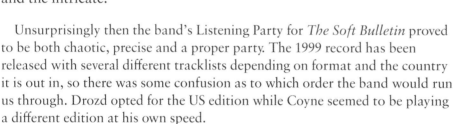

@waynecoyne

.. at the time we were so immersed in our own trip..just self indulgent self creating .. but it's the only way you can do it… we were making music that we knew WE liked.. but there would be times when we thought: we've lost our minds.

↑

Wayne's world. Steven
Drozd, Coyne and
Michael Ivins.

### 1. RACE FOR THE PRIZE

☑ **@waynecoyne**

2 scientists are racing for the cure that is the prize, theirs is to win, if it kills them... It was (at first) meant to be the opening track for Zaireeka [the band's previous album, an experimental release that came on four CDs to be played simultaneously]. Like, BLAM a new world has arrived – a new way to live. It's such a triumphant beginning. But then it just seemed to render the song toooo weird putting it into that fucked-up format of Zaireeka so we kept saving it. So it wasn't till AFTER Zaireeka was done that (with great relief) we started to really get the vibe of what we were doing. Steven had Race For The Prize (wasn't called that) for a bit and he kept re-working the arrangement on his 4-track cassette machine, he stumbled upon the warbly string sound and I was like oh yeah!! Now I get it!!!

### 2. A SPOONFUL WEIGHS A TON

☑ **@waynecoyne**

I didn't have ALL the lyrics for A Spoonful Weighs A Ton. I went to sing the end (which I didn't know what I was gonna sing) and I sang out of nowhere "the sound they made was love". There were times during the recording of A Spoonful that we would get toooo dramatic with too much "over the top" strings and timpani and stuff, we trimmed it back. We were looking for a combination. Walt Disney meets LED Zeppelin. Ha.

### 3. THE SPARK THAT BLED

☑ **@waynecoyne**

Spark That Bled is the perfect collaboration/combination of Steven and mine's different ways of coming up with songs. It is literally pieces put together. I had these 3 different bits that I thought told a "kind of story of an idea that you can't let go of" and MY parts were very very simple and I think in different keys.

### 4. THE SPIDERBITE SONG

☑ **@stevendrozd**

A tearjerker! Classic Wayne lyrics

### 5. BUGGIN'

☑ **@waynecoyne**

Buggin was a little folk song I had for a little while... I think it's always good to have a song about insects, it makes things not sooo serious.

### 6. WHAT IS THE LIGHT?

☑ **@waynecoyne**

What is the light... the way it connects to The Observer track was the way we had it even on the very first demo 4-track. And that little beat puff.. poof.. puff.. poof.. took [producer] Dave Fridmann a while to be satisfied with its sound. He ran it through a Moog patch, I think...

### 7. THE OBSERVER

☑ **@stevendrozd**

It's hokey to say I'm proud of something but I thought we went next level on this one! Wayne's beautiful/eerie gtr melody. Brian Wilson chords in the middle. The middle of The Observer is among my fave moments we've ever made.

### 8. WAITIN' FOR A SUPERMAN

☑ **@waynecoyne**

The opening line of Superman, is it gettin heavy??? I asked you a question, is it gettin heavy?? Jeeez... Once you stumble upon such a great opening line ya can't fuck it up .. Well, ya hope ya don't fuck it up... At the time we were so immersed in our own trip, just self indulgent self creating, but it's the only way you can do it. We were making music that we knew WE liked, but there would be times when we thought we've lost our minds.

Blood ties. Coyne's nun glove puppet was a consistent performer/prop at Flaming Lips shows before the band upgraded to their now-famous bubble balls.

The Flaming Lips certainly made their mark with *The Soft Bulletin*. Not only was the record a breakthrough for the band, but creatively it inspired many.

### 9. SUDDENLY EVERYTHING HAS CHANGED

**@stevendrozd**

Wayne always says the middle instrumental interlude on Suddenly... is where it sounds most Soft Bulletin-esque. Going for late 60s movie soundtrack vibes.

**@waynecoyne**

That first elongated section is pure Steven at his most expressive. It's just unspeakable how it really does feel like a "feeling" instead of sounding like music. And Steven taking that last verse and making it so introspective, my original demo just had each singing segment as the same chords each time. His ability to turn my crude storytelling into sumthin sooo stunningly emotional and beautiful.

### 10. THE GASH

**@stevendrozd**

Oh here comes Armageddon... haha The Gash. We worried we took it too far. Now I'm glad we did all of it.

### 11. SLOW MOTION

**@stevendrozd**

Ok! Slow Motion! An early one that Wayne and I traded back on in fall '96. Cool bass moves by Michael.

### 12. FEELING YOURSELF DISINTEGRATE

**@waynecoyne**

I remember coming up with the chorus and thinking it's just too much. That I didn't really want to say that "out loud". Like, it was fine to say to yourself but, ya can't really say that into the world.

**@stevendrozd**

Feeling Yourself Disintegrate was one of the very last songs done for Bulletin. Summer '98. We felt we got as much emotion out of stuff and this was almost a step back. Feeling Yourself Disintegrate is one of my fave Wayne songs. My [prog rock guitarist] Steve Howe-ish gtr solo at the end was 2nd take!! We were listening to a lot of Marvin Gaye What's Going On and King Crimson!

### 13. SLEEPING ON THE ROOF

**@stevendrozd**

I was so happy with this. Still am. Sounds hokey but I'm very pleased with it! There's a 20 minute version on a 4track cassette somewhere. The outro? That's a refrigerator firing up.

# You Can't Hide Your Love Forever
## Orange Juice
Polydor, 1982

What a year 1982 was for Orange Juice. Coming off the back of helping to define the fledgling indie sound with their early singles for influential Scottish label Postcard, the Glasgow band released two albums within 12 months. In November 1982 *Rip It Up* would create one of the most iconic indie moments ever with its title song, just eight months after they would make a lasting impression on the sound and look of British music with this their debut album, *You Can't Hide Your Love* Forever. With a competitive spirit spurring on Edwyn Collins (guitar/vocals – **@EdwynCollins**), James Kirk (guitar/vocals) David McClymont (bass) and Steven Daly (drums – **@Steveplustax**), the record fizzes with ideas and styles, stitched together by jangly guitars, crooned vocals and glorious harmonies. So here is the Listening Party for what is possibly the only album in the world that observed an official, in-studio pause in proceedings to mark Charles and Di's royal wedding… Clearly, you really can't hide the love.

PHOTOGRAPHY:
Jill Furmanovsky

---

**LISTENING PARTY
9 APRIL 2020**

### 1. FALLING AND LAUGHING

☑ **@EdwynCollins**
When I was 17, walking on the beach in Brora, thinking about how bad my songs were. I wanted to be a muso, but I thought they were sub-standard. Either then or shortly afterwards, I came up with Falling and Laughing. "This is more like it," I thought.

### 2. UNTITLED MELODY

☑ **@Steveplustax (Steven Daly)**
Great song—quite underrated. Always thought it had a wee touch of Big Star's third. The drums were recorded on a four-bar loop. Primitive sampling, innit. Nice of Edwyn to let the wee man [David McClymont] do a bass solo over his.

### 3. WAN LIGHT

☑ **@EdwynCollins**
James Kirk was a 20th century Lord Byron. Evidence – rhyming "steed" and "heed." I loved his archaic turn of phrase, don't you Steven? Do you know what 'wan' means, young people? Do you?

☑ **@Steveplustax**
James Kirk was a most unusual cat, a true original. When James first played us the song, it was only a couple of minutes long. Edzo came up with the "Is this what life is all about?" section to stick on the end. #ValueForMoney ("Wan" means "one" in Glaswegian.)

### 4. TENDER OBJECT

☑ **@EdwynCollins**
James used to call me a tender object. He was mocking me, of course. So I put it in a song, so there! I like the guitar solo, I was getting better.

### 5. DYING DAY

☑ **@EdwynCollins**
I still play this in my set. In fact, I've always played it. It has so many chords, it's crazy, but it's a catchy tune, decent words, I've never gone off it. We were great at this live.

### 6. L.O.V.E. LOVE

🔵 **@EdwynCollins**
And it's L.O.V.E!!!!!! Yikes, we had a cheek. I struggle a bit with this. I like the backing track but my vocals are shit. I must have liked it at some point.

### 7. INTUITION TOLD ME (PART 1)

🔵 **@Steveplustax**
Edwyn mentioned Gershwin as one of his influences. They were a Manchester band, right?

### 8. UPWARDS AND ONWARDS

🔵 **@Steveplustax**
Backing vocals by [Scritti Politti's] Green Gartside. When he showed up at the studio, it was absolute scenes. The staff thought they were getting a visit from Princess Di!

### 9. SATELLITE CITY

🔵 **@EdwynCollins**
This is a mess, these horns are ridiculous. I highly recommend you don't listen to this version. This was not bad when we did it live. Listen to the Glasgow School version instead, from the demo album, Ostrich Churchyard.

### 10. THREE CHEERS FOR OUR SIDE

🔵 **@Steveplustax**
James [Kirk] in excelsis. I'm not crying you're crying.

🔵 **@EdwynCollins**
Very good lyrics. "We sit here, in torpor, by our old fireside; and just agree to differ, three cheers for our side." What can I say? James is a genius. Dodgy backing vocals though. Some strange things happened.

### 11. CONSOLATION PRIZE

🔵 **@Steveplustax**
Stephen Pastel [Stephen McRobbie of fellow Glasgow-based indie band The Pastels] said something kind of insightful in an OJ radio documentary. He said that the group was actually kind of avant garde. "Avant garde boy band" – I quite like that… Platinum logic! There is it on the outro, the birth of Madchester indie! Our gift to you.

### 12. FELICITY

🔵 **@EdwynCollins**
Whhoah Whhoah!!! Felicity! James wrote it and let me sing it. Thank you James. I came up the whoa whoa whoa bit, for dramatic effect.

### 13. IN A NUTSHELL

🔵 **@EdwynCollins**
It's a pretty song but quite vicious. I wish I could remember who I was angry at. I like the line about looking behind the iron curtain. James was such a good lyricist, I think he made me try hard to match up to him. We were vibing off each other, you know? Although it was always a James song or an Edwyn song, we did write bits together and come up with suggestions for each other. It's a really long time when you're young kids. We knew each other, all our good points, really well, and we made each other laugh. We had the time of our lives.

⬇

Orange Juice in 1982, the last time Edwyn Collins (centre) listened to *You Can't Hide Your Love Forever* before the Listening Party.

# *The Three E.P.'s*
## The Beta Band
Regal, 1998

Individually, EPs Champion Versions, *The Patty Patty Sound* and *Los Amigos del Beta Bandidos* were releases that commanded attention. Visionary yet lo-fi, organic yet experimental, each four-song release from The Beta Band offered an insight into this mysterious group from Fife who were pushing boundaries and emotions. Yet when combined as a single, album-length release in 1998, an alchemy occurred. Despite covering a period that went from bedsit home recordings to state-of-the-art studios, and the band's changing membership – co-founder Gordon Anderson would later front the much admired The Aliens and bassist Steve Duffield would leave frontman Steve Mason (**@SteveMasonKBT**) and keyboard player John Maclean (**@johnbetamac**) during the period, while drummer Robin Jones and bassist Richard Greentree would join – there is a shimmering cohesiveness to *The Three E.P.'s*. Golden guitars mesh with homemade production techniques, field recordings with hypnotic beats, creating a 12-track record that is deep and dark, yet immediate and brimming with blissful feeling. John Cusack famously sells five copies of the album in the film version of High Fidelity just by playing opening track Dry The Rain. Sharing stories and jogging one another's memories on the way, Mason and Maclean threw a Listening Party that truly sold the magic behind *The Three E.P.'s*.

ARTWORK:
Brian Cannon

⊕

(Left to right) An early mock-up of the Champion Versions EP sleeve; John Maclean recording B + A; the band in 2001.

## 1. DRY THE RAIN

✅ **@SteveMasonKBT**

Was the first song of mine we worked on. This really captures that time for me. Just the 3 of us with Gordon coming in and out of the picture. Very simple time. Very creative. I love this song.

## 2. I KNOW

✅ **@johnbetamac (John Maclean)**

The was one of the very few songs I wrote and 'sang'. Me and Steve made it in a few hours – I lay down the samples and beats and vocal, I think the bass was a sample too - and Steve laid down the guitar in one take.

## 3. B + A

✅ **@SteveMasonKBT**

The demo of this is a monster but we really really struggled in the studio to get it right. Called in [The Verve's] Nick McCabe to help out.

## 4. DOGS GOT A BONE

✅ **@SteveMasonKBT**

Another favourite. So simple. Me, Robin and Gordon wrote it sitting on John's bed. Trading lines. I always forget how great this is. Our stuff got real complex after the 3 E.P.'s but these simple tracks are amazing.

## 5. INNER MEET ME

✅ **@SteveMasonKBT**

I dreamt this song and woke up and quickly recorded it on a tape player. Dream was I was in the centre of our universe and the planets were singing me this song.

## 6. THE HOUSE SONG

✅ **@johnbetamac**

This was really for the live shows. We had the acoustic guitars and bongos and bird song, but we were also all ravers and hip hop heads too.

## 7. MONOLITH

✅ **@johnbetamac**

I think this was a result of my obsession with Chill Out by the KLF – I lined up 30 samples on my keyboard and we miked up the entire studio and just did whatever for 16 minutes – no overdubs, no edits. Then we all had 4 faders each and whatever happened, happened and we mixed it once. I had this crazy sticker system colour coded for playing live, with a sample on each key I could hit in time with Robin's drumming to keep nothing sequenced – all organic.

## 8. SHE'S THE ONE

✅ **@SteveMasonKBT**

Even though it's called She's The One this song was about me and Gordon. I really missed him and his talent around this time. I was panicking inside. And out actually.

## 9. PUSH IT OUT

✅ **@johnbetamac**

If Patty Patty EP was us getting together as a live band, Los Amigos was us getting to grips with studio recording and a massive percussion budget from EMI, so we hired tuned sleigh bells and any strange instrument we could get our hands on.

## 10. IT'S OVER

✅ **@johnbetamac**

I'm not sure where the lyrics came from, I didn't have a book or anything, I was thinking about what you think of yourself and what people think of you. About reassurance too, I think.

## 11. DR. BAKER

✅ **@johnbetamac**

I remember Steve producing this one – the plate reverbs and stripped back sound – I came up with a very simple piano hook, staying within my playing ability.

## 12. NEEDLES IN MY EYES

✅ **@SteveMasonKBT**

Brilliant, nice simple song. Recorded outside on the harbour wall at Sawmills. We all swapped instruments. So loose and fragile. Me and Rich had a massive fight the night before, so tension was HIGH! Really added to the vibe.

# *Different Class*
## Pulp
Island, 1995

☇ As inspirations go, *Different Class'* influences are a set apart – and with the storytelling eye of Jarvis Cocker, a lyrical director able to cut seamlessly from cold voyeurism to the intimate heart of the action, Pulp's fifth album truly lived up to its title.

Having finally achieved success with preceding album *His N Hers* following nearly a decade of unappreciated effort on the indie circuit, there was a possibility fame could have gone to the Sheffield band's head. After all, two songs destined for this album were virtually debuted during Pulp's headlining set at Glastonbury 1995 when the group stood in for The Stones Roses at the last minute. Yet that experience, and these songs, served to connect Jarvis Cocker, Russell Senior (guitar/violin), Candida Doyle (keyboards), Steve Mackey (bass), Mark Webber (guitar/keyboards – **@pulp2011**) and Nick Banks (drums – **@TheRealNickBank**) to the people in a unique way. From its kitchen-sink dramas and after-hours tales, to hopeful love songs and anthems inspired by living your life your own way, *Different Class* is a record that has filled dancefloors, and soundtracked weddings.

"All the stuff that I write about is taken from my own life anyway," explained Jarvis on the album's release, inadvertently capturing why audiences connected with Pulp so passionately. "I thought to myself that I was actually working undercover, trying to observe the world, taking notes for future reference, secretly subverting society. And one day, when the time was right, I would come out of the shadows and pounce on the world." And pounce Pulp certainly did – for this Listening Party Banks and Webber took stock of what puts this record in a *Different Class*.

PHOTOGRAPHY:
Donald Milne

**@TheRealNickBank**
From the [Mis-Shapes] video. The local misfits meet the "townies" down the "disco" and the revolution begins.

✔ **@pulp2011** (Mark Webber)
I guess this is something like a call to arms from us to all the other freaks & weirdos. (Like you lot.)

⊕

(Below)
**@TheRealNickBank**
We often got mixes through the recording on good old cassette.

(Below right)
**@TheRealNickBank**
El Jarv, looking like something from a teen love story mag – he was one years and years ago in fact – though only once. Horrid shirt. His speciality.

## 1. MIS-SHAPES

☑ **@TheRealNickBank**
What an opener, a call to arms, a rallying cry, now is the time to storm the barricades; it's our time. If you ever been bullied, called a weirdo, hit, spat at for being, looking or feeling different... this is your tune!

☑ **@TheRealNickBank**
Candida recalls: Most of the LP was written above Nick's mum's pottery warehouse in Catcliffe on the outskirts of Sheffield, towards Rotherham. In a railway arch, we could only use it after 4pm which suited us as early starts just didn't happen.

## 2. PENCIL SKIRT

☑ **@pulp2011 (Mark Webber)**
Fade in? How radical. Better to fade in than to fade out.

☑ **@TheRealNickBank**
Has quite a claustrophobic feel at the start. The tension builds nicely. Close miked singing drawing you in to Jarvis' pervy world. Mucky. We often got mixes through the recording on good old cassette...

## 3. COMMON PEOPLE

☑ **@TheRealNickBank**
CP is a song that can only have been written from an outsider's perspective. Especially moving from Sheffield to London. You meet some right types, and it often amplifies your background and circumstances. It can often seem like us and

them. Always great to play live and is rightly seen as our 'signature' choon. When it was played at Glasto '95 was the first time we experienced the whole crowd singing along and it was a very special moment.

## 4. I SPY

☑ **@TheRealNickBank**
Over dramatic? Nah!! Lush orchestration provided by Anne Dudley who has done loads of famous soundtracks and worked with everyone from Elton to us!

☑ **@pulp2011**
Anne conducted strings for a great version of I Spy on Later with Jools Holland. We later asked her to play the lead piano on This Is Hardcore after Jarvis, Mark, Candida and Chris Thomas had all failed to make the grade.

## 5. DISCO 2000

☑ **@TheRealNickBank**
Album version of course – the single was a remixed version by Alan Tarney who did loads of Cliff Richard classics and A-Ha stuff – super cheesy! Right up our strasse! Prefer the LP version though, got loads more grit, etc. Easiest video we ever did as we are represented as the cardboard cut outs as used on the Diff Class cover – didn't even have to turn up!!

*Handwritten track listing:*

Pulp

SIDE A
1. Pencil Skirt   2/3/95 (Rough)
2. Ska   7/3/95 (Rough)
3. Mile End-   9/3/95 (V. Rough)
4. Common People   4:07
   7" MASTER
5. Common People   5:41
   LP MASTER
6. Common People   6:25
   Club MASTER

SIDE B
1. Monday Morning   4:15
   (SKA Song) MASTER
   29/3/95
2. Underwear-   4:0
   Prod MASTER
3. BAR Italia   ☕
   (Rough mix 1) 24/3/95
4. Microstop
   (Rough Mix 2) 2/3/95
5. Pencil Skirt - MASTER   3

**B MAG**
TOUTE LA MUSIQUE

**PULP**
JARVIS COCKER
SEX, POP
& ECSTASY

**DIFFERENT CLASS**

NOUVEL ALBUM
SORTIE LE 30 OCTOBRE

ⓡ ISLAND

JOE STRUMMER PARLE

## 6. LIVE BED SHOW

☑ **@pulp2011**

This is a great song. An opening instrumental verse with Jarvis lead guitar part was edited out of the LP version but appeared on a b-side. A few years later we indulged ourselves in concert with a long disco outro tagged onto the end. I bought an MXR Phase 90 pedal to use on this song. Made me feel like I was in Led Zeppelin. Which reminds me … The man we bought our Mellotron from said it was the actual one used on "Stairway to Heaven". No doubt this is what every Mellotron salesman says. I was living in above a chip shop on Hornsey Road at this time. Sharing a flat with Chris & Simon from Menswear!!! Fortunately they were also busy, so we were rarely home at the same time. This is where I slept in the corner of my room.

## 7. SOMETHING CHANGED

☑ **@pulp2011**

Something Changed was an old song that Jarvis dredged up and we all dusted off. There's a rehearsal tape of a previous incarnation of Pulp attempting it circa 1984. No, that's not a typo in the year! This was the first time I sat down to really try and write a guitar solo, in the days before we recorded the demo at Axis in Sheffield. Didn't turn out so bad.

☑ **@TheRealNickBank**

A love song, simple as that but so very effective. Written years before, I think, with help from Jarvis's sister, Saskia. Again a superbly lush orchestration from Anne Dudley, it really fits the song plus heavy use of the ol' 12 string. Many Pulp fans have told us they either had this as the first dance at their wedding or even walked down the aisle to it.

## 8. SORTED FOR E'S & WIZZ

☑ **@TheRealNickBank**

In the late 80's we did quite a bit of raving – living in a 14th floor squat in Camberwell… and at times it really did feel like the world could change. I didn't, and all got a bit messy really. This song came out of that 'experience'. This was a phrase Jarv heard once whilst out at a said 'rave' and it stuck. Even though the song did get up the nose of the tabloids back in the day… it is really more of an anti-drug song emphasising the inevitable come downs that follow over use.

→

The cover of the Daily Mirror, 20 September 1995.
**@TheRealNickBank:** The tabloids didn't like it [Sorted For Es N Whizz]… so what?

**BAN THIS SICK STUNT**

Chart stars sell CD with DIY kids' drugs guide

DRUGS ROW: Singer Jarvis Cocker

**EXCLUSIVE**
By KATE THORNTON

POP idols Pulp were blasted last night for offering teenage fans a DIY guide on hiding illegal drugs.

Anti-drug campaigners branded the instructions on the band's new single a "sick stunt".

The sleeve of their CD Sorted for Es and Wizz, released on Monday, carries a diagram of how to make a special

● Turn to Page 4

↑

Common People.
Jarvis Cocker and
Candida Doyle in
1995.

**@pulp2011**

We were recording Top of the Pops the day it all kicked off. Island Records brought in a specialist tabloid consultant (!) to advise Jarvis on how to respond & handle it all. This was all new for us.

### 9. F.E.E.L.I.N.G.C.A.L.L.E.D.L.O.V.E.

**@TheRealNickBank**

I remember Jarvis buying a knackered 'Synare' synth drum from a junk shop and bringing it to rehearsal and asking if I could do some kind of drum start incorporating the 'synare' This song came out of that really.

### 10. UNDERWEAR

**@TheRealNickBank**

Underwear was one of the first tracks we recorded for the record I think…. it was a long time ago… More grubby musings from JC. Firm fan favourite and always good to play live, plenty of light and shade, quiet and loud bits.

### 11. MONDAY MORNING

**@TheRealNickBank**

The bit after "Stomach in chest out, etc…" Was always a bit of a lottery when playing live as Jarvis liked to stretch that bit out for some dramatic tension and the cue to come back in was that Jarv would leap in the air and we all had to come in as his feet hit the floor. Surprisingly it nearly always went right…

### 12. BAR ITALIA

**@TheRealNickBank**

Homage to the famous Soho, London Coffee Bar on Frith Street. After a heavy night 'Out' the waifs would often end the night here with a sobering coffee. Brilliant place that opened late or early, depending on how big the night had been. I never particularly went as I would never end the night with a mere coffee.

# Dog Man Star
## Suede
Nude, 1994

It might seem obvious to say where you are standing really alters your perspective, but it's strange how often it applies to how we hear music, too. To the fans and their contemporaries, Suede's opus-like second album *Dog Man Star* is a remarkable triumph. Ambitious and epic, it took the London band's chemical noir-indie and unfurled it across the night sky with lung-busting vocals, epic guitar solos and expanded instrumental horizons that seem to have put Brett Anderson (vocals), Bernard Butler (guitars), Mat Osman (bass – **@MatOsman**) and Simon Gilbert (drums) on a new creative level. However, for the band and the album's producer, Ed Buller (**@Ed_Buller**), at the time there was a sense of a missed opportunity. Claiming his ambitions for the record had been thwarted, Butler left the band towards the end of the sessions, while the others have since spoken about their studio regrets and the changes they would like to have made. Yet despite this apparent blemish, *Dog Man Star* not only remains an impressive album, but one that is truly loved. For the Listening Party, Osman and Buller reunited on Twitter to offer a frank, yet finally celebratory, insight into a record that for all its so-called flaws, truly soars.

**PHOTOGRAPHY:**
Joanne Leonard

**SLEEVE DESIGN:**
Brian Cannon

(→)
Tagging the Asphalt World.
Graffiti featuring Suede's
second album title in 1994.

→

@jo_napoli
Derby assembly room 1996 was pretty good.

(Below) Introducing the band who recorded *Dog Man Star*, Brett Anderson, Bernard Butler – who would leave during the recording session – Mat Osman and Simon Gilbert.

### 1. INTRODUCING THE BAND

⊘ **@MatOsman**
Inspired by a trip to a Japanese temple with famed Manics photographer Mitch Ikeda. That's a miked up Leslie cabinet and some fretless bass. All piano is Bernard I think. Ed Buller might have played a bit. Bit of Alice in Wonderland in there.

### 2. WE ARE THE PIGS

⊘ **@MatOsman**
Now there's a riff! The chorus lyrics actually predate Suede. From Brett's teenage band The Pigs. The record company BEGGED us not to make it the first single. They wanted Wild Ones. Should have been, in retrospect. Best solo on the record coming up. The Kick Horns sleazing it up a bit too.

⊘ **@Ed_Buller**
A great little guitar solo. Not sure if that Brass worked, wanted Peter Gunn [the Henry Mancini composed theme for the US television series].

⊘ **@MatOsman**
Nah, I love those horns

### 3. HEROINE

⊘ **@MatOsman**
About as gothy as we got I reckon. I mean, if you're going to steal... Great middle eight – what an odd key change. Fuck I'd forgotten how atonal that end was.

### 4. THE WILD ONES

⊘ **@MatOsman**
I always feel like this song belongs to you lot more than us. It's the one song that lives out there in other people's lives. I don't know if anyone's ever mentioned what an obvious influence [Jacques Brel's] Ne Me Quitte Pas is on Wild Ones. The long version of this is out there somewhere. It's lovely but I'm so glad we cut it to Motown-song length. A Japanese fan once sent us a message that read 'punk rockers hair and songs should be short'. Sweet strings. Not too fussy.

### 5. DADDY'S SPEEDING

⊘ **@MatOsman**
Now this I love. Though I don't think I'm actually on it. Brett had a book with the crashed James Dean Porsche pic long before this track. The thing is, when we came to play this live for the Dog Man Star shows, it's actually a really simple song. It's the arrangement and production that makes it feel so strange. So many little lines tucked away behind the sound. That little orange phaser really got a workout on this one. Brett is as obsessed with cars as only a non-driver can be [ironically, the singer's dad is a taxi driver]. Genuinely the worst sense of direction of any human being I've ever met.

### 6. THE POWER

**@MatOsman**

I think I'm the only one in the band who really likes The Power. I think it's such a clever song about the relationship between a band and its fans. There's a kind of subtle, consensual S&M thing going on. And it mentions Cathay [European historical name for China], like we're bewhiskered Victorian explorers.

**@Ed_Buller**

Shame, this had big Promise. Needed Bernard.

### 7. NEW GENERATION

**@MatOsman**

Basically our Motown attempt.

**@Ed_Buller**

A song with TWO, count em, TWO choruses. Poor Brett. Bernard refused to change the key so he is singing right at the top of his range, had to help him on only one note though! Such a great song. SUCH an awful MIX. I'm full of shame.

**@MatOsman**

Man the acoustic guitar is LOUD in this. Brett's easily the best whistler in the band [and features towards the end of the track]. Coulda been a professional.

### 8. THIS HOLLYWOOD LIFE

**@MatOsman**

I remember hearing the guitar riff and just being 'let me at it'. So great to play live this. I remember a stripper in San Francisco saying this and *She* were the best Suede songs to strip to. Which is nice.

### 9. THE 2 OF US

**@MatOsman**

2 Of Us is a bit special. Bernard's piano playing always made for really classic songs. Something about the simplicity. My favourite lyric on the album. That sweet spot between despair and romance. This is the track you hired a tap-dancer [to provide percussion] for, right Ed Buller?

**@Ed_Buller**

Yes... Not my finest moment.

**@MatOsman**

Title written that way is a Prince ref, obviously. *Sometimes It Snows In April* was a total influence.

### 10. BLACK OR BLUE

**@MatOsman**

Right I'm really not sure about the instrumentation on this. Autoharp? This was pretty much done by the time I came to play on it. Just trying to find a line through massed guitars. So liquid those guitars. The structure of this and 2 of Us is really clever; verses get shorter and choruses expand. Does something to your sense of time.

### 11. THE ASPHALT WORLD

**@veriteehill [fan]**

The song I've been waiting for...Asphalt World!! There are so many beautiful lyrics in this song that create such vivid imagery. I've always been curious about "a dove in her head", I like to think it represents peace.

**@MatOsman**

Sadly not... it was a brand of ecstasy!

**@veriteehill [fan]**

Ooooooo thank you so much for clearing that up!!! I was always curious about that lyric. I am clearly not versed on my ecstasy brands.

**@MatOsman**

For some reason this whole song plays in my head if I drive along The Westway at night. Taxi song. Someone on the Insatiable Ones [Suede fan] forum actually worked out what that snippet of film dialogue was from. It was just whatever was playing at the time, not chosen for its significance. [It is Lauren Bacall in 1954 film Woman's World]

### 12. STILL LIFE

**@MatOsman**

Most of this orchestration is Ed Buller's doing. It's so un-rock. I mean, its great. But it's kind of hilarious too. Maybe we should have kept the orchestra for just the outro. Total baller move. Phew. I need a lie down. That was fantastic.

New Generation. "It was our imperial phase," Brett Anderson later said of *Dog Man Star*. "Everything we were writing felt like gold dust. But we knew people were listening and with that comes hubris."

# *Up The Bracket*
## The Libertines
Rough Trade, 2002

**PHOTOGRAPHY:**
Roger Sargent

There is something both timeless and unique about The Libertines. On one hand they are a classic "band of brothers". A camaraderie born right from the off when Carl Barât (vocals/guitar – **@CarlBaratMusic**), Peter Doherty (vocals/guitar – **@PeteDoherty**), John Hassall (bass – **@JohnCoryHassall**) and Gary Powell (drums – **@gdogg27**) would all wear the same red tunics for gigs and photoshoots, while co-frontmen Pete and Carl would often share spittle-flecked mics at gigs, leaving many listeners in the early days trying to guess who was singing what on their frenzied, vivid, yet charmingly melodic songs. At the same time, each of The Libertines – as the name suggests – is a true individual. All have their own groups outside the band, some run record labels, others have appeared in opera. One has been hounded by the law and the tabloids, while another was recently blanked at his own gig by a senior politician who had addressed the band's crowd before they played. They have harmonised and fought with each other, but the lesson from Peter and Carl is that you might not always be friends with your best friends, but you need them. Stick with those you love.

The Libertines' album *Up The Bracket* is the artistic expression of this brilliant contradiction, so when it came to the Listening Party it was inevitable there would be multiple Twitter accounts busy swapping broadsides *and* recollections. Still there is no better, or more honest, way to chart the organised chaos that created The Libertines' generation-influencing debut album.

@PeteDoherty (Peter Doherty)

## Boys In The Band

Horrorshow. Carl Barât in the band's shared Bethnal Green flat, christened the Albion Rooms. The scene of many "guerrilla gigs", visitors claimed the pile of washing-up was particularly epic.

## 1. VERTIGO

**@PeteDoherty**

I remember vividly and fondly getting the tube to the studio from the original Albion Rooms, Teesdale Street. The sessions always had a strict break at 6pm so Mick Jones [member of The Clash and producer for Up The Bracket] could watch the last night's episode of Eastenders which he religiously recorded - we had dinner and played ping pong.

**@CarlBaratMusic**

Hitchcock and Hancock were the inspirations here, plus a girl I met on a canal boat when I was 15, Karima. Stories of hapless romance, forever walking under ladders, like calamity James from the Beano, or wailing beneath balconies, and finding bravery in unlikely places.

## 2. DEATH ON THE STAIRS

**@CarlBaratMusic**

This has always been my favourite song of ours. I was too drunk to stand in the Albion Rooms and @petedoherty made me write a riff to the verse chords, he recorded it on his Nokia 3310 as the answerphone message so's we were able to remember it the next day and finish the song. The lyrics came from an old poem we wrote and a little added inspiration from the Times Literary supplement we kept next to the toilet.

## 3. HORRORSHOW

**@CarlBaratMusic**

Still too much of a horror to play, this one sometimes. Fucking fast. We filmed an amazingly bad video in the 90's of this in St Pancras Graveyard and an abandoned mental hospital in Dalston with Pete's then girlfriend. It looked like a student re-make of Nosferatu.

## 4. TIME FOR HEROES

**@CarlBaratMusic**

This one does what it says on the tin, brings back too many memories to possibly do justice here, riots and dreams etc... I remember when I met @GrahamCoxon and he told me he'd seen me on Top of the Pops and had loved my 'anti guitar solo'. I've no idea what he meant but I was fucking happy. I still fuck up the anti solo pretty regularly as it goes.

## 5. BOYS IN THE BAND

**@PeteDoherty**

I remember recording Boys In The Band. Everything was so fucking loud I had to stuff Tampax in my ears.

**@CarlBaratMusic**

This one takes me back to the time when we were working behind the bar at Filthy McNasty's and the Vodka And Cokes [The Libertines' rhyming slang for labelmates The Strokes] had hit it big and we felt a little left out.

## 6. RADIO AMERICA

**@CarlBaratMusic**

Such a sweet and innocent ditty and a nod to The Libertines' skiffly beginnings, taken with a massive dose of drugs'n'liquor.

### @JohnCoryHassall

Listen hard for when @CarlBaratMusic falls asleep during recording and his head bumps on the mic.... he, he, he.

## 7. UP THE BRACKET

### @PeteDoherty

Written in Dalston Lane at Maraid's gaff was about standing up to muggers and has a secret coded bar chord historical theme. Take a certain La's track – possibly/possibly not the melody always finds me (Timeless Melody) – for the verse. Insert a chorus straight out of The Smiths' I Want The One I Can't Have and stream through the core a defiant lyrical theme akin to Hard To Explain' by the Vodka And Cokes [The Strokes].

### @gdogg27 (Gary Powell)

Think this was the track that kind of gave us our sound. Plus we spent so much time by the Caledonia Road it ain't funny!

## 8. TELL THE KING

### @JohnCoryHassall

This is one of my favourite songs. This is all recorded pretty much live apart from vocals and some guitars.

### @gdogg27

Took about three days to record! I couldn't play it in time! Kept quiet about it though and no one gave me any jip about it either!!!

## 9. THE BOY LOOKED AT JOHNNY

### @CarlBaratMusic

The Boy Looked at Johnny... Rotten, not [Razorlight frontman] Borrell. I remember one of the technicians at the rehearsal room sneered 'Don't you know who I think I am' at me. He was right. Love the li-de-di moment. Actually quite pertinent if a Londoner happens to find themselves homesick in the Big Apple.

## 10. BEGGING

### @CarlBaratMusic

These little kids on a Kings Cross estates used to take the piss out of us as we sauntered by in our charity shop finery en-route to rehearsals shouting 'You lot are begging mate.'

## 11. THE GOOD OLD DAYS

### @CarlBaratMusic

Still as true as the day she was penned. These are the good old days. It's a fucker they changed Bodecia's name to Boudica though. Really fucks the song up if you sing it like that.

## 12. I GET ALONG

### @CarlBaratMusic

So proud of how this one came out. Mick Jones nailed it – and so did Bernard Butler [who did a version for a standalone EP]. You can hear my whisky bottle (Famous Grouse) being chucked in the metal ashtray at the end of the take. Job well done.

### @PeteDoherty

We wrote and recorded and released Up The Bracket whilst thinking we were getting on and getting old – in fact, in reality, we were younger than the dew drops on winter lawn and frozen just as fast.

*Up The Bracket*, up the road. The Libertines playing live in Peterborough in 2002, while below the raucous Rangers engage in some team bonding in Southend, the same year.

Bilo & Biggles, AKA Pete and Carl onstage.

# *Our Favourite Shop*
## The Style Council
Polydor, 1985

⚲ Being in an era-defining band that both charts, entertains and informs the culture around you is a once-in-a-lifetime thing. Unless you are Paul Weller. After The Jam rattled cages in the late '70s and early '80s with their precision mod songs, their frontman disbanded the group at their commercial peak and returned a year or so later with The Style Council. Drawing on the more playful and international side of modernism, the group, driven by his collaboration with organist Mick Talbot, used a wider palette than Weller's first band. European chic meshed with English vaudeville, sounds from South America merged with '80s pop signatures, while a lightness of touch went hand-in-hand with politically informed lyrics. Arguably *Our Favourite Shop* is The Style Council's masterpiece, where all these elements balanced perfectly. "I think of sunshine when I think of *Our Favourite Shop*," suggested Weller during this Listening Party. "The subject matter's pretty grim but it's off-set with some beautiful tunes and melodies."

Naturally for a record that boasts so many different aspects, the people joining its playback were suitably varied. Weller, who does not usually tweet himself, used the account of Tim's record label, O Genesis Recordings (**@OGenesisRecords**), to share his thoughts. Style Council drummer Steve White (**@DrummerWhitey**) was also on hand, as was Simon Halfon (**@Halfon**) who designed the album's sleeve. Teenage fan of the record, now political journalist, John Harris (**@johnharris1969**) added his insight, while The Style Council's historical (if any group has an historian it has to be this one) Mr Cool's Dream (**@MrCoolsDream**) provided context and character.

PHOTOGRAPHY:
Olly Ball

SLEEVE DESIGN:
Simon Halfon

Men of great promise. An autographed Polaroid of Weller and Talbot from 1985.

✔ **@OGenesisRecords** (Paul Weller)

I felt we covered a lot of the styles of music we were into – Latin, jazz, soul and R&B, pop etc. But we covered those styles successfully I think, because the album still has a great cohesive sound and shape to it.

Holiday shopping. The Style Council's Paul Weller, Dee C Lee and Mick Talbot in 1985.

LISTENING PARTY
**15 APRIL 2020**

### 1. HOMEBREAKERS

✔ **@OGenesisRecords (Paul Weller)**
My fave tune on the album. It was Mick's tune and I did the lyric for it. Love the atmosphere on it. Mick's voice really works on it too.

✔ **@DrummerWhitey**
Superb lyrics, brave and fearless opener , heartfelt vocals, get on your bike said Sir Norman Tebbitt.

### 2. ALL GONE AWAY

✔ **@OGenesisRecords**
I felt we were writing about what was happening in our country but that's what music had always done. That's in all folk music around the world. As a source of information issued as entertainment.

### 3. COME TO MILTON KEYNES

✔ **@DrummerWhitey**
Come to Milton Keynes, music hall whimsy and satire – the burghers of MK were very upset.

✔ **@OGenesisRecords**
So many great musicians on this record. John Mealing the arranger was just so clever and really got the ideas. Lots of very good brass players too.

### 4. INTERNATIONALISTS

✔ **@MrCoolsDream**
An anthem, or as near to possible to one. biting lyrics, great drumming and a great end to the live set.

### 5. A STONES THROW AWAY

⊙ @JohnHarris1969

I can't emphasise enough how this record spoke to/educated/soundtracked the life of so many politicised young people (like me, aged 15) in 1985. I used to read the quotations on the sleeve most days. And this song in particular.

### 6. THE STAND UP COMIC'S INSTRUCTIONS

⊙ @OGenesisRecords

I felt we covered a lot of the styles of music we were into – latin, jazz, soul and R&B, pop etc. But we covered those styles successfully I think, because the album still has a great cohesive sound and shape to it.

### 7. BOY WHO CRIED WOLF

⊙ @Tim_Burgess

Lush orchestrated strings and squelchy synths - lovely vocals by [Style Council co-vocalist] Dee C. Lee – a real favourite.

### 8. A MAN OF GREAT PROMISE

⊙ @DrummerWhitey

Once again beautiful lyrics with lament and poignant meaning supported by a dark yet bittersweet orchestration. All those little chimes...

### 9. DOWN IN THE SEINE

⊙ @DrummerWhitey

What pop drummer gets to play in 3/4 and with brushes, and then a verse in French! Get in.

### 10. THE LODGERS (OR SHE WAS ONLY A SHOPKEEPER'S DAUGHTER)

⊙ @Halfon

What a tune – 80s and it's summer...

### 11. LUCK

⊙ @MrCoolsDream

That young romantic Paul Weller liked to write a love song...

↑
Snap! Paul Weller was keen to embrace the visual side of the band, as art director Simon Halfon revealed during the Listening Party, even going so far as to build their own 'shop' in a photo studio for the album artwork.

## 12. WITH EVERYTHING TO LOSE

✓ **@DrummerWhitey**
The juxtaposition of the Latin groove and really hard hitting lyrics could have not worked but this is genuine political comment on an album that went to no 1!

## 13. OUR FAVOURITE SHOP

✓ **@DrummerWhitey**
Big fat instrumentals! Mick Talbot's one of the best Hammond players ever!

## 14. WALLS COME TUMBLING DOWN!

✓ **@Halfon**
What are track – Instant Karma for the 80s. Steve White doing the job of two drummers at once. Design-wise we were really given the freedom to just do as we pleased – there was no plan – just having fun and wind up the wrong (or right) people...

✓ **@DrummerWhitey**
Probably one of the best pop singles ever?

Shipshape. Weller, Lee and the rest of the band on set to film a video for The Lodgers (Or She Was Only a Shopkeeper's Daughter) in 1985. "For me, Our Favourite Shop is the best we did," Weller told the Llistening Party of his band's efforts on this record.

# *Dogrel*
## Fontaines D.C.
Partisan, 2019

❦ The first thing that hits you about Fontaines D.C.'s music is the snarling energy that informs every song. The second thing, almost simultaneously, is the poetry that rests on these serrated edges. Sharp and to the point, both lyrically and musically, the Dublin band are a true collision of anger and beauty. Capturing this spirit on record, not to mention the flows of emotion that ebbs from youthful disillusionment to tender affection, was no straightforward task. Fortunately the band – Grian Chatten (vocals), Carlos O'Connell (guitar – **@FontainesDublin**), Conor Curley (guitar/piano), Conor Deegan III (bass) and Tom Coll (drums – also **@FontainesDublin**) – formed a partnership with wonderfully unconventional – and acclaimed – producer Dan Carey (**@SpeedyWunder**). Famed for his unorthodox sessions in a converted church with unusual instruments, disco lights and laser illuminations, Carey set about capturing Fontaines D.C. on record by recording the band live to tape – a rare occurrence in the age of computer-driven, digital recording. This old-fashioned approach proved the perfect method for distilling the essence of a band who hit you with their freshness. Fittingly then, Carey joined the Fontaines' O'Connell and Coll to shed some light on an album that was – partially at least – recorded in the dark (with lasers).

PHOTOGRAPHY:
Bruce Davidson

SLEEVE DESIGN:
Matt de Jong

The famous Fender Mustang guitar, owned by producer Dan Carey and used on 90 per cent of the album.

(Bottom row, left to right) The album was recorded live to tape, an unusual practice with the advent of digital studios, but key to the record's atmosphere; Grian Chatten in the studio; Dan Carey, working his magic.

**LISTENING PARTY**
**16 APRIL 2020**

(Top row, left to right) Carlos O'Connell, stepping up; Grian Chatten and Dan Carey in the studio; from the Too Real photoshoot.

### 1. BIG

✅ **@FontainesDublin**

Tom: Big was the first tune we recorded in Dan's studio in Streatham. We recorded the album in 15 minute blocks to tape so the whole thing is made up of blocks of 2 or 3 songs with the idea being trying to re-create what a live gig is like.

✅ **@SpeedyWunder (Dan Carey)**

Deego [Conor Deegan, bassist] said that Grian asked him to write a bassline that sounded like he'd been hit on the head with a brick.

### 2. SHA SHA SHA

✅ **@FontainesDublin**

Tom: My favourite overdub on the album is me hitting a spring suspended from the roof of the studio with a stick that Dan somehow mic'd up. You can hear it in the chorus if you really listen.

### 3. TOO REAL

✅ **@FontainesDublin**

Tom: This is my favourite tune to play live.It's such a fun one to play on the drums. This is Dan's beautiful old Rogers kit I recorded Dogrel with.

✅ **@SpeedyWunder**

We recorded it on 2 rolls of tape partly for sound but partly so we didn't keep multiple takes. if anything went wrong we went back to the start of the tape and wiped it

### 4. TELEVISION SCREENS

✅ **@FontainesDublin**

Carlos: Listened to this song for the first time in years the day of the anniversary [of the release] this week. So pleased with the sound we got here. Favourite thing about it is the sound of Dan's 1965 Mustang with the pickups out of phase. I used that guitar on 90% of the album.

71

### 5. HURRICANE LAUGHTER

**@FontainesDublin**

Tom: I remember Grian writing this tune on my couch in the Liberties in Dublin in what must have been late 2016. I didn't think I'd be talking about it on Twitter years later.

**@FontainesDublin**

Carlos: One of my favourite overdubs on the album is the Clavioline, big part of the low end over Hurricane. Organic subs. Though Tom in this might be better, whatever it is that was going on there.

### 6. ROY'S TUNE

**@SpeedyWunder**

It's worth pointing out that most of the instrumental tracks were recorded live – mostly in one or two takes, and we just had one track left on the tape for vocals, so Grian did most of those in one take too. I was also really keen for all the lyrics to be very audible, so I mixed the vocal very separate from the music. Some people didn't like it at the time.

### 7. THE LOTTS

**@FontainesDublin**

Carlos: Best recording on the album. Dan is a genius.

**@SpeedyWunder**

When all the instrumentals and vocals were recorded then we edited them into one long piece and mixed that. Rather than doing it as individual songs.

**@FontainesDublin**

Tom: We were in the rehearsal room every day for the summer of 2018 writing and I'm pretty sure this was the last tune written during those sessions that made it on the record. The arpeggiator at the end is one of my favourite moments on the album.

### 8. CHEQUELESS RECKLESS

**@FontainesDublin**

Tom: We wrote it as a B-side to Boys In The Better Land and didn't think much of it at the time until our manager convinced us to put them out as a Double A-Side.

### 9. LIBERTY BELLE

**@FontainesDublin**

Tom: This was our first ever single that we put out ourselves. It'll always hold a very special place in my heart.

**@FontainesDublin**

Carlos: Liberty.. It's all been said about this one.

### 10. BOYS IN THE BETTER LAND

**@FontainesDublin**

Tom: Dan decided to put his lasers on in the studio when we were tracking this and the energy that added to the room was unreal.

**@SpeedyWunder**

This was one that we recorded in the dark with lasers and a smoke machine.

**@FontainesDublin**

Carlos: Fender Deluxe reverb from 75 and the famous Framus Curley bought in Berlin in 2016 was what I used to get that intro sound on Boys.

### 11. DUBLIN CITY SKY

**@FontainesDublin**

We recorded this tune with the lasers on as well weirdly enough.

**@FontainesDublin**

Carlos: Dublin City Sky… same sky wherever you are really. This is the sky over Sunny Hill Road, where the album was recorded. I miss this view, as I miss Dan and the rest of the boys now that we're apart. Love ye all. Thanks to everyone who's supported this band.

Fag break: Tom Coll, Conor Deegan and Grian Chatten.

Boy In The Better Band. Conor Curley.

# *Version*
## Mark Ronson
Columbia, 2007

Making mixtapes, or more recently playlists, for your friends – or would-be "special" friends – is a time honoured tradition. However super-producer Mark Ronson (**@MarkRonson**) took the idea to the next level making his mixtape of treasured songs *with* his friends. Snatching time during sessions with world famous artists, or calling in favours to his own studio, the British-American pulled together *Version*, his brass-and-breakbeat adored covers album, over several years. Naturally then having made a mixtape for the world, it duly fell on Mark Ronson to finally write the accompanying note in tweet form explaining the reasons behind his track choices… and also discuss how the album yielded one of the definitive moments of Amy Winehouse's brief but bright career. This is the definitive version.

**PHOTOGRAPHY:**
David Hughes

**SLEEVE DESIGN:**
Village Green

LISTENING PARTY
**16 APRIL 2020**

### 1. GOD PUT A SMILE UPON YOUR FACE (FEATURING THE DAPTONE HORNS)

**@MarkRonson**
This was my favourite song off of A Rush Of Blood [To The Head, Coldplay album] for sure. I was a big fan of Parachutes and probably bought this the day it came out … the change when it goes to the chorus ("now when you work it out…") always kills me – harmonic delight and shit.

### 2. OH MY GOD (FEATURING LILY ALLEN)

**@MarkRonson**
I was still living in NYC so I was pretty far behind on the UK indie stuff but when I heard Employment [by Kasier Chiefs, see pages 122–125], man, I was knocked out. The lyrics were so biting but not mean. I was just starting to work with Lily and the kind of very UK-viewpoint that both their lyrics represented to me made it obvious to ask Lily. I loved her voice, I could honestly listen to her sing the phone book. Or at least up to the Rs.

↑

@MarkRonson The first time I met Johnny Marr was in the lobby of the K west hotel. I was so nervous. He was lovely and we got to play this song [Stop Me] 6 years later with Nile Rodgers at a gig in Montreux. I'm also a proud owner of his signature guitar.

### 3. STOP ME (FEATURING DANIEL MERRIWEATHER)

⊘ **@MarkRonson**

When I think of Stop Me right now, I'm hearing all the jangly wall of sound of Johnny Marr's guitars in all the instrumental sections, and I can get chills just thinking about it.

### 4. TOXIC (FEATURING OL' DIRTY BASTARD & TIGGERS)

⊘ **@MarkRonson**

Everyone knows Toxic is one of the best pop songs of the past 30 years. Everyone knows because everyone always says it. But it's true. Apparently it was written for Kylie but then Britney recorded it and it was nearly left off her album because her label didn't like it.

### 5. VALERIE (FEATURING AMY WINEHOUSE)

⊘ **@MarkRonson**

I was working on Version and then recorded half of Back To Black with Amy in the middle. Me and Amy were so tight by the end, both as friends and musical cohorts, that it seemed weird not to have her on Version.

### 6. APPLY SOME PRESSURE (FEATURING PAUL SMITH)

⊘ **@MarkRonson**

I discovered this song while DJing at Ibiza Rocks in the summer of '06 with Zane Lowe. We were going song for a song in a sort of DJ battle and he threw this on. And I watched the entire crowd sing as if it meant EVERYTHING to them.

### 7. INVERSION

⊘ **@MarkRonson**

This is an interlude. I guess I had a few chord progressions and melody ideas lying around while making this album that I wanted to get off my chest.

### 8. PRETTY GREEN (FEATURING SANTIGOLD)

⊘ **@MarkRonson**

I was obsessed with this song from seeing The Jam perform it on an old American talk show called Tom Snyder. All of Weller's sneer and the rhythm section, oof. I played it for Santi and we printed up lyrics and recorded it in the same night.

### 9. JUST (FEATURING ALEX GREENWALD)

⊘ **@MarkRonson**

I was always so obsessed with the two guitar harmony that happens in the middle of the Radiohead version (Jonny Greenwood is a genius, we all know that) that I thought I'd start my version with an extended interpretation of it, where it kind of becomes a distant cousin of I Want You Back [by the Jackson 5].

### 10. AMY (FEATURING KENNA)

⊘ **@MarkRonson**

Kenna is my dear friend. He makes so much good music and does so many good things for the world like climbing Kilimanjaro. Yes, he climbed Kilimanjaro to raise awareness for clean water, he came up with Chad and Pharrell and all his records have been super influential.

### 11. THE ONLY ONE I KNOW (FEATURING ROBBIE WILLIAMS)

⊘ **@MarkRonson**

Some Friendly [see pages 16–21] was me and my friends' favourite album for a year. And we all felt so cool that we (a bunch of early teenaged NYers) knew about this cool UK indie band. Years later, I found out Robbie Williams loved it too. No surprise there. While working on his record he was kind enough to lend his lovely pipes here.

### 12. DIVERSION

⊘ **@MarkRonson**

This is an Interlude Pt 2. My manager was like, "we need SOME publishing on this album, bro".

### 13. L.S.F. (LOST SOULS FOREVER) (FEATURING KASABIAN)

⊘ **@MarkRonson**

I discovered Kasabian's Club Foot at a Soul Record Store in SOHO. I LOVEd the breakbeatiness of it. Everything on that first album spoke to me so much. This wasn't a cover as much as a remix. I really love Kasabian.

### 14. OUTVERSION

⊘ **@MarkRonson**

This is the last interlude. Something a little soulful and soothing. This has been a lot of fun. So much love to everyone.

# Rattlesnakes
## Lloyd Cole & The Commotions
Polydor, 1984

Music loves a college drop-out. Kanye West made a whole album about it, and if Lloyd Cole (**@Lloyd_Cole**) had hung on to get his degree in literature and philosophy there would have been a big hole missing in British pop music. Studying in Glasgow just as the city became the innovative epicentre of indie, Derbyshire-born Cole, along with Commotions Blair Cowan (keyboards), Lawrence Donegan (bass), Neil Clark (guitar – **@ClarkNeilRobert**) and Stephen Irvine (drums) tapped into the jangly guitar atmosphere that illuminated the Scottish scene but added a warm pop heart and some considerable lyrical athleticism of their own as they made their debut with *Rattlesnakes*. Indeed, while Cole might not have got his degree, he had not been slacking as references to Norman Mailer, Grace Kelly, Joan Didion and Simone de Beauvoir pepper the record in a natural, never in a show-offy, way. **@Tim_Burgess**: "I had a list in my head of the people namechecked on this album. Pre-Google it was a case of keeping an eye/ear out for who Simone de Beauvoir, Leonard Cohen or Arthur Lee were. I thought that if Lloyd knew about them, then I should too." Now you don't even need to search, as Cole and Clark took to their keyboards for a listening party that brought all of *Rattlesnakes'* element together, surprising its makers in the process.

PHOTOGRAPHY:
Robert Farber

SLEEVE DESIGN:
Da Gama

(Below left) Lloyd Cole's handwritten lyrics for 2CV, probably written 10,000 feet above the ground...

(Below) Going underground. The Commotions on influential British TV show *The Tube* in 1984.

Causing a commotion. Lloyd and the band in 1984.

### 1. PERFECT SKIN

✔ **@Lloyd_Cole**

We recorded Perfect Skin, Forest Fire and (b-side) You Will Never Be No Good with Paul Hardiman in early 1984 at The Garden studio in Shoreditch. We returned in the early Summer to record the rest, which took a month or so. We stayed in a flat Polydor rented for us in Maida Vale. The Garden was owned by John Foxx from Ultravox at the time. He sold it to Matt Johnson (The The). Not sure if Matt still owns it.

### 2. SPEEDBOAT

✔ **@Lloyd_Cole**

Not sure if anyone in the band noticed, but nobody told me – I had stolen the bassline from What Presence? by Orange Juice. I was mortified when I realised, but it was too late.

### 3. RATTLESNAKES

✔ **@Lloyd_Cole**

Neil's song. His riff. I wrote the vocal melodies and my other input was to come up with the idea of the strings playing a sort of reverse of the guitar, starting on the high note, not the low one. Brilliant bass playing on this.

### 4. DOWN ON MISSION STREET

✔ **@Lloyd_Cole**

My favourite arrangement is Down On Mission Street. I don't think I gave [string arranger] Anne [Dudley] any direction on that one. When they swell up and take over after the vocal, it's pretty magical.

### 5. FOREST FIRE

✔ **@Lloyd_Cole**

My two Forest Fire memories are Neil recording the guitar solo, with three amps and tape on the floor for feedback sweetspots, and mixing, there was no automation, Stephen and I had to open and close channels to mute the drum hits we decided we didn't want. Stressful but fun! This still sounds as fresh as day one and I have hairs on my back misbehaving.

### 6. CHARLOTTE STREET

✔ **@Lloyd_Cole**

My favourite drumming on the record. It's just a single tom, but it makes the track IMHO. Stephen was and probably still is a great drummer, but man, is he loud. It was a mostly true tale that really happened in Camden Market near Upper St. Charlotte St just sounded better.

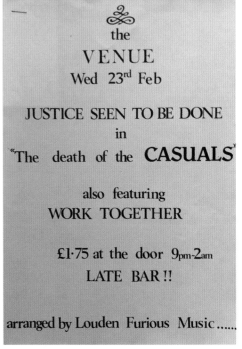

the
## VENUE
Wed 23rd Feb

JUSTICE SEEN TO BE DONE
in
"The death of the CASUALS"

also featuring
WORK TOGETHER

£1·75 at the door 9pm-2am
LATE BAR!!

arranged by Louden Furious Music......

←

Marking their Marq. The Commotions onstage at London venue the Marquee.

(Below) @Lloyd_Cole Before the Commotions, Blair and I had a band called the Casuals. Neil helped out on guitar. Maybe 2 or 3 months after our debut concert I decided to change things & morph into The Commotions, but then an actual concert promoter contacted me & wanted to promote a Casuals show so we played a farewell show. The death of The Casuals.

→

**@Lloyd_Cole**
Rattlesnakes was the 3rd single from the album. I was outvoted. I voted for Heartbroken. Touring non-stop needed to record a b-side. 1 day in Rockfield with Paul. Sweetness was the only song recorded between Rattlesnakes and Easy Pieces and remains our best b-side IMO.

## 7. 2CV

◎ **@Lloyd_Cole**
We were flying up and down from Glasgow to London a lot, for TVs and promo stuff that Spring and Summer. I'd never been on a plane before. Jet Set! I wrote, or finished writing a few of the songs in flight. 2 CV for sure. A lot of the songs here are inspired by my year in London after A Levels. My failed attempt to study Law. They were far more autobiographical than I would admit, at the time.

## 8. FOUR FLIGHTS UP

◎ **@Lloyd_Cole**
Lawrence and I were the two big Dylan fans in the band and we decided to have a go at a Bob Dylan's 115th dream type thing. According to the notes I just dug up, it was briefly entitled 2nd Hand Bookshop. We dodged a bullet there.

## 9. PATIENCE

◎ **@Lloyd_Cole**
Blair's song. The oldest song on the album written Summer '83, I think. Last but one track on side 2 is always where you put the track you think is weakest. It has been argued that there isn't a weak track on Rattlesnakes. But there could have been...

◎ **@ClarkNeilRobert**
I played a hamfisted solo on this. Telecaster straight into the desk.

## 10. ARE YOU READY TO BE HEARTBROKEN?

◎ **@ClarkNeilRobert**
The acoustic is double tracked. Guitar was a cheap, but good sounding Ibanez.

◎ **@Lloyd_Cole**
This is the song that really got us started. We already had Patience, but we didn't really have an identity. It was written to be the b-side of an indie single. It took us a day. A-side took a week. It took a while to admit that it was better. Then we were off. We had had a small hit, and a near miss. Our expectations were not high. We knew the record was good, but so what? We had a band bet - where would the album enter the charts? I dared for #20, or so. Everyone else guessed lower. It went in at 13 & stayed in the top 100 for a year. Rattlesnakes took us all over the world. The touring only stopped when we had to make a follow up. New York. Chris and Tina [Frantz and Weymouth from Talking Heads] came to see us! Really! 1984-1985 was exhausting and fantastically exciting. We had done it. We were famous. People liked our music, some people loved it. Almost everyone eventually came around to liking Rattlesnakes. Not John Peel. He described us as the Leicester City of bands - In the first division, but should probably be in the second. Weren't Leicester Liverpool's bogey team in the 80s?

# I Should Coco
## Supergrass
Parlophone, 1995

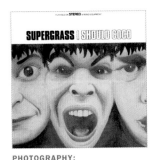

**PHOTOGRAPHY:**
Paul Stanley

**SLEEVE DESIGN:**
The Designers Republic

📌 "Golly, you've got to be fast with this record," tweeted Supergrass bassist Mick Quinn (**@MonkeyBasket**) as he tried to type and keep up with his band's debut album. Yet the frenetic time signatures are only the start of the speed that *I Should Coco* moves at. Inspired by an irrepressible youthful enthusiasm, Quin, Gaz Coombes (vocals/guitar) and Danny Goffey (drums) filled their first LP with stacks of ideas, textures, words and energy. There are glam-rock stomps, 30-second horror film soundtracks, wistful acoustics and – in the form of chiming single Alright, in particular – the encapsulation of youth on record. Yet there is also an almost unnerving precision about *I Should Coco*. There is no spare meat, no waffle, this is a record that gets in, explodes joyously, and gets out. It's no wonder that despite frontman Coombes only being in his teens when the record was released they were fast-tracked to indie pop glory.

✔ **@Tim_Burgess**

We hung out a few times with Supergrass I remember. One mad one at a hotel in San Francisco with a guitar-shaped swimming pool. Blur were staying there too, it was like a copy of the NME that had come to life.

→
Strange ones, Gaz Coombes and Mick Quinn backstage at Moles in Bath in 1995.

### 1. I'D LIKE TO KNOW

⊘ **@MonkeyBasket (Mick Quinn)**

Cor, what an opener. That's Sam Williams (producer) playing Vox Continental. Someone left it in the studio from a previous session and we couldn't resist "borrowing" it.

### 2. CAUGHT BY THE FUZZ

⊘ **@MonkeyBasket**

Released on Backbeat records, July '94. Dave Norland ran Backbeat from his bedroom in a squat off Iffley Road. The label financed on a £600 donation from Phil Collins.

### 3. MANSIZE ROOSTER

⊘ **@MonkeyBasket**

All three of us had to jump up and down on a big wooden box to get banging enough in the verses.

### 4. ALRIGHT

⊘ **@MonkeyBasket**

What can I add here? Gaz is smaking the piano, I'm bending the notes.

### 5. LOSE IT

⊘ **@MonkeyBasket**

Bit of a style shift. Wrote this riff on acoustic guitar and it used to go into the chorus chords of [second album title track] In It For The Money. Pulled them apart and saved some of it for the next album.

### 6. LENNY

⊘ **@MonkeyBasket**

A firm set list favourite right from the start, writing this kick started *I Should Coco*.

### 7. STRANGE ONES

⊘ **@MonkeyBasket**

Loosely based on the homeless regulars from my café job before the band made it. They'd spend most of the day in there with us slipping them free drinks. During the breaks you'd get collard to share their conspiracy theories. Very entertaining.

### 8. SITTING UP STRAIGHT

⊘ **@MonkeyBasket**

This song got faster the more we played it. If we'd started writing it at this speed I could probably have used a lot less notes.

### 9. SHE'S SO LOOSE

⊘ **@MonkeyBasket**

Blew a small part of the budget recording live cellos on this.

### 10. WE'RE NOT SUPPOSED TO

⊘ **@MonkeyBasket**

Have you got any mandies? Always liked the version we did live when we could afford a horn section.

### 11. TIME

⊘ **@MonkeyBasket**

Love how Gaz changes on this, and always fun playing it live and hearing the vocals float out into the room.

### 12. SOFA (OF MY LETHARGY)

⊘ **@MonkeyBasket**

A slowed down version of Alright. It's the same chords practically.

### 13. TIME TO GO

⊘ **@MonkeyBasket**

About to go down the pub and waiting for everyone to put their coats on. Picked up the guitar and banged this out in 10 seconds. Time to go.

⊕

Not Sitting Up Straight. Danny Goffey onstage at Moles in Bath in 1995.

# *Love*
## The Cult
Beggars/Sire, 1985

⚓ Having emerged from the ashes of bands Southern Death Cult, and then just plain old Death Cult, *Love* might, on the face of it, seem an unlikely album title for The Cult. In fact, not only are the muscular rockers not as fearsome as their past names suggest, but the band that has been built around shamanlike frontman Ian Astbury and riff lord Billy Duffy (**@TheBillyDuffy**), has always been open and approachable. For starters this, the band's second album, boasts the global hit She Sells Sanctuary suggesting The Cult has the ability to make *something* of a connection, while on a personal level, despite the dark glasses and black clothes, the gothic-tinged rockers enjoy a reputation for being very welcoming. @**Tim_Burgess**: "The Cult invited The Charlatans to play at Gathering Of The Tribes 2 in massive amphitheatres in California. When we arrived in LA, Ian was there to meet us. Such a dude, he didn't have to do that. We went to his house in the Hollywood Hills and we watched videos of Free and had our hair cut." Billy Duffy was similarly obliging with his commentary for *Love*.

**PHOTOGRAPHY:**
Andrew MacPherson

**LISTENING PARTY**
**19 APRIL 2020**

### 1. NIRVANA

◉ **@TheBillyDuffy**
One HUGE thing is that [She Sells] Sanctuary was recorded with Nigel Preston on drums and earlier than the rest of Love in a separate session. Big Country's Mark Brzezicki did the album session as Nige had been "let go" at that point. #Dontdodrugskids. Mark is a creative drummer and really pushed us on musically. The drum beat he used on Nirvana is derived from 1970s RnB and is known as the "Pea Soup"... I kid you not!

### 2. THE BIG NEON GLITTER

◉ **@TheBillyDuffy**
This was clearly a go at a good old-fashioned glam rock stomp of a song. We can't do this without giving a very special mention to Martin Mills from Beggars Banquet. Having signed Southern Death Cult originally, he was happy to support Ian and I getting together for Death Cult all on a handshake initially!

### 3. LOVE

◉ **@TheBillyDuffy**
What appeals to me about the track Love and makes it my favourite Cult song ever is because it has a unique atmosphere. It's a lucky combination of all the elements and how they came together including, I believe, "more cowbell". It all creates a beautiful tension. I think it was my call for the title of the album Love and TBH a bit of a two fingers to the UK music press who were less than in Love with us at the time.

### 4. BROTHER WOLF; SISTER MOON

◉ **@TheBillyDuffy**
Jamie did a great job of doing the (keyboard) strings on this. There's a thunderstorm on the track which was actually a recording of a real storm that happened while we were at Jacobs recording.

## 5. RAIN

✓ **@TheBillyDuffy**

By the time of recording Love, Sanctuary had already been in the charts for quite a few weeks and we were determined not to be a one hit wonder. So, we worked really hard with Steve Brown on making Rain very "hooky" to be the follow-up single. When you have 20/30 ideas it's helpful to get us all on the same page early on by using working titles, hence this started out as White Wedding, then became Sad Rain, before finally becoming Rain.

## 6. THE PHOENIX

✓ **@TheBillyDuffy**

During the recording Phoenix was known as Stooges and clearly it's hugely influenced by I Wanna Be Your Dog – but not just that track. The whole attitude of the Stooges' and the repetition of simple chord changes with elements coming in and out. The Stooges approach to songwriting was very blue collar but in a way genius in its simplicity and a big part of what appealed to me.

## 7. THE HOLLOW MAN

✓ **@TheBillyDuffy**

I'd always felt later on that The Hollow Man and The Smiths' What Difference Does It Make have some similarities, same key, similar chords... not sure what me and Johnny [Marr, Smiths guitarist] were channelling at that time.

## 8. REVOLUTION

✓ **@TheBillyDuffy**

After I'd created the tune the first words Ian came up with were for the chorus. It was such a strong hook that we just took it from there. It's still one of my favourite Cult songs and definitely in my top 10.

## 9. SHE SELLS SANCTUARY

✓ **@TheBillyDuffy**

The She Sells Sanctuary session was only done initially to do a one off single with producer Steve Brown. He had recently worked with Wham! and knew how to make a pop single so with it charting we went on to do Love with him. There was a swimming pool at the studio when we were working on Love and I remember drinking champagne in there when we found out Sanctuary had gone Top 30 in the UK charts! It was a massive thing to get on Top Of The Pops in those days.

## 10. BLACK ANGEL

✓ **@TheBillyDuffy**

Ian and I had been listening to David Bowie's Port Of Amsterdam quite a bit and it certainly influenced the feel on Black Angel. Looking back I think Black Angel was more of a song that represented where we had been with [debut album] Dreamtime where rockier songs like Love and The Phoenix were looking forward to the next phase... We weren't signed in the USA at the time of Sanctuary as Beggars hadn't found the right partner label there. We came close to signing to A+M but they cooled interest. Then when we heard that the legendary Seymour Stein of Sire Records had seen the Sanctuary video and wanted to meet. Sire had an amazing roster of artists all curated by Seymour personally plus had distribution with Warner Brothers Records in the US so we felt it would be a great fit for the band... perfect in fact. He proposed flying over to meet us in the studio during the Love recording and we were well up for it! So he came, we met for dinner and we loved him... hello Sire Records!

Black Angels. The Cult's creative powerhouse Billy Duffy and Ian Astbury.

# *Real Life*
## Joan As Police Woman
Reveal Records, 2006

For most people, real life is a sometimes beautiful, sometimes scary blend of our inner thoughts and external encounters we experience as we make our way through the world. *Real Life*, the debut album by Joan Wasser (**@JoanPoliceWoman**) under her performing name Joan As Police Woman, touchingly captures that mix. At the point she recorded this album, Wasser's life had ranged from the vivid to the heartbreaking, experiencing moments of great openness and deep contemplation. She credits her adoptive childhood for inspiring her "very extroverted" personality, which led her to music and performance.

**PHOTOGRAPHY:**
Conrad Ventur

Arresting. Joan (Wasser) As Policewoman.

LISTENING
PARTY
**19 APRIL
2020**

### 1. REAL LIFE

✅ @JoanPoliceWoman

Recorded by Jack McKeever at his White Room studio (recently closed) on the Lower East Side on his upright Steinway, an instrument I particularly love. Strings recorded by myself and Jeff Hill, bassist by trade but played cello and bowed upright for this occasion. I wrote this song for a poor soul who I met for five minutes and decided was "The One". After he received the song he said "but Joan, I don't want to be reckless with you", a response that was so responsible and respectful that I didn't even know what to do with it at the time.

### 2. ETERNAL FLAME

✅ @JoanPoliceWoman

What about that drum fill!? That's the GREAT Ben Perowsky, who I somehow convinced to play with me after playing solo for a while and so badly needing a drummer. I had seen him play and literally felt like he lifted me off the ground. Ben, thank you forever for playing with me. You changed my life. That's the total bad ass Rainy Orteca on the bass guitar. Singing the super-low and some of the high vocals is Joseph Arthur, a good friend and amazing musical mind. He really added such a vibe to this song. His vocal range is insane. This song was recorded by Bryce Goggin at Trout Recording in Brooklyn, the studio that is still my primary place for making records. Early on (before I was even playing live) Bryce told me to come to his studio when I was ready to make my own album. I called him when I was ready to make my EP and he's a huge part of the reason I am making records at all. Bryce told me the music was good enough. THANK YOU BRYCE!!

### 3. FEED THE LIGHT

✅ @JoanPoliceWoman

Bryce's engineer, Adam Sachs, recorded this song. It's just Joseph Arthur and I singing and playing everything. I played the bass, strings and guitar. He played the drums and the piano.

## 4. THE RIDE

### ⊘ @JoanPoliceWoman

I wrote this song with the idea that I'd write a song for Whitney Houston to sing. I thought I might not even include it on the album as I didn't know if it fit. I am glad I did. When Ben and I started playing together I said "you know I'm going to want you to cover some of the harmony vocals" and he just looked at me with the expression "NO". He sings the backup vocals with me. His voice is PERFECTION. I'm startled at how relaxed I sound. Bryce helped with that. I remember talking about Al Green sounding like he had just rolled out of bed. The initial idea I had for this record is that I wanted to make my version of Let's Stay Together by Al Green.

## 5. I DEFY

### ⊘ @JoanPoliceWoman

I remember sitting at Anohni's upright in her (then) tiny apt. and started playing the piano riff that was to become I Defy. The song came together quickly. It was one of those that felt written already and just had to be pulled out of the ether. I began playing in [Anohni's previous group] Antony And The Johnsons in 1999. It was a rough time for me and the songs and ensemble and of course, THAT VOICE, helped me greatly. There was this space that needed a solo that I was at a loss for. Bryce, got on the piano and threw down this gorgeous burst of energy/chaos that was done in 10 seconds. I adored Eyvind's viola playing and had him into the studio to do free improv with me. He's one of the only people who can actually quote Plato with some dignity.

## 6. FLUSHED CHEST

### ⊘ @JoanPoliceWoman

Yes, this song I wrote about Jeff Buckley! [Wasser's boyfriend. The singer-songwriter drowned in 1997] "Morning bird, I'll wait for you, how could I not?"

## 7. CHRISTOBEL

### ⊘ @JoanPoliceWoman

That's Joseph Arthur's voice again. Wow! This is so fast! Haha. The words in my mind were "why won't you fall in love with me?" but I didn't think I could get that into a song without it sounding... lame? But then, I just did it and gave up thinking

about it. Glad I did. I had a lot of fun recording this distorted violin solo, THIS IS NOT GUITAR!!

## 8. SAVE ME

### ⊘ @JoanPoliceWoman

That drum part is NOT DELAY, it's Ben playing the part as if it were delayed. THAT'S HOW COOL HE IS! I was so tired of my thoughts and had to get these thoughts out in a song rather than doing something really stupid. I would write about my escaping my thinking a couple of albums later on The Magic. That's Rainy whispering "Save Me" THE BEST. Segue by Eyvind Kang and I, both on viola to clear the air, a bit of a prayer.

## 9. ANYONE

### ⊘ @JoanPoliceWoman

I wanted to write a straight-up soul ballad. Anyone is what happened. "So try me please I'm a better dancer than it seems the lightest floating feather is how I feel when I'm with you." Charlie Burnham, the great violinist, sang the harmony vocals with Ben. "I like whole pies underdone a little"... I remember thinking, can I include that lyric?

### ⊘ @Lloyd_Cole

I think before this record was a musician first and a singer second. This turned that on its head. Just my take. I've only ever asked two singers to sing on records with me. Tracey Thorn and Joan. Also, Joan As Policewoman is funny, charming and generous. Just for the record.

### ⊘ @JoanPoliceWoman

THANK YOU LLOYD! so are you but I won't tell anyone!

## 10. WE DON'T OWN IT

### ⊘ @JoanPoliceWoman

I wrote this for my friend [singer-songwriter] Elliott Smith, who had died a few years previously. I watched what happened with his friends and the press and was so saddened. I had experienced a similar situation when Jeff died in '97. I'm sure I acted insane as well. But to see it from the outside, with Elliott, gave me some much-needed insight. WOW. That was a stroll down memory lane. I am sending all my love to everyone who listened in. Makes me feel so much less alone!

# *Don't Try This At Home*
## Billy Bragg
Elektra, 1991

The beautiful thing about Billy Bragg (**@BillyBragg**) is everyone thinks they know what he's all about. Politically charged, on the nose musically, his "Bard Of Barking" nickname conjures up an immediate image of a man commanding the stage alone. Yet pinning down Bragg's essence is easier said than done. From his early protests, via his '80s pop collaborations with the late Kirsty MacColl, to reconstructing unrecorded Woody Guthrie songs with alt-country heroes Wilco on the Mermaid Avenue albums, yes, he's the "Bard", but he is also so much more too. His 1991 album *Don't Try This At Home* makes this point loudly. There are protest songs, but there are also tracks about losing his father, war and some big tear-jerkers about Bragg's then recent break-up. Musically too the album includes both country-ish twangs, recorded with members of R.E.M, and a protest anthem-come-pop banger made in collaboration with Johnny Marr. Bragg took us through the many facets of *Don't Try This At Home* with his Listening Party, as followers discovered the true meaning behind his often poignant lyrics.

**SLEEVE DESIGN:**
Caramel Crunch

@ChorizoGarbanzo
Here's @BillyBragg & me at Bracknell Folk Festival, summer 1991. He insisted the photo was taken in front of these Clash singles & instead of saying "cheese" we're saying "socialism".

## 1. ACCIDENT WAITING TO HAPPEN

⊘ @BillyBragg

Accident Waiting to Happen is one of several songs on the album that I wrote in a dropped D tuning – normal tuning but the bottom E string dropped to D. I stole it off folk singer John Faulkner when the two of us were on tour in the DDR in 1987 – I gave him a thank you in the sleeve notes!

## 2. MOVING THE GOALPOSTS

⊘ @BillyBragg

Moving the Goalposts is about love against the backdrop of the changing world following the fall of the Berlin Wall. Gennady Gerasimov was the spokesman of the Soviet Foreign Ministry tasked with explaining glasnost and perestroika to the West. I had been to the USSR a couple of times in the late 1980s and I'd never seen a Soviet bureaucrat wearing Italian shoes and talking in such media friendly terms. His demeanour in tv interviews was a sign that change was coming to Russia.

## 3. EVERYWHERE

⊘ @BillyBragg

Greg Trooper wrote Everywhere with Sid Griffin and when Greg opened for me on tour in America, the song was a highlight of his set. The internment of 120k people of Japanese ancestry by the US during WWII is a wretched blot on American history.

## 4. CINDY OF A THOUSAND LIVES

⊘ @BillyBragg

When I first went to the US opening for Echo & The Bunnymen in 1984, I was obsessed with buying postcards. One that really struck me was a weird photo of a child with a pig's snout. That the picture was called Untitled #140 was even more intriguing. The only clue as to the meaning of the image was the name of the artist, Cindy Sherman. It turned out that not only was Cindy responsible for the image, she was also the subject. The grotesque figure was a self portrait, as were all of her photos.

## 5. YOU WOKE UP MY NEIGHBOURHOOD

⊘ @BillyBragg

Lori Taylor worked in the Smithsonian Institute in Washington DC in the Folkways Records archive. She invited me to come to their offices and see some of Woody Guthrie's drawings they had in their collection. An image of a large woman swinging her hips in a dance with the words 'you woke up my neighbourhood' beside her stayed with me. A while later in Athens Georgia, Peter Buck had some chords and asked me if I had any words... I guess you could say that Neighbourhood was a Guthrie/Bragg collaboration that pre-dated Mermaid Avenue by several years.

## 6. TRUST

⊘ @BillyBragg

The AIDS epidemic – and the stigma attached to it – was a big issue in the late 80s. I wanted to write about it and, with Trust, I ended up doing so in a manner that could also refer to an unplanned pregnancy.

## 7. GOD'S FOOTBALLER

⊘ @BillyBragg

When Wolverhampton Wanderers striker Peter Knowles gave up football to become a Jehovah's Witness in 1970, it shocked many. I was fascinated by the fact that he sought redemption somewhere other than the football pitch.

## 8. THE FEW

⊘ @BillyBragg

We were doing an overnight drive when the lyrics to The Few began to form in my mind. Everyone else was asleep apart from the driver and my guitar was in the back with the gear, so I had to take emergency action. In order not to lose the lyrics while they were flowing, I decided to utilise the tune of another song to hang them on Bob Dylan's Desolation Row.

## 9. SEXUALITY

⊘ @BillyBragg

There always seemed an undertow of puritanism in official reactions to AIDS as if the idea of people expressing themselves sexually was disgusting. I wanted to write something that celebrated sexuality and outed myself as an ally to the gay community.

Billy Bragg onstage in
The Hague in 1991.

**@BillyBragg**
I met Mary Ramsey when
she was playing violin with
10,000 Maniacs. I was
backstage before the show
and heard her warming up
down the corridor by playing
Vaughn Williams' Fantasia
on Greensleeves. The next
day she was in the studio
recording Rumours of War
with me, which includes,
at my insistence, a melodic
quote from Vaughn Williams.
Mary is now the lead singer
of 10,000 Maniacs.

@BillyBragg
Dolphins features the wonderful Danny Thompson on double bass. Talking him through the song, I asked if he'd heard the Tim Buckley live in London version? "I played on it" was his withering response.

### 10. MOTHER OF THE BRIDE

@BillyBragg
Mother of the Bride should really have been on Worker's Playtime as it's ostensibly about the breakup that inspired most of the songs on that album. Although, I never did feel sorry that we didn't get married.

### 11. TANK PARK SALUTE

@BillyBragg
My father died in 1976 when I was 18 and I never spoke to anyone about it until I wrote Tank Park Salute in 1990. So when people say that it helped them to come to terms with their loss, I tell them it had the same effect on me. Thanks for all your kind words about Tank Park Salute. It's a song that means a great deal to me. It was my Mum's favourite of my songs too.

### 12. DOLPHINS

@BillyBragg
Dolphins features the wonderful Danny Thompson on double bass. Talking him through the song, I asked if he'd heard the Tim Buckley live in London version? "I played on it" was his withering response.

### 13. NORTH SEA BUBBLE

@BillyBragg
North Sea Bubble is one of three songs produced by Johnny Marr at his Clear Studio outside Manchester in October 1990. The other two were Sexuality and Cindy Of A Thousand Lives.

### 14. RUMOURS OF WAR

@BillyBragg
I met Mary Ramsey when she was playing violin with 10,000 Maniacs. I was backstage before the show and heard her warming up down the corridor by playing Vaughn Williams' Fantasia on Greensleeves. The next day she was in the studio recording Rumours of War with me which includes, at my insistence, a melodic quote from Vaughn Williams. Mary is now the lead singer of 10,000 Maniacs.

### 15. WISH YOU WERE HER

@BillyBragg
Deep down inside, I always wanted to be Smokey Robinson. Lorraine Bowen of Crumble Song fame not only coached me to sing on this song, she also formed and led the backing group.

### 16. BODY OF WATER

@BillyBragg
Somewhere over the spring of 1991, what began as a single album morphed into a double that featured something never heard on a Billy Bragg LP before – a few real pop songs. We had a start, a middle but no end. So late in the mixing we went back in and recorded Body Of Water. Wiggy provided the tune, I decided to write some meaningless lyrics and for once got to play lead guitar. If you chase the fade you can hear we're all a bit demob happy.

# *Bring It On*
## Gomez
Hut, 1998

Very few teenage bands ever make it beyond the end of school. None then use the furtive first recordings made in these groups to make a Mercury Prize-winning album. Except Gomez that is. After Ian Ball (vocals, guitar – **@iballmd**), Paul "Blackie" Blackburn (bass – **@GomezTheBand**), Tom Gray (vocals, guitars, keyboards – **@MrTomGray**) and Olly Peacock (drums, synths, computers) bonded over recording songs on a four-track tape recorder in a parental garage – later to be joined by new uni friend Ben Ottewell (vocals, guitars – **@OttewellBen**) – the group would devote their spare time making increasingly ambitious songs via a host of lo-fi but effective production techniques. Added to this passion for painstaking home recording (the band would repeatedly get as much as they could on each of their four tracks, before "bouncing" their work down to a single track and then add more) is their rare love and knowledge of blues songs, meaning nobody else sounded like Gomez – well not outside the Mississippi Delta.

ARTWORK:
Paul Collins & Reggie Pedro

While making *Bring It On*, Gomez were always pushing what could be achieved on a home recording set-up, years before computer technology made it practical.

After a bidding war that involved (a losing) Madonna, their new label decided the "demos" would become the mainstay of their debut album *Bring It On*, complemented by some extra recording done with producer Ken Nelson at Liverpool's Parr Street Studios. The album not only won the aforementioned Mercury in 1998, but more notably earned praise from John Lee Hooker who said of Bring It On: "I've dun listen through this record time and again and I can't find no defect whatsoever." A unique album obviously means a unique Listening Party too. Bring it on…

**@MrTomGray**

I remember John Peel coming up to me at a gig looking sheepish. I'm like, surely the godfather of weird can't like my band. He's like "errr my daughter is a big fan can I get an autograph". You win and lose some.

## 1. GET MILES

**@MrTomGray**
First song we ever recorded as a 5 piece and this is the actual recording of the first time we got through it all the way.

## 2. WHIPPIN' PICCADILLY

**@GomezTheBand** (Paul Blackburn)
This song is about going to see Beck at Manchester Academy on the Odelay tour.

**@iballmd** (Ian Ball)
I sound about 12. Pretty early in the album for a tuba.

## 3. MAKE NO SOUND

**@iballmd**
First tune recorded in an actual studio. You can tell the difference when someone who knows what they're doing gets involved. Thanks to the evergreen [producer] Ken Nelson.

## 4. 78 STONE WOBBLE

**@MrTomGray**
I think, technically, the first Gomez song. Started in 1995. Me and Ol were fucking around with old records. The gristle is playing off my grandma's old dansette.

## 5. TIJUANA LADY

**@iballmd**
Lords, this song. I apologise, we were hungover.

**@OttewellBen**
I remember Ian's mother hating my voice, particularly on the song Make No Sound. Believe it was written, probably recorded too, by your pool table – no match for that reverb!

## 6. HERE COMES THE BREEZE

**@MrTomGray**
So the rest of the lads had finished a version of this song that was really lovely and then I decided to make a racket. Apologies. Bally was a very willing co-conspirator.

## 7. LOVE IS BETTER THAN A WARM TROMBONE

**@ottewellben**
My favourite part of the record. Excavated from the very first time we all played together.

## 8. GET MYSELF ARRESTED

**@MrTomGray**
Oh no, me singing before I'd learnt to sing. Here we go. We wrote this about a lad I went to Uni with. You'll feel weird when you learn that a few months later he spent 3 months in prison. #foresight

## 9. FREE TO RUN

**@iballmd**
Seriously, no-one owned a guitar tuner??

## 10. BUBBLE GUM YEARS

**@MrTomGray**
Here comes 20 year old me doing his best (worst) Randy Newman. I remember John Peel coming up to me at a gig looking sheepish. I'm like, surely the godfather of weird can't like my band. He's like "errr my daughter is a big fan can I get an autograph." You win and lose some.

## 11. RIE'S WAGON

**@MrTomGray**
So Rie's Wagon, was a shit car that belonged to our mate Anne-Marie. Was it a Vauxhall? I think it was a Vauxhall? First song since [Paul McCartney's Bond theme] Live And Let Die that employed the disturbingly annoying reggae section.

## 12. THE COMEBACK

**@GomezTheBand**
Only band in history to start their career with a comeback.

**@iballmd**
The tuba finishes it off, very nice.

# *My Love Is Cool*
## Wolf Alice
Dirty Hit, 2015

⚓ Fast, brittle, yet tender when they need to be, Wolf Alice are a band that captures the emotional impact of a modern world tossed and turned by social media and memes, unrequited love and selfies. Fronted by singer/guitarist Ellie Rowsell, along with guitarist Joff Oddie, bassist Theo Ellis (**@SteadyTheo**) and drummer Joel Amey, the London band served up a choppy tumult of thoughts and feelings with their rocky debut album, *My Love Is Cool*. It is a record that proves to be both affecting and accessible, yet also moves quickly, constantly driving forward. In fact it is an album that goes so fast, that Ellis discovered there was "Not even time for a fag" when he offered his personal tour through *My Love Is Cool* via a Listening Party. What there was time for though was a couple of quizzes, which ended with the bassist giving away rare vinyl. There are no prizes on offer now, save the reward of enjoying a stunning debut album.

**PHOTOGRAPHY:**
Rachel Thomas

**SLEEVE DESIGN:**
Samuel Burgess-Johnson

→ Super cool. Frontwoman Ellie Rowsell.

## 1. TURN TO DUST

**@SteadyTheo (Theo Ellis)**

Cue moody intro. Is it a synth, is it a guitar? It's motherfucking Joff. We spent a good few days trynna figure out what tuning the guitar parts were in the original demo. Not sure we ever actually got it right.

## 2. BROS

**@SteadyTheo**

I am always two seconds from playing the wrong note at this point. Ten grand who knows what 43 is symbolic of?

**@driiveblind [fan]**

The 43 bus!!

**@SteadyTheo**

You win.

## 3. YOUR LOVES WHORE

**@SteadyTheo**

God love Mike Crossley's vista light drum kit for sounding so naughty, one for the tech heads. I actually love this tune, not really much insight but yeh what a banger.

## 4. YOU'RE A GERM

**@SteadyTheo**

We made a zombie apocalypse music video to this and our sound engineer slept through axe murders and window smashing for a chilled 16 hours.

## 5. LISBON

**@SteadyTheo**

I'd like to think me and Joel did this in one take but I'm probably wrong. RUN RUN RUN AWAY (to the kitchen it's a fucking lockdown baby).

## 6. SILK

**@SteadyTheo**

We spent about 4000 hours in this caf just next to Livingston studio and also met our beloved [sound engineer and tour manager] Johnny Haskett.

## 7. FREAZY

**@Tim_Burgess**

I watched Wolf Alice at a festival a couple of years ago and their connection with the audience was unique. They have something extra special.

## 8. GIANT PEACH

**@SteadyTheo**

If you have nothing to do tomorrow then this is a good time to smash the house up when it drops.

## 9. SWALLOWTAIL

**@SteadyTheo**

I'd quite like to have a drink at the top of the Shard but appaz its proper expensive. Joel has been getting free drinks off this tune for years!

## 10. SOAPY WATER

**@1p4YourTruth [fan]**

One of the few tracks I've never heard live. The only track not played at my first gig in Sept 2015. Crowdsurfing occurred.

**@SteadyTheo**

We tried to play this live once, with me and Joff playing mainly foot synthesiser, didn't last long tbh.

## 11. FLUFFY

**@SteadyTheo**

A lot of people think this song is about a cat I used to have called buddy. Forgot we tried to slip in some kind of spoken word.

## 12. THE WONDER WHY (INCLUDES HIDDEN TITLE TRACK MY LOVE IS COOL)

**@Tim_Burgess**

When I saw Wolf Alice I realised I had met Joel before and seen a couple of the bands he'd been in. I was happy he was in a band making such a fantastic noise.

**@SteadyTheo**

I miss Ellie. I miss Joel. This has been emotional I miss you all and really loved listening to My Love Is Cool with you.

# *Dig Your Own Hole*
## The Chemical Brothers
Freestyle Dust/Virgin Records, 1997

Today DJs are superstars (as The Chemical Brothers later predicted themselves on Hey Boy Hey Girl). They play stadiums, they fly on private jets and there's even a Twitter account retweeting this glamorous set when they petulantly moan about executive lounge WiFi (@DJsComplaining). Yet when Tom Rowlands (@ChemBros) and Ed Simons (@EddyChemical) released their second album in 1997 DJ/producers were largely regarded as tecchie weirdos, confined behind the decks or locked in studios. *Dig Your Own Hole* was in many ways the record that helped bring dance music to the global audience who needed it. The Chemical Brothers' debut, 1995's *Exit Planet Dust*, had established the landscape of fresh beats, vintage samples and clever collaboration, this record stamped it on the wider consciousness, primed as it was to take on rock for the hearts and minds of the world's moshpits. "This album was really shaped by touring *Exit Planet Dust* and going to lots of new and exciting places, playing live a lot and wanting our music to sound incredible out of a big PA. We were also buying lots of weird records in Japan and the US," explained Rowlands at the start of *Dig Your Own Hole's* Listening Party. "My main association with the writing of the album was intense touring in America. Thinking about long fun days of crate digging in dusty old record shops before the gig, then crazy adventures and club-hopping with people we met after the shows," added Simons.

The Listening Party was also a collaborative blast, as the duo were joined by guest vocalist Beth Orton (@Beth_Orton), their manager Nick Dewy (@NickDewey0) and their then press officers and confidents, now authors, John Niven (@estellecostanza) and Robin Turner. "The shift between *Exit* and *Dig* was so huge," suggested Turner. "*Exit* had been incredible gigs at the Astoria with Keith Flint dancing on stage. *Dig* was headlining the Other Stage at Glastonbury." There may have been no festivals in 2020, but the Listening Party for *Dig Your Own Hole* kept that spirit alive (and there wasn't one moan about WiFi).

**SLEEVE DESIGN:**
Negativespace

⊕

Tom and John Niven shared by **@ChemBros** during the Listening Party.

## 1. BLOCK ROCKIN' BEATS

### @ChemBros (Tom Rowlands)

Block Rockin' Beats was made to play on a Saturday night when we were DJing in London. It was made for a very specific dance floor so it was wild to see it go off and connect around the world.

### @estellecostanza (John Niven)

24 years on and Block Rocking Beats intro still be jumping them neck hairs...

## 2. DIG YOUR OWN HOLE

### @ChemBros

This song began life as a remix for Bjork's Hyperballad. She was very much not in to it. I think her words were "I will not have a slap bass on my record" which is fair enough. I found a DAT of it the other day and she was right, it was not good. She saved us.

### @EddyChemical

Dig Your Own Hole was graffiti outside the studio we worked in, Dig Your Own Hope. Wanted to create that sense of collision, abandon, wildness, synths drums beyond control.

## 3. ELEKTROBANK

### @ChemBros

The intro features the legendary DJ Kool Herc on the mic. The recording was made at a concert we played at @IrvingPlaza in NYC in 95. Our amazing promoter Matt Silver had the idea of asking DJ Grand Wizard Theodore and "inventor of hip hop" DJ Kool Herc to warm up for us. We loved this idea and it was a rocking night. Also has Keith Murray doing the "psychedelic fuckin" vox. Remember telling Radio 1 that he was saying "funkin" so they could play it – he wasn't, but they did!

## 4. PIKU

### @EddyChemical

Piku is the name of a rowing boat we rowed in France, our Rosebud, if you like. Wow those drums! Steve Dub at the controls.

## 5. SETTING SUN

### @ChemBros

Was so exciting to work with Noel Gallagher on this song. This song was engineered by John Dee, one of the few songs we've recorded not to have been worked on with Steve Dub. I remember John playing it to his mum when it went to No. 1. His mum was not keen. This record is fully off its axis.

→ Superstar DJs. Chemical Brothers' Tom and Ed making the best of it at the incredibly wet, cold and muddy Glastonbury 1997.

@NickDewey0

I remember hearing Chris Evans play this on the Radio 1 breakfast show one morning. He took it off half way though and just said it was a racket or some such nonsense. Had to play it as it was number one UK.

## 6. IT DOESN'T MATTER

@EddyChemical

Might be my fave Chems track. Buddhist non attachment set to a disco beat and the baddest bass drum.

@ChemBros

The bass drum to rule them all. This song samples Lothar And The Hand People's It Comes On Anyhow. I had bought this 60s record on tour in the US and was immediately obsessed with how the voice sounded. When we got the groove working the sample made total sense in its new context. Sounds incredible in a night club.

## 7. DON'T STOP THE ROCK

@EddyChemical

Don't Stop The Rock jazz drums bit taking me straight back to the DJ booth at Gurnmills. [Turnmills night club in London]

## 8. GET UP ON IT LIKE THIS

@EddyChemical

I remember we used to love to listen to Hip Hop Radio in NYC and that was one of the aims to keep a sense of a mix show. You can hear the radio mix show influence on Get Up On It Like This.

## 9. LOST IN THE K-HOLE

@EddyChemical

Have been subsequently told that a K hole doesn't sound like this. We were imagining a cavernous duvet den…

## 10. WHERE DO I BEGIN

@ChemBros

It was great to work with Beth Orton again after making Alive Alone together on the first album [Exit Planet Dust]. I had the words written but knew it would be so much better with her singing. Her voice is so beautiful on this song.

@Beth_Orton

Love this song. Loved singing it. Love you dudes. Which is my favourite Chemical Brothers track I sing on? I love them like my babies and can't compare, but I love the way Where Do I Begin boots off.

## 11. THE PRIVATE PSYCHEDELIC REEL

@ChemBros

The song to finish the album, nowhere to go after this. Was definitely inspired by seeing Mercury Rev in concert. There was a moment in their gig when the band lined up on the front of the stage and just created this whirl of sound, a big wall of noise and melody. Wanted this feeling – but in our world.

@EddyChemical

PPR! Surrender to the Void, this time is yours.

A promo for The Private Psychedelic Reel shared during the *Dig Your Own Hole* Listening Party.

The schedule for the US tour shared during the *Dig Your Own Hole* Listening Party.

## THE BAND

TOM ROWLANDS
ED SIMONS

## THE CREW

TOUR MANAGER - STUART JAMES
LIGHTING DESIGNER - CHRIS CRAIG
LIGHTING TECH - TBC
BACKLINE/MIDI TECH 1 - AARON CRIPPS
BACKLINE/MIDI TECH 2 - MATT COX
SOUND ENGINEER - JOHN JACKSON
SWAGMAN - BRADTON FOGERTY
TRUCK DRIVER - MICK KIRKCALDY
BUS DRIVER - TBC
VEGETABLE VISION - ADAM SMITH
VEGETABLE VISION - NOAH CLARK

## THE CHEMICAL BROTHERS
## USA - SPRING '97

**APRIL**

| | | | | |
|---|---|---|---|---|
| WED | 23 | TRAVEL TO USA | | |
| THU | 24 | DALLAS | BOMB FACTORY | with The ORB |
| FRI | 25 | | | |
| SAT | 26 | CHICAGO | ARAGON | with The ORB |
| SUN | 27 | MINNEAPOLIS | FIRST AVENUE | |
| MON | 28 | | | |
| TUE | 29 | DENVER | OGDEN THEATRE | |
| WED | 30 | | | |

**MAY**

| | | | | |
|---|---|---|---|---|
| THU | 1 | SALT LAKE CITY | BRICKS | |
| FRI | 2 | LAS VEGAS | THE JOINT | with The ORB |
| SAT | 3 | | | |
| SUN | 4 | SAN FRANCISCO | KAISER | with The ORB |
| MON | 5 | | | |
| TUE | 6 | | | |
| WED | 7 | SEATTLE | UNION STATION | |
| THU | 8 | VANCOUVER | THE RAGE | |
| FRI | 9 | | | |
| SAT | 10 | LOS ANGELES | SHRINE EXPO | |
| SUN | 11 | | | |
| MON | 12 | BOSTON | AVALON | with The ORB |
| TUE | 13 | TORONTO | THE WAREHOUSE | with The ORB |
| WED | 14 | MONTREAL | METROPOLIS | |
| THU | 15 | | | |
| FRI | 16 | PHILADELPHIA | ELECTRIC FACTORY | |
| SAT | 17 | NEW YORK | MANHATTAN CENTRE | |
| SUN | 18 | | | |
| MON | 19 | | | |
| TUE | 20 | ATLANTA | MASQUERADE | |
| WED | 21 | TAMPA | RITZ THEATRE | |
| THU | 22 | RETURN TO UK | | |
| FRI | 23 | | | |
| SAT | 24 | BRIGHTON | ESSENTIAL MUSIC FESTIVAL | |

# *Leftism*
## Leftfield
Hard Hands/Columbia, 1995

A mix of cutting-edge music production and some original, organic voices, Leftfield's *Leftism* is an ever-shifting sonic experience. Inspired by sound systems and club nights, old reggae records and punk venom, the debut album from duo Neil Barnes (**@Leftfield**) and then creative partner Paul Daley not only set new standards for electronic records, but its shape and form attracted the ears of music fans not so familiar with the rare tech-and-dub pressings that inspired the duo.

"We had to buy a second copy of this album," Beta Band frontman, now solo singer-songwriter, Steve Mason tweeted of *Leftism* during its Listening Party. "Amazing work, a total influence."

He wasn't alone as the cavalcade of dancing GIFs – including kittens with glow sticks – that occupied Barnes' tour through the album proved.

"This album is what #TimsTwitterListeningParty is all about," tweeted Tim Burgess as memories and celebrations were shared for each of the record's tracks. "It's a brilliant album, but gets a boost from all of us listening. And knowing that Leftfield are among us, well that is pretty special, right?" Special, and sonically spectacular.

**SLEEVE DESIGN:**
Blue Source

**@Leftfield:**
Leftism 22 tour. The band backstage at Barrowland, Glasgow, May 2017. With all these amazing guys who I miss massively at the moment.

(Below) Neil Barnes hosting the Listening Party.

## 1. RELEASE THE PRESSURE

◉ **@Leftfield (Neil Barnes)**

Trance hall is taking over inna your area. RTP features heavenly voice of [reggae singer] Earl Sixteen, originally released as 1st single on our own label Hard Hands In 1992.

## 2. AFRO-LEFT

◉ **@Leftfield**

[Electronic artist Neil] Cole (Djum Djum) helped me get my first single Not Forgotten onto [influential dance label] Rhythm King Records. Then he came up with his own language which duels with the [Brazilian single-stringed instrument] berimbau on Afro-Left, played amazingly by [jazz saxophonist] Kevin Haynes. There's only one Djum Djum and he came from space.

## 3. MELT

◉ **@Leftfield**

Melt was built from a selection of samples from 1980s influenced jazz and ambient records reflecting our obsession to make Leftism a journey that defied contemporary views of what a dance album should sound like.

## 4. SONG OF LIFE

◉ **@Leftfield**

SOL features the voice of Yanka Rupkina a Bulgarian singer from trio Bulgarka. We dedicated this to old friend Steve Waters who was a massive support to us in the early days.

## 5. ORIGINAL

◉ **@Leftfield**

Here we go! Eyes shut. Lights pulsating. Adam [Wren, now full member of Leftfield] laughing at me on stage. Memories. Original features Toni Halliday from Curve. I was a big fan of Curve. We loved taking people with nothing to do with dance music and putting them in different environments.

## 6. BLACK FLUTE

◉ **@Leftfield**

The first of two bangers in a row. Such a happy memory touring Leftism in 1996.

## 7. SPACE SHANTY

◉ **@Leftfield**

A cosmic inspired 303 and bass drum banger we conceived on a journey through the cosmos late one night. Dulcimers and rave meet sequenced arps. No sleep on this one.

## 8. INSPECTION (CHECK ONE)

◉ **@Leftfield**

We were influenced by [reggae artist] Danny Red's track Riddim Wize. Our A&R man, the sadly missed Mick Clark, sorted it out. Again twisting it up and mixing genres. Heavy acid line again.

## 9. STORM 3000

◉ **@Leftfield**

Back to breakbeats. But twisting it up with our beloved chroma Polaris keyboard making the weird almost jazz feel that the track has. An Electric storm across the universe.

## 10. OPEN UP

◉ **@Leftfield**

What more can I say, [Sex Pistols and Public Image Ltd frontman] John Lydon is a genius. The demo was done in 1990 but it took three years to get John into the studio to do it. John was an absolute dream making this. Open Up amazing recording experience.

## 11. 21ST CENTURY POEM

◉ **@Leftfield**

Our dystopian view of the future made with the wonderful and inspirational [poet] Lemn Sissay. 21st Century Poem morphs and twists halfway and we spun it all in backwards to create the feeling of the album drawing to a close and the journey ending.

## 12. [POSSIBLE PULL QUOTE]

◉ **@Leftfield**

Making Leftism was a joyous experience. It wasn't easy. It pushed us both to the limit but represented me and Paul in a magic space. Together in our own creative world. And I'm forever touched and moved that so many share that space with us.

# *Since I Left You*
## The Avalanches
Modular Recordings/XL Recordings, 2000

**ARTWORK:**
Fred Dana Marsh

Rumours of The Avalanches' debut had been circulating for a while before its actual release. Founded by Robbie Chater (**@TheAvalanches**) and Darren Seltmann in the mid-'90s, and later joined by Tony Di Blasi (also **@TheAvalanches**) on keyboard, label folk and DJs shared horror stories about this Australian band's record that had used so many samples it would never be cleared legally and then, *remarkably*, it was… even the track "borrowing" a bit of Madonna! However, if a record built by blending together so many different sources sounded potentially technical and cold, the resulting *Since I Left You* was anything but. A cavalcade of sounds, songs and spoken words, assiduous studio work and new recordings by the band allowed The Avalanches to make their samples their own, colouring their debut with emotions and feelings straight from their hearts. "I remember the first time I heard the title track, I was aware it was made up solely of samples and it blew my mind," recalled influential DJ Erol Alkan during the Listening Party. "The marriage of different sources were [sic] blended so tastefully, and with so much respect. It was very loving as well. There was something *very* special at the heart of it. When I had eventually heard each of the source tracks, they all sounded empty and paled to *Since I Left You*. That's kind of the highest compliment you can give but no slight on the original records".

→ Live At… The Concord. The Avalanches launch *Since I Left You* live in Brighton in 2000.

All things splice.
Robbie Chater knew
he had found The
Avalanches' sound
when "I'd written a
proper pop song
entirely from
samples".

## 1. SINCE I LEFT YOU

⊘ @TheAvalanches

Robbie: This track was the culmination of years of experimentation, finding a unique sound, it was the first time I thought, "Yes, I've done it! I've written a proper pop song entirely from samples intro, chorus, bridge, everything."

## 2. STAY ANOTHER SEASON

⊘ @TheAvalanches

Tony: We were so excited that Madonna let us clear this sample. Apparently it was the first one she's ever cleared.

## 3. RADIO

⊘ @TheAvalanches

Robbie: Ahh this track still sounds great, it was like a Phil Spector wall of sound but in a club. That's what was in our hearts Phil Spector, The Beach Boys, Mercury Rev, The Bomb Squad, Tribe Called Quest, De La Soul, Camp Lo.

## 4. Two Hearts in ¾ Time

⊘ @TheAvalanches

Robbie: This song was lovely because the four of us randomly found one of the four main elements each, and it fitted together perfectly. I remember with most of the songs all the songwriting royalties went to the sampled artists, leaving us with very little. John Cale was so fucking cool about his sample though – he insisted he take less, and that we should get the same % as him.

## 5. Avalanche Rock

⊘ @TheAvalanches

Robbie: I had the Raekwon 'avalanche rock' sample hanging around forever. Then Basement Jaxx came out with Remedy with all those little self referential interludes. We played that record endlessly. I can really hear it when I listen to our album now.

## 6. FLIGHT TONIGHT

⊘ @TheAvalanches

Tony: I recall Robbie chopping up The Count from Sesame Streets voice as samples for this one, and using them throughout the song for vibe. They ended up working so well I always get a chuckle when I hear it.

## 7. CLOSE TO YOU

⊘ @TheAvalanches

Tony: Ahhh so great to hear our heroes [hip hop duo] Sonny Cheeba sampled on there! We came full circle when we worked with them in person on Because I'm Me on Wildflower.

## 8. DINERS ONLY

⊘ @TheAvalanches

Robbie: I got a real kick out of using the sound of champagne glasses here, and of course the Moog machine record was a nod to The Beastie Boys and Get It Together. Mario C was always super supportive when we were kids and just starting out.

## 9. A DIFFERENT FEELING

⊘ @TheAvalanches

Robbie: Our psychedelic take on some of the house records that were coming out of France at the time and, of course, a sample of the one and only Carl Craig's incredible Paperclip People record.

The ARIA Music Awards in Sydney, October 2001, where the band picked-up four awards for *Since I Left You*.

## 10. ELECTRICITY

✔ @TheAvalanches

Tony: We got an opera singer in to sing this melody idea we had. We kept asking her to not sing as polished and sophisticated, but she couldn't do it! So we just let her sing in her natural operatic voice and surprisingly it ended up working really well.

## 11. TONIGHT

✔ @TheAvalanches

Robbie: This was really late in the process, although I'd had the piano sample for years. I recorded it with my hand on the turntable and it warped like that as I sampled it into the AKAI s9000. I lost the record [I sampled it from] on tour with Public Enemy in like '97 and to this day don't know what it was from, all I had left was the floppy disk labeled "sad piano".

## 12. PABLO'S CRUISE

✔ @TheAvalanches

Robbie: This was Darren's collage, although it was really long initially, we edited it down so in the end it served as a kind of introduction to Frontier Psychiatrist.

## 13. FRONTIER PSYCHIATRIST

✔ @TheAvalanches

Robbie: I'd had the bombastic Enoch Light spaghetti western kinda loop for years, and was always trying to turn it into like a super banging hip hop tune, but it just wasn't going anywhere. One day I came across the Wayne And Shuster comedy album [In Person Comedy Performance] and a little lightbulb went off in my head. I'd combine it with the spaghetti western sample and make a surreal scratch/comedy song.

## 14. ETOH

✔ @TheAvalanches

Robbie: I was on a real roll by now and these songs just flowed so effortlessly. I never thought much of Etoh at the time, it was so simple, I made it as if in a dream, Summer Crane too. It still surprises me how many people say it's their favourite track.

## 15. SUMMER CRANE

✔ @TheAvalanches

Robbie: I haven't listened to this for years. Sounds like a snippet of Carousel in there? Ahh that Francoise Hardy sample!

## 16. LITTLE JOURNEY

✔ @TheAvalanches

Tony: I think this was one of the last songs finished. Robbie had put it together really quickly. Just a beautiful example of pure creative expression.

## 17. LIVE AT DOMINOES

✔ @TheAvalanches

Robbie: The demo of this was absolutely mind bending, but we could never get it to sound as good once we took it into the proper studio to mix. You can hear the influence of the Roule and Crydamoure [French house] labels here.

## 18. EXTRA KINGS

✔ @TheAvalanches

Robbie: This was us using junk shop records to naively try and make huge sounds like My Bloody Valentine albums. I loved finding that Donny Osmond sample to finish the album, the way he echoed the vocal line from the opening song "ever since the day I left you…"

Recording Summer Crane at Sing Sing Studios, Melbourne in January 2000.

✔ @TheAvalanches

## Still sounds really good. Lovely to be here sharing it with you all.

# *Last Splash*
## The Breeders
4AD, 1993

PHOTOGRAPHER:

⚑ While having technically started life as a side-project of the Pixies (see page 240–241), *Last Splash* is the album that ensured The Breeders were no mere branch of someone else's rock family tree. Formed in 1989 by Kim Deal during down-time with her first group to make use of the songwriting ideas she couldn't get recorded, when Pixies became inactive in the early 1990s the class of this album elevated The Breeders from being a footnote in someone else's story to the authors of their own destiny. Awash with guitar fuzz, hard drums, popping bass grooves and bright melodies, *Last Splash* is a blast of cool, clipped grunge, that even provided one of the movement's greatest anthems, the juddering Cannonball. A favourite of everyone from Nirvana (who took the band on tour) to dance-punks The Prodigy (who "borrowed" S.O.S.'s guitar loop for Firestarter), *Last Splash* has proven a consistently influential record for fans and other bands alike. With Deal (guitar and vocals on this record – **@TheBreeders**), her sister Kelley Deal (guitars – **@KelleyDeal**), Jim MacPherson (drums – also **@TheBreeders**) and Josephine Wiggs (bass – **@JosephineWiggs**) – including co-producer Mark Freegard (**@Mark_Freegard**) – all logging on to Twitter to tell The Breeders' story, this was one Listening Party to really dive in to.

➔ Do you love me now? Kim and Kelley Deal playing live for MTV in 1993.

A good Deal. Kim Deal's Pixies side-project quickly became her main band.

LISTENING PARTY
26 APRIL 2020

### 1. NEW YEAR

**@TheBreeders**

Jim: This is the first song I ever demoed with Kim. CroMag Studios in Dayton, Ohio 1992. When we listened back to it, Kim turned off all the lights and lit up a big joint.

**@Mark_Freegard**

The intro was originally the middle 8 - we re arranged in the mix I think – at The Record Plant, Sausilito, the swirling guitars are randomly chopped up 1/4inch tape.

**@KelleyDeal**

The track of weird noises was created by recording some "rad" guitar onto 1/2" (1/4"?) tape, marking favourite bleeps, cutting those out, then reassembling them as a guitar track.

### 2. CANNONBALL

**@TheBreeders**

Kim: That squealing is my vocal microphone feeding back. I was using my brother's harmonica mic plugged straight into my Marshall amp. Cuz what else are you gonna do with your brother's harmonica mic?

**@JosephineWiggs**

The stops in Cannonball didn't exist when we recorded it – they were made post-production – using the mute buttons on the mixing desk. They came as a bit of a surprise I can tell you.

**@KelleyDeal**

I remember hating the dress I wore for parts of the video that Kim Gordon and Spike Jonze made for this song – but I didn't want to complain to Kim Gordon. Who would really?

**@JosephineWiggs**

I did. I kept pointing out that I was the only one with a fan blowing their hair and wasn't that weird?

**@TheBreeders**

Jim: For Cannonball I used a Gretch 1982 snare drum 8"x14" recorded at Coast Studio San Francisco, CA

**@TheBreeders**

Kim: The wind chimes that you hear at the end of the song were mine that I had hanging on my porch in Dayton, Ohio. Do I remember thinking "The wind chimes!" "Musn't forget to put those in the box truck for the 2,388 mile drive out to San Francisco" No. But there they are.

### 3. INVISIBLE MAN

✅ **@Tim_Burgess**

Love the chord changes to invisible Man. Kim and Kelley move so sweetly with the vocals.

### 4. NO ALOHA

✅ **@TheBreeders**

Kim: Thank you to [singer-songwriter] Chuck Prophet for letting us borrow some of his guitars. And thank you [guitarist] Nick Kizirnis for his help with the demos.

✅ **@KelleyDeal**

I think I played a lap steel that Chuck Prophet loaned us for the pretty intro slide.

✅ **@Mark_Freegard**

Two different versions chopped together. Love this edit. I gave Kim tape delay – she loved it.

✅ **@TheBreeders**

Jim: This is the second song I demoed with Kim. No Aloha is my favourite sounding demo from the Last Splash sessions.

### 5. ROI

✅ **@JosephineWiggs**

I was mucking around on the drums in Kim's basement one day, playing this drum riff & a "jam" must have started (this doesn't happen very often…) and Roi was the result… In the studio, I felt a bit self-conscious taking over the drum-stool from Jim – he is such a great drummer and I'm just a hack really.

✅ **@TheBreeders**

Kim: Roi is one of my favourite songs on the album. Thanks Ed Lacy [from Ohio] for letting me use your 1972 Minimoog Model D.

✅ **@KelleyDeal**

I love how my Strat and Kim's gold top sound together on this song.  Lovely and rackety.

### 6. DO YOU LOVE ME NOW?

✅ **@TheBreeders**

Kim: I recorded these vocals with my head stuck under a piano lid with a weight on the foot pedals. I thought it sounded dreamier.

### 7. FLIPSIDE

✅ **@TheBreeders**

Jim: I went to a [session drummer] Kenny Aronoff's drum clinic at Gilly's nightclub in Dayton, Ohio. I was so inspired I called Kim and showed her the idea that became Flipside

✅ **@TheBreeders**

Kim: [4AD designer] Vaughan Oliver kept putting naughty bits on my albums; using a receptionist's areola in the typography for Safari, wearing a huge phallus for Pod. So the album is called Last Splash. "Please, Vaughan." "Please don't put any ejaculations…nuthin!" "I don't want any naughty bits on this."

✅ **@JosephineWiggs**

Such a blisteringly fast song—always a challenge for me to play – hence all the live footage with my foot on the monitor – it made it easier. It wasn't 'til we did the 2013 reunion that Kim mentioned a tip "if you get the angle of the pick like THIS, it's easier to play fast." Thanks Kim.

### 8. I JUST WANNA GET ALONG

✅ **@KelleyDeal**

My memory is that Kim asked me to sing this song the day we recorded it at Coast.

✅ **@JosephineWiggs**

Do you *really* have a memory of that?  Or did you just ask Jim?

✅ **@KelleyDeal**

Ha! No Jo. I remember stuff…

✅ **@TheBreeders**

Jim: This is the first song we recorded for the album at Coast Recorders in San Francisco.

### 9. MAD LUCAS

✅ **@TheBreeders**

Jim: I asked Kim if I could make these drums sound like the Charlie Brown Christmas album.

✅ **@KelleyDeal**

Kim sang through my lovely Montgomery Ward tremolo amp.

@Mark_Freegard
Mad Lucas has the most beautiful rhythm guitar sound on the record.

## 10. DIVINE HAMMER

@TheBreeders
Jim: We demoed this song at Coast. I sang lead vocals. Kim thinks I'm lying to her.

@TheBreeders
Kim: Jim is lying to me.

## 11. S.O.S.

@TheBreeders
Kim: Dot dot dot, dash dash dash, dot dot dot. The guitar lead is playing Morse code for SOS.

@KelleyDeal
Had to bring my sewing machine to the studio to work on my quilt.... as one would. Kim recorded it through my Marshall amp and that's the sound that starts off the track

@TheBreeders
Jim: Solo drum section was plugged into a Leslie Rotating Speaker. This is the section The Prodigy used for Firestarter.

## 12. HAG

@JosephineWiggs
We ran out of time at Coast Recorders, and had moved to the Record Plant to mix, so vocals on Hag were recorded by Andy Taub at Muther's Recording ... Sean Hopper's studio (keyboardist in Huey Lewis and the News) down the street from the houseboats we lived in in Sausalito.

@KelleyDeal
I feel like some of the chords of this song were left in a motel room in Vail, Colorado.

## 13. SAINTS

@TheBreeders
Kim: When Jim was keeping beat on the hihats I kept bugging him to open his cymbal so it sounded like War Pigs. You know we re-recorded this as a single with [Dinosaur Jr's] J Mascis. I think it turned out really good.

## 14. DRIVIN' ON 9

@TheBreeders
Kim: Dear Dom Leone [from folk trio Ed's Redeeming Qualities] wrote this, RIP 1989.

@TheBreeders
Jim: This was the last drum take for Last Splash. This was recorded down the road at Brilliant Studios. While I was recording, Kim was air drumming and dancing along to illustrate how she wanted the breakdown to feel.

@KelleyDeal
I played the little guitar leads on a mandolin. Also Chuck Prophet's... thank you Chuck!

## 15. ROI (REPRISE)

@TheBreeders
Kim: Why did we have a reprise anyway? Kelly said "I'm thinking Pink Floyd...Animals...?"

Best in breed. Jim MacPherson, Kelley Deal, Kim Deal and Josephine Wiggs.

# The Trials Of Van Occupanther
## Midlake
Bella Union, 2006

With its blissful harmonies, horizon-spanning atmospheres and pastoral jangle, Midlake's *The Trials of Van Occupanther* is not just a beautiful record in its own right but an important musical bridge. Inspired by a range of vintage sounds, Tim Smith (vocals/guitar – **@TimSmith_Harp**), Eric Pulido (guitars – **@EBTheYounger**), Eric Nichelson (keys), Paul Alexander (bass) and McKenzie Smith's (drums – **@McKDeezy**) second album not only added a splash of modern colour to a previously neglected corner of Americana, but also helped mark out a musical space that kindred folk-rock spirits could thrive in.

"As far as lyrics/themes go for the album, they simply came from images/scenes in my mind, like a movie clip/snapshot in which to write from," wrote main songwriter and then Midlake frontman Tim Smith of the inspiration for this approach, as he opened *The Trials Of Van Occupanther's* Listening Party. "I could easily picture each song and wrote from that viewpoint rather than directly from my own life. I've always been interested in creating a world with music. Not just songs (ones that sound completely different from each other) but an overall cohesive feeling. I care less about surprising the listener than I do of creating a place for them." Smith eventually left the Texan band, handing over the group's reins to Pulido in 2012, so it proved a pleasure to return to the golden pastures of *The Trials Of Van Occupanther*.

PHOTOGRAPHY:
Tim Smith

SLEEVE DESIGN:
Tim Carter

(→)
In this camp. Eric Nichelson, Eric Pulido, Tim Smith, Paul Alexander and McKenzie Smith backstage in Brighton in 2006.

## 1. ROSCOE

⊘ **@TimSmith_Harp**

I'd made a short home demo (probably of just the first verse) to see what the band thought of this new idea. The demo though, to my ears, sounded just a bit too similar to Radiohead meets Fleetwood Mac. So I was somewhat hesitant when sharing it with them. No matter though, they liked it and so did I.

## 2. BANDITS

⊘ **@TimSmith_Harp**

I was really into Jethro Tull during that time. When writing it I was trying to keep Tull in sight. Of course, the finished song sounds nothing like Tull. Not sure what happened there…but still it turned out alright.

## 3. HEAD HOME

⊘ **@TimSmith_Harp**

Writing a chorus for Head Home was very difficult for some reason. Must've taken a couple weeks to find it. Finally came one afternoon after being inspired listening to a certain song… yep Fleetwood Mac's Rhiannon… now you know.

## 4. VAN OCCUPANTHER

⊘ **@TimSmith_Harp**

About a year before the actual recording of it, I'd drawn a little sketch of Occupanther flying which provided the idea for the song. Some outcast guy being picked on by the mean ol' townsfolk.

## 5. YOUNG BRIDE

⊘ **@TimSmith_Harp**

Remember writing this on a toy keyboard, just two chords, back and forth, very quietly in my apartment so as to not disturb the neighbours.

⊘ **@McKDeezy (McKenzie Smith)**

Many people think was recorded in some high end studio with tons of vintage gear. It was actually recorded in our living room with a very basic and minimal recording set up.

## 6. BRANCHES

⊘ **@TimSmith_Harp**

McKenzie's dad came to the studio around this time to record some jazz standards and rented a baby grand piano. I used it one night to record Branches. You can hear the sustain pedal felts in the quietest sections. Thankful it was there!

## 7. IN THIS CAMP

⊘ **@EBTheYounger (Eric Pulido)**

I remember we thought In This Camp was going to be a single when recording it… or maybe just me! It wasn't, some other tunes came after it that were a bit stronger, but I always loved this one.

## 8. WE GATHERED IN SPRING

⊘ **@EBTheYounger**

Someone asked about keys on this one and I'm pretty sure it was the MS2000 right guys? There were so many random keyboards around on the first 2 records especially.

## 9. IT COVERS THE HILLSIDES

⊘ **@TimSmith_Harp**

My Yacht Rock phase. Some Christopher Cross in there. ;-)

## 10. CHASING AFTER DEER

⊘ **@TimSmith_Harp**

Inspired by one of my all-time favourite albums, Isle Of View by Jimmie Spheeris.

## 11. YOU NEVER ARRIVED

⊘ **@TimSmith_Harp**

This song is stranger than I remember. Kinda sad, kinda humorous. Thank you all for making this album more important than I ever dreamt it would be!

**@TimSmith_Harp:** Here's what remains of the head [from the album cover]. It would tour w/us & be displayed on stage at shows. Originally had a baked clay nose but at some point a fan decided they must have it… and so he lost his nose. Replaced with duct tape until it retired.

# The Boy With The Arab Strap
## Belle & Sebastian
Jeepster, 1998

Belle & Sebastian had been somewhat overlooked ahead of the release of *The Boy With The Arab Strap* in 1998. Word of mouth around their first two records was spreading, but it was with this, their third album, that the cardigan-clad titans reached a wider world. Often associated with an indie tweeness, *The Boy With The Arab Strap* is anything but. Filled with beautifully drawn narratives, there is a deftness yet muscularity to the bounding keyboards and spinning guitars that imbue this record with a sinister joyfulness. Frontman and main songwriter Stuart Murdoch (**@Nee_Massey**), keyboard player Christopher Geddes (**@BeansGeddes**) and violinist, flautist and singer Sarah Martin (**@BellesGlasgow**), all tweeted their own distinctive memories of the recording process during the Listening Party, guiding us through the album that helped to take Belle & Sebastian to some unexpected places. "You may remember, this was our latest record when we surprisingly won the Best Newcomer award at the Brits," recalled Martin. "We partied in our kitchen that night!" What a brilliant career…

PHOTOGRAPHY:
Stuart Murdoch

@martin_j_wilson [fan]
I think the first time
[I saw Belle &
Sebastian] was
a good one.

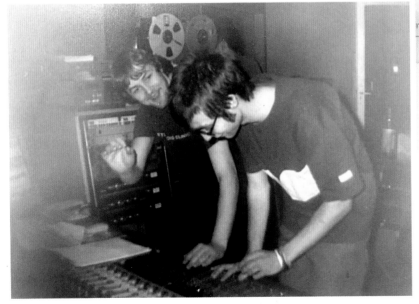

THE ZODIAC
190 COWLEY ROAD     OXFORD      Tel: 01865 726336

SATURDAY   2  AUGUST  1997

BELLE AND SEBASTIAN

£5.00 In Advance    £6.00 On Door

rs Open 8.30pm                Ticket No 165

LIVE MUSIC BEGINS 30 MINUTES AFTER DOORS OPENING

@BellesGlasgow: This
was all before the
desk in Cava studios
had automation.
These pics were from
*a* mix (possibly not
*the* mix) of The
Rollercoaster Ride.

LISTENING
PARTY

**27 APRIL
2020**

(↑)

Vocalist and cellist
Isobel Campbell
and Stuart Murdoch
onstage in New York
in 1997.

### 1. IT COULD HAVE BEEN A BRILLIANT CAREER

⊘ **@Nee_Massey (Stuart Murdoch)**
This is first time I've listened to this LP for many
years, and the one thing I felt about it was that it
was the one when the band announced itself. As
a result, I think it has a special flow that we
perhaps struggled to replicate. You can't plan for
these things though, you just cease the moment.

### 2. SLEEP THE CLOCK AROUND

⊘ **@BeansGeddes (Christopher Geddes)**
The arpeggio that goes all the way through this
tune is from a Roland Jupiter 8 that I paid £1000
for. It seemed a massive amount at the time, but
now you're lucky to find one for ten times that.

### 3. IS IT WICKED NOT TO CARE?

⊘ **@BellesGlasgow (Sarah Martin)**
We made a video for this song, and it ended up
including album cover art.

### 4. EASE YOUR FEET IN THE SEA

⊘ **@Nee_Massey**
Ease Your Feet was one that was recorded in
the church hall, you can hear the ambience in the
recording, and Richard counting to himself on the
break!

### 5. A SUMMER WASTING

⊘ **@Nee_Massey**
This was an ancient song, the oldest we'd
recorded up to that point, describing the summer
of '87, in which I failed my higher ordinary physics
for the fourth time, and gave in to music.

### 6. SEYMOUR STEIN

⊘ **@BeansGeddes**
[Record exec] Seymour Stein took us out for a
curry at a place called the Creme de la Creme,
it was an old art deco cinema, since demolished
for flats.

@BellesGlasgow: We went to a fox rescue sanctuary to take photos for the album sleeve. Wasn't the plan to call the album "Belle and Sebastian Support The Work Of The Clydeside Hunt Saboteurs", @nee_massey?

@nee_massey: That was [subsequent album] "fold your hands" I think!

## 7. A SPACE BOY DREAM

**@BeansGeddes**

I was listening to a lot of hip hop at the time, so probably wanted to get some harder drums on one of our tunes than we normally had. I don't think we'd really planned for this to go into the jam bit, it just happened spontaneously when we were recording it.

## 8. DIRTY DREAM NUMBER TWO

**@BellesGlasgow**

I think Stuart forgot to sing that spoken bit, so I suppose that was the first time my voice was committed to tape. I thought DD#2 was one of the best things we'd done then.

## 9. THE BOY WITH THE ARAB STRAP

**@Nee_Massey**

People ask us if we ever get sick of playing Arab Strap, personally I don't. It's fun, the crowd make it fun.

## 10. CHICKFACTOR

**@Nee_Massey**

Remember that movie Betty Blue? Think I ripped the piano off from the main theme for Chickfactor, but once it's in the mix nobody cares.

## 11. SIMPLE THINGS

**@BeansGeddes**

I stole the one note piano part from The Stooges. I thought it was the kind of thing I'd get told to stop doing but they just mixed it so quietly that you can't hear it!

## 12. THE ROLLERCOASTER RIDE

**@BeansGeddes**

I'd forgotten this started with a break. Sample it, somebody! We did a version of this with loads of synths and dubby effects which at the time I was absolutely raging that we didn't use, to the point of nearly quitting the band over it. With a bit of distance this version is probably better though.

# *English Tapas*
## Sleaford Mods
Rough Trade Records, 2017

**PHOTOGRAPHY:**
Simon Parfrement

⚑ A seemingly angry man accompanied by another who stares into his laptop while sipping beer might not seem the most promising of musical propositions. It certainly didn't appeal to many record labels in the early days, but Sleaford Mods have always had the faith to do things their own way. Justifying their self-belief, Jason Williamson ("shouting" – **@SleafordMods**) and Andrew Fearn's ("laptop") politically charged electronics have increasingly resonated with music fans, seeing them grow from an initial word-of-mouth phenomenon to a global proposition this, their (count 'em) ninth album, *English Tapas* proved to be a "state of the nation/state I'm in" step up. True to their self-driven, ahead of the curve form, the Mods not only embraced the Listening Parties early on, but methodically set themselves up to do one per week during the first lockdown, charting each of their records every Thursday in the spring of 2020. Their rundown of *English Tapas* was typically sharp, incisive and to the point – but then beats and brevity is what Sleaford Mods are all about.

Just Like We Do. Jason and Andrew along with the Nottingham bus adorned with English Tapas' artwork, as captured in the Bunch Of Kunst documentary (and shared by the filmmakers during the Listening Party).

# SLEAFORD MODS

See w
Ticket
It's th
any re
notify
must b

LISTENING
PARTY
**30 APRIL
2020**

⊕

The Mods performing
*English Tapas* for
an Irish audience
in 2017.

## 1. ARMY NIGHTS

✓ **@SleafordMods (Jason Williamson)**

Bit new model army this which obviously I didn't mind. Track covers my interest in all things gym. How the idea of exercise gets sniffed at as some vanity thing. So what. It beats taking crack.

## 2. JUST LIKE WE DO

✓ **@SleafordMods**

Fan favourite. Hadn't realised at the time but the bass is very close to Cameo's Word Up.

## 3. MOPTOP

✓ **@SleafordMods**

[Boris] Johnson a running theme throughout our recording career. You could see from as far back as his mayor of Lon role and how a lot of folk, intelligent ones included, praised him. Worrying, back then. Clearly very corrupt.

## 4. MESSY ANYWHERE

✓ **@SleafordMods**

My personal fav. Really liked the talking heads feel and George Harrison style backing vox.

## 5. TIME SANDS

✓ **@SleafordMods**

Another drug hell track. The song discusses getting a train from Kings Cross off my head which isn't an alien experience for anyone really but I thought it was an interesting way to portray the continued self destructive habits of myself and a lot of people.

## 6. SNOUT

✓ **@SleafordMods**

English street music for 45+ year olds. Again as in most of the stuff we do it attacks the zombified oppressed. Those who can't even fucking see who's driving them off a cliff.

## 7. DRAYTON MANORED

✓ **@SleafordMods**

Andrew came up with the idea of the door sound as you walk into the off licence. Fucking brilliant. Made the track.

## 8. CARLTON TOUTS

✓ **@SleafordMods**

Another tune knee deep in W/C code and habit. Ugly pubs full of high vis jackets and Stone Island (before it got trendy) shite shops and a co-op. Dog groomers. Tattoo parlour. Massage parlour. Etc.

## 9. CUDDLY

✓ **@SleafordMods**

Andrew pulling this one out the bag near the end of the album sessions. Took me about 90 minutes to get a vocal. I followed the rhythm more with this instead of floating a rant over the top. Very Specials like.

## 10. DULL

✓ **@SleafordMods**

We don't do positivity. That's about as useful as them fucking rainbows on people's windows currently. No disrespect but fireguard/chocolate.

## 11. B.H.S.

✓ **@SleafordMods**

This is a classic. This tune is irresistible in every way. For me it sits alongside most stuff I've been influenced by.

## 12. I FEEL SO WRONG

✓ **@SleafordMods**

The vocal is a bit Paul Weller but a good version of him I think. Ha,ha. I've done some dodgy ones. Andrew's music sometimes just gets ya scratching ya head. He pulls these wildcards out and it just shifts the landscape.

# High Land, Hard Rain
## Aztec Camera
Rough Trade Records, 1983

If early 1980s indie was defined as much by its jangly guitars as the independent record labels who released the records, then Aztec Camera was the band who at once defined and then reinvented the genre with their debut album. Released by Rough Trade, *High Land, Hard Rain* was driven by frontman Roddy Frame's dexterous guitar playing. Yet his urgent vocals and sharp songwriting took the fledgling indie sound somewhere else. Inspired by old jazz records and a pop sensibility, the Scottish group's debut *High Land, Hard Rain* is a timeless affair of bright emotions, chiming chords and irresistible rhythms that opened up whole new worlds for its listeners. Roddy Frame (**@RoddyFrame**), along with drummer David Ruffy (**@DaveRuffy**), offered some Hard insight into Aztec Camera's debut.

**ARTWORK:**
David Band

Release! Aztec Camera performing live at at Liverpool's James Byrom Hall in 1983.

### 1. OBLIVIOUS

⊘ @RoddyFrame

Written in Highlands Avenue, Acton. Bit of a Reginald Perrin vibe. Sunny. Semi Tudor. Heard the Stone Poneys in Alan Horne's van. Hence beat of a different drum. The guitar solo mimics the trumpet in Alone Again Or by Love. Is that David Ruffy's 808 claves I hear? More clavé! Campbell [Owens, bassist] keeping it sparse. Sounds like there's enough going on, to be fair. Haha.

### 2. THE BOY WONDERS

⊘ @RoddyFrame

Folky intro with Dave giving a bodhran vibe on the toms – then a kind of "Clash on a 12 string" riff under the verses. Written in East Kilbride. Remember the exact moment I was walking up my street and thought "I know... we need shouting!"

### 3. WALK OUT TO WINTER

⊘ @RoddyFrame

I was finding lots of nice chords for the first time and very into clean glacial tones. Roland Jazz chorus amp (60, nothing flash yet). Durutti Column. Clean and wintry vibes. The opposite of bluesy valvey authenticity, I guess.

### 4. THE BUGLE SOUNDS AGAIN

⊘ @RoddyFrame

Memories of the Equi cafe [in Sauchiehall Street, Glasgow] and rehearsing in the old art school buildings under the M8 flyover. Acoustic guitars attracted me because they were strictly taboo in our indie world. Apart from Paul Weller's brave, beautiful English Rose, which I just loved, they were frowned on.

### 5. WE COULD SEND LETTERS

⊘ @RoddyFrame

For the solo, [producer] John Brand handed me this Spanish guitar he'd brought and said "make me cry!" that's true. I remember just improvising a solo in each take til we got a good one. Just me and John, in the dark late at night. Amazing memories.

### 6. PILLAR TO POST

⊘ @RoddyFrame

Our vision of indie Motown. With a Clash poster on the wall. Haha. We loved singles. I spent my Saturdays trawling the singles boxes in Impulse records. Punk and beyond was all about seven inches.

⊘ @DaveRuffy

Thank you Mr Frame, that was the first track we recorded together. it was the first Rough Trade single I believe...

### 7. RELEASE

⊘ @RoddyFrame

Got Wes Montgomery's [jazz album] While We're Young from the local library. And found out all I could about him. He played with his thumb rather than a plectrum, so as not to disturb the neighbours. I loved his sound.

### 8. LOST OUTSIDE THE TUNNEL

⊘ @RoddyFrame

Wrote this back in my pre Aztec band Neutral Blue, which was John Maciness's band. With David Mulholland and Eddie MacPhail. Sounds like I was listening to The Cure!

### 9. BACK ON BOARD

⊘ @RoddyFrame

I think inspired by a Scottish piper souvenir Amazing Grace lyric tea towel I had hanging up. Amazing words to that hymn of course.

### 10. DOWN THE DIP

⊘ @RoddyFrame

Written more as a gesture, than a song. Just a way to end the album with a little intimacy. There was a pub called the Diplomat in East Kilbride so that must be where I got the idea. Nice cross fade by John Brand. Back in the days of splicing tape and blades! And there you have it!

⊕

The Boy Wonders. Roddy Frame onstage fronting Aztec Camera in 1983.

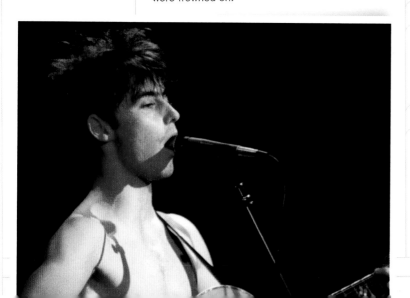

# Holy Fire
## Foals
Transgressive/Warners, 2013

**SLEEVE DESIGN:**
Leif Podhajsky

⚘ Having twisted and turned with the math rock of their debut *Antidotes* and created blissfully immersive spaces with trance-like songs on *Total Life Forever*, it wasn't obvious Foals needed to add anything else to their rock'n'roll armour. Then their third album, *Holy Fire*, arrived with a new elemental force that really shifted the Oxford band up a gear: swagger. The enticing and hypnotic deftness remained, the big atmospheres and visionary lyrics too, but Foals had added a confidence and a robustness that gave their songs a volume and invulnerability that confirmed them as a true 21st-century rock band. *Holy Fire* was an assured yet artistic statement from Yannis Philippakis (vocals/guitar – **@Foals**), Jack Bevan (drums – also **@Foals**), Jimmy Smith (guitar/synths), Edwin Congreave (synths/keyboards) and then bassist Walter Gervers. The band's Philippakis and Bevan joined the Listening Party, and as you would guess from an album with so much swagger, the *Holy Fire* playback got raucous.

**LISTENING PARTY**
**4 MAY 2020**

### 1. PRELUDE

✅ **@Foals**
Yannis: We wanted a swampy & intense intro like entering a weird jungle. Always felt like an opener, even when it was called Pavlov's Dog.

### 2. INHALER

✅ **@Foals**
Jack: This track was actually a combo of a few different ideas and we couldn't quite crack it. It nearly didn't make the record but we had a breakthrough towards the end of recording. I remember taking this home and playing it to Kit (our percussion player, who I was living with at the time) and he just said "fucking hell".

### 3. MY NUMBER

✅ **@Foals**
Yannis: Have a dance... bust the room up. Feel good. Probably the funkiest track we've ever written.

### 4. BAD HABIT

✅ **@Foals**
Yannis: I wanted to be super vulnerable with the lyrics on this one, regret and guilt and mortality.

### 5. EVERYTIME

✅ **@Foals**
Yannis: The song started out as our idea of a Fleetwood Mac track. We were excited about how poppy it was.

### 6. LATE NIGHT

✅ **@Foals**
Jack: I recorded this track with a broken kick drum pedal and you can hear it squeaking if you really listen.

### 7. OUT OF THE WOODS

✅ **@Foals**
Yannis: Always made me think of the Pacific highway cruising down, wind blowing, with friends imaginary or otherwise!

@Foals

Jack: It has a lightness to it that I love and it's very positive.

## 8. MILK & BLACK SPIDERS

@Foals

Yannis: Yannis: We wanted the song to move from paranoia and darkness into this beautiful positive place. The lyrics to this hung on the line 'you're my compass and my sea'. I was at the start of a new long-distance relationship, confused and a bit lost. This song was the expression of that. Like a message in a bottle.

## 9. PROVIDENCE

@Foals

Yannis: I wanted to tap into a deranged gospel preacher vibe. Jack looked like he was gonna explode doing the mental drum solo thing.

@Foals

Jack: Flood let me improv the big fill three times, then pick one. I still don't really know what my arms were thinking. Live it is slightly different every single time.

## 10. STEPSON

@Foals

Yannis: Me and jimmy tracked this at night with a load of wine in low light and we didn't listen back to the takes. Great for this time of night. This one is for all the dads out there...

## 11. MOON

@Foals

Yannis: I'd seen the movie Melancholia [by Lars von Trier] at the cinema and came back to the studio feeling dark and spooked. Jimmy was messing with these chords so I made a rhythm on my loop pedal and the lyrics poured out. I wanted it to be like a painting of the apocalypse.

Burning ambition. Foals frontman Yannis Philippakis took the band's incendiary live performances to a new level with *Holy Fire*. Often literally.

# Welcome To The Pleasuredome
## Frankie Goes To Hollywood
ZTT, 1984

⚔ Pop band? Art project? Progressive force? There has been a lot of theorising and mythologising about Frankie Goes To Hollywood – not least by the band themselves – but with their debut album Holly Johnson (vocals – **@TheHollyJohnson**), Paul Rutherford (backing vocals), Brian Nash (guitar), Mark O'Toole (bass) and Peter Gill (drums) justified much of what has been ascribed to them. Boasting a 13-minute title track, instrumentals, a Bruce Springsteen cover, a modern-day torch song in The Power Of Love, pioneering production and an irresistible, sexually vibrant pop song banned by the BBC in the form of Relax, *Welcome To The Pleasuredome* is a sprawling epic Samuel Taylor Coleridge, author of equally sprawling epic Kubla Khan, would approve of. Yet, during the 1980s, with the threat of intercontinental nuclear armageddon informing some of the lyrics and, in Johnson, a man who instinctively understood gay culture, which was only just starting to make its way out of the shadows, *Welcome To The Pleasuredome* is far from a frivolous affair. This is a record that set out to rewire civilisation, yet Johnson's Listening Party toned down the fanfare of its birth and eschewed the rhetoric, instead offering some enigmatic pointers to help you relax and immerse yourself in this wonderful record. Welcome…

**ARTWORK:**
Lo Cole

→ The lads are here. Frankie's Holly Johnson and Paul Rutherford.

## 1. THE WORLD IS MY OYSTER (INCLUDING WELL, SNATCH OF FURY)

**@TheHollyJohnson**

Well.... The World Is My Oyster. It certainly felt like it at the time. Young, dumb and full of… well you know. Life goes on day after day. Liverpool seemed a long way from home at this point in time.

## 2. WELCOME TO THE PLEASUREDOME

**@TheHollyJohnson**

To me the whole of side one is just surfing on a wave of bass and drum machine. Keep moving on… Errrrrrrrect! VE Day …. The War Is Won! Supernova!

## 3. RELAX (COME FIGHTING)

**@TheHollyJohnson**

Relax not the classic seven-inch mix, but one you didn't have.

## 4. WAR (…AND HIDE)

**@TheHollyJohnson**

Side Two It is then. I was fumbling with my flies obviously! Yeahhhhhhhhhhh Ha!

## 5. TWO TRIBES (FOR THE VICTIMS OF RAVISHMENT)

**@TheHollyJohnson**

ENJOY!  Two Tribes, sock it to me biscuit!

**@TheHollyJohnson**

Are we living in a land where sex and horror are the new gods?

## 6. FERRY (GO)

**@TheHollyJohnson**

It's a covers band from the Cavern all of a sudden. [The track is a cover of Gerry & The Pacemakers' *Ferry Cross The Mersey*] Signing on was all we had in 1983.

## 7. BORN TO RUN

**@TheHollyJohnson**

[A Bruce Springsteen cover] What can I say. The Boss is The Boss.

## 8. SAN JOSE (THE WAY)

**@TheHollyJohnson**

Sublime: San Jose by Bacharach and David arranged by Anne Dudley. A Las Vegas lounge version recorded while the Notting Hill Carnival raged outside the studio on a sunny Saturday in 1984.

## 9. WISH (THE LADS WERE HERE)

**@TheHollyJohnson**

Love Has Got A Gun was the title of this song always was always will be to me.

## 10. THE BALLAD OF 32

**@TheHollyJohnson**

Time to pour yourself a drink or roll one of those cigarettes… and disappear to the dark side of the room? Hallucinating some poor girl under the piano, she's lost something. I wonder what?

## 11. KRISCO KISSES

**@TheHollyJohnson**

You can take it, take it up, Buttock-Up.

## 12. BLACK NIGHT WHITE LIGHT

**@TheHollyJohnson**

Are Dire Straights in the next studio? Is it a Danielle Steel Novel? Or just The Other Side Of Midnight ?

## 13. THE ONLY STAR IN HEAVEN

**@TheHollyJohnson**

Grace Jones liked this one allegedly. "Everybody Create, before it's too late" is my favourite line.

## 14. THE POWER OF LOVE

**@TheHollyJohnson**

It's not just for Christmas, it's for life. Thank you all for listening  and giving me so much love over the years. Thanks to everyone who worked on this record and made it what it was. Make Love Your Goal!

## 15. "…BANG"

**@TheHollyJohnson**

Frankie Say… No More.

# *Employment*
## Kaiser Chiefs
B-Unique, 2005

When the newspapers are using your song titles for headlines (I Predict A Riot…) and football fans are adapting your songs on the terraces ("Oh my God I can't believe it… we've never been this good away from home"), it is safe to assume your music is having a cultural moment. Emerging out of a lacklustre melee of British guitar music at the start of the 2000s, Leeds' Kaiser Chiefs brought tunes, wit and anthemic ambition. Their debut album *Employment*, not only propelled the band's songs to household-name status, but also lit a fuse for a new wave of six-string-led creativity. Since 2005 the band have gone on to tour the world, judge the TV show The Voice and star at Live8, although the original line-up of Ricky Wilson (vocals – **@RickOnTour**), Simon Rix (bass – **@curlywand**), Nick "Peanut" Baines (keyboards – **@PeanutKaiser**) and Alan "Whitey" White (guitars – **@WhiteyKaiser**) shifted slightly after drummer Nick Hodgson (**@NickJDHodgson**) left the band not entirely un-acrimoniously in 2012, leaving VJ Mistry to jump behind the kit. However, such is the communal spirit of the Listening Party that all band members – past and present – joined together to give us some gainful *Employment* along with album producer Stephen Street (**@StreetStephen**).

ARTWORK:
Cally at Antar

Anyone got any dice? **@fulliautomatix6** shared the board game-styled special edition of Employment that came with Kaiser Chiefs monopoly money during the Listening Party.

✔ **@Tim_Burgess**

I love the fact Nick Hodgson is joining his old Kaiser Chiefs bandmates for the listening party. Got me emotional here fellas.

122

Team mates. Nick "Peanut" Baines, Andrew "Whitey" White, Ricky Wilson, Nick Hodgson and Simon Rix.

LISTENING PARTY

13 MAY 2020

### 1. EVERYDAY I LOVE YOU LESS AND LESS

**@RickOnTour (Ricky Wilson)**
I wasn't up for EILYL&L being the first track... but I like that now. Starting with a break-up. Dead easy to write... everything just had to rhyme with 'less'.

### 2. I PREDICT A RIOT

**@curlywand (Simon Rix)**
This was the first song we recorded for the album and the first time with Stephen Street. We met him on The Ordinary Boys tour in June 2004 at the London gig which was at Kings College. That gig was also memorable for our stage time being before doors.

### 3. MODERN WAY

**@NickJDHodgson**
So fast for a slow song. I remember playing an early version of Modern Way to Simon and Ricky in my flat in Headingley [Leeds]. But the chorus came in rehearsal and I remember riding about on BMXs with Ricky after, going on about it. Big song.

**@PeanutKaiser (Nick Baines)**
My synth beeps were referred to as Nintendo-esque in a review somewhere. I like that.

**@StreetStephen**
Modern Way, a fantastic song, needs more cowbell though!

### 4. NA NA NA NA NAA

**@curlywand**
We were doing lots of little one-off gigs by the time we wrote this song. Where you have 25 mins to win the crowd over. We wrote this either just before or just after one of those at Dublin Castle with Bloc Party and Dogs. The idea was just something energetic with something simple to sing that everyone could "get".

### 5. YOU CAN HAVE IT ALL

**@curlywand**
One of my favourites. Band wise we all thought this was a single. Prob single 4. For us early influences were post punk and 2 Tone and Beach Boys, but my favourite band was Super Furry Animals and I thought this was something close to something they would write.

### 6. OH MY GOD

**@NickJDHodgson**

Trivia fans...The original lyrics to the pre chorus were "It don't matter to me, cos all I wanted to be. Was left to my own resources, like only fools and horses." So we tried to replicate it and soon it was the chorus. I read John Peel's obituary in the build up before the last chorus.

### 7. BORN TO BE A DANCER

**@curlywand**

After our first indie release of OMG, we were going to do a second release with [label] Drowned In Sound, we were keen on Born To Be A Dancer but our label boss at that time Sean was insistent we had to write something else something as good as Oh My God. Fortunately for us we went away and wrote I Predict A Riot. Unfortunately for Sean it was so much "as good" that we ended up releasing it elsewhere. I'm always grateful for the advice though.

### 8. SATURDAY NIGHT

**@curlywand**

When we played this at our first ever gig Ricky had a megaphone (and I was wearing sunglasses indoors). It wasn't very pretty and both were very quickly dropped. The song stuck around though. Graham Coxon's motorbike at the start. Big Horns in the Chorus.

### 9. WHAT DID I EVER GIVE YOU?

**@PeanutKaiser**

Nice bit of Hammond there. I played that intro riff and Nick liked it and then the song grew quickly from there. I think it was a 'maybe' for the album but once recorded, it earned its place. I like the vocals on this.

### 10. TIME HONOURED TRADITION

**@curlywand**

We started with this idea that the band was going to be quirky British sing-along. But then we kept doing these low chanty vocals that we thought were kinda of Russian. So it became another thing in the Kaiser Chiefs sound collection. I always remember [journalist] Tim Jonze from NME who was a massive Kaiser Chiefs supporter in the early days, he gave us single of the week and a load of other press that really pushed us on our way. He hated this song...

I predict a riot. The band signing copies of their album at HMV in London.

### 11. CAROLINE, YES

**@curlywand**

When we played this at our first gig it was called Hail To The Chief. Which was a play on the Radiohead album title, so we changed it for a play on a Beach Boys song that seemed more congruous with our sound and what we were doing.

### 12. TEAM MATE

**@WhiteyKaiser (Alan White)**

Team Mate's reverse guitar is actually me playing the song backwards. I start at the end of the song and then move my fingers away from the guitar. Inspired by '109.PT2' by The Charlatans.

**@curlywand**

We all always imagined this to be the last song. I was really skeptical about all the backwards guitar stuff being a bit corny and done by Oasis, but I was in fact wrong.

**@PeanutKaiser**

Steve Harris really liked my delicate piano on this. I was a relatively new keyboard player at the time and compliments like that gave me a lot of confidence. I always remember that.

**@NickJDHodgson**

This song started off on a Hammond Organ that took up a lot of space in our storage space. My dad loved this song and said it pointed to where we might go next. I love Ricky's vocal.

The Voice. Kaiser Chiefs frontman Ricky Wilson in the thick of the action at Brixton Academy.

# *Lovelife*
## Lush
4AD, 1996

 Having been described as "shoegaze pioneers", Lush looked up to take in life around them when they came to make their fourth album, *Lovelife*. Inspired lyrically by the fallout of broken relationships, the record also boasted snappy pop hooks that chimed loudly with the growing confidence British bands were acquiring in the mid '90s after several years of domination by their American peers. Not a pure Britpop blast – although it does feature a cameo from Jarvis Cocker – the band still retained their dreamier side, with Miki Berenyi (lead vocals/guitar – @Berenyi_Miki), Emma Anderson (guitars/vocals), Phil King (bass) and Chris Acland (drums) creating a record that reflected its times but was still quintessential Lush.. "Oh bloody hell - just spilt wine all over my keyboard!" tweeted Berenyi as *Lovelife's* Listening Party got underway. Never mind, getting together with some friends over a good bottle is always the best way to take stock of your *Lovelife*.

**PHOTOGRAPHY:**
Ichiro Kono

**SLEEVE DESIGN:**
v23

Ciao! Emma Anderson, Miki Berenyi, Phil King and Chris Acland.

@Berenyi_Miki
The Single Girl video was excellent fun. We had two actors from Four Weddings & A Funeral (couldn't quite stretch the budget to Hugh Grant/ Kristen Scott Thomas)...

## 1. LADYKILLERS

@Berenyi_Miki
I'm always asked to name the men in Ladykillers but nope, not gonna because honestly it could've been written about any number of people.

## 2. HEAVENLY NOBODIES

@Berenyi_Miki
I do love a bar-chord riff! Played on my lovely [12 string Gibson guitar] Firebird which is still (just about) in one piece.

## 3. 500 (SHAKE BABY SHAKE)

@Berenyi_Miki
Emma wrote this song about the Fiat 500. She'd just passed her test and wanted to own one.

## 4. I'VE BEEN HERE BEFORE

@Berenyi_Miki
One of the many songs on the album about relationship ups and downs and breakups. Partly why we called it Lovelife.

## 5. PAPASAN

@Berenyi_Miki
Papasan is another breakup gone bad (I was even more of a dickhead than he was) but hey, that's all long ago and we're friends again now.

## 6. SINGLE GIRL

@Berenyi_Miki
The Single Girl video was excellent fun. We had two actors from Four Weddings & A Funeral (couldn't quite stretch the budget to Hugh Grant/Kristen Scott Thomas) and a whole bunch of our mates.

## 7. CIAO!

@Berenyi_Miki
Also known as The Jarvis Duet. Jarvis agreed to do Ciao, possibly because the demo made him laugh (I sang his 'low' vocal parts and sounded like a depressed frog). Jarvis came to the studio, had a few nips of brandy to calm his nerves, then did the whole thing in 2 takes.

## 8. TRALALA

@Berenyi_Miki
Emma's lyrics were inspired by the character from Last Exit To Brooklyn (not sure whether from the book or Jennifer Jason Leigh's brilliant performance in the film).

## 9. LAST NIGHT

@Berenyi_Miki
This was my top choice for the single that never was. Actually getting rather blissed out listening to this song.

## 10. RUNAWAY

@Berenyi_Miki
Lyrics were about a friend who struggled with drug addiction – a brilliant person becoming much less so.

## 11. THE CHILDCATCHER

@Berenyi_Miki
If you've even wondered what Phil is narrating under the middle 8 section of The Childcatcher, it's this poem – The Bloom of Youth – by Billy Childish. It felt suitable paedo-ish.

## 12. OLYMPIA

@Berenyi_Miki
I remember really struggling with the vocal. They put a guitar tuner on the mixing desk and I had to sing it over and over until it registered in the right spot. Pretty much killed the whole fucking song for me.

# *Olympian*
## Gene
Costermonger/Polydor, 1995

By shifting guitar music from the cultural fringes to the mainstream – inadvertently or otherwise – Britpop memories tend to focus on Blur, Oasis and Pulp. However, while the brilliance of those acts certainly deserves the spotlight, it is often forgotten just how rich British music was in the mid '90s, regardless of it being either a true scene or just a happy collision of talents. London band Gene seem to be one of the most overlooked of the era. Despite regularly bothering the charts and selling out tours, Martin Rossiter (vocals – **@MartinRossiter**), Steve Mason (guitar), Matt James (drums – **@MusicMattJames**) and Kevin Miles' (bass) smouldering emotions and stylish, soulful indie has been downgraded beyond their hardcore of fans. Which is what made the Listening Party for Gene's debut, *Olympian,* a truly unique celebration. The playback connected many listeners who were reminded about how overlooked Gene were and what a lost gem their debut was. And it made the band themselves appreciate the record even more as they revisited it for the first time in years. "What I like about *Olympian* as an album now is it's the sound of a band with ambition," wrote Rossiter, who, together with James, offered a tour round the album. "Sometimes fulfilled sometimes not, but it was the ambition that mattered." What also mattered was the Olympian playback took place on the night of the Gene frontman's 50th birthday making this a true Listening PARTY although he was giving out rather than receiving presents. "Can we make Tim Burgess a saint, please?" Martin Rossiter tweeted later. "Saint Tim has a ring to it." A birthday, a lost classic revived and a canonisation? Well, good things do come in threes…

**PHOTOGRAPHY:**
Kevin Westenberg

**SLEEVE DESIGN:**
Andy Vella

@Tim_Burgess

I have good memories of the shows that we played with Gene – Charlatans fans really enjoyed them and they were sound people. Can't ask for more than that.

↓

Matt "The Hat" James (left) and Martin Rossiter (right) meet "the biz". @MartinRossiter The exact moment we signed to Polydor.

### 1. HAUNTED BY YOU

**@MartinRossiter**
The bass is what drives this, Kev is a very under rated bass player. He reminds me of McCartney – strikes a good balance between melody, harmonic foundation and groove.

**@MusicMattJames**
Working title was Chimney. Breezy opener and a real live rabble rouser in the early days. Didn't hugely catch that on the record IMO. Was one of the last to be written and hadn't been demoed many times like other tunes.

### 2. YOUR LOVE, IT LIES

**@MartinRossiter**
I always loved the line "I'll take your arms and tend you like a vine." It felt like a lyric that a proper writer would pen.

**@MusicMattJames**
Classic early Gene I love Steve's jazzy plucking and Mart's voice has a lovely kinda young purity about it? Hard to articulate but it's very charming and throughout the LP. Chorus always got the crowd going as is very well telegraphed!

### 3. TRUTH, REST YOUR HEAD

**@MusicMattJames**
My fave on the LP still gives me goosebumps listening to it and still sounds amazing. Verse influenced by Under The Bridge [by Red Hot Chili Peppers] which Steve bloody loved. In fact the working title was Chilli Tune!

**@MartinRossiter**
Steve worked so hard on the guitar parts for this – he used to take his guitar with him when he had a bath. I love how melodic the guitar is, like a second vocal.

### 4. A CAR THAT SPED

✅ **@MartinRossiter**
I'd just watched Truly, Madly, Deeply on the telly when I wrote this. I liked the idea of a dead partner still being able to communicate with their ex. It's the dead partner telling the living to move on and have a life.

### 5. LEFT-HANDED

✅ **@MusicMattJames**
We felt we needed rockier tracks as live we were much more like that. The lyrics are great, but prob would not make my LP now. The demo was more Led Zep.

### 6. LONDON, CAN YOU WAIT?

✅ **@MartinRossiter**
I remember a reviewer knocking this song for the use of 'kith and kin because it was antiquated. Well I say to him, "Beest gone, thou art not at Tim's Twitt'r Listening Party."

✅ **@MusicMattJames**
Total class song that has/will stand test of time. Music was inspired by Faces' Cindy, but Mart's vox style puts it in very different place. Great build, great lyrics, great crescendo. We played this throughout our whole live career which says a lot.

### 7. TO THE CITY

✅ **@MartinRossiter**
When did fade-ins stop being de rigueur? Again Matt and Kev joined at the hip, at their best they felt like a four armed rhythm machine.

✅ **@MusicMattJames**
Love the piano doubling the bass, feels like a very gloomy Madness.

### 8. STILL CAN'T FIND THE PHONE

✅ **@MartinRossiter**
A single in Germany, if I remember correctly. Sales in double figures, that showed 'em. Steve did a cracking job of fitting super musical parts around the vocal, the riffs are delicious. Matt's rarely heard but dulcet tonsils on backing vocals.

**@MartinRossiter**
Around this time I did some work with Greenpeace, who's the beardy guy on the left in the red jacket?

My kith and kin.
Matt James, Martin
Rossiter, Steve Mason
and Kevin Miles.

→

**@MartinRossiter**
From the same [1993]
notebook here are the
lyrics from For The
Dead. [The single did
not feature on
*Olympian*, although
both Matt James and
the singer suggested
during the Listening
Party that was a
mistake.]

✓ **@MusicMattJames**
Love this! When we went into the studio it sounded
like tomorrow never knows. It came out like
Everybody's Talkin by Harry Nielsen!

### 9. SLEEP WELL TONIGHT

✓ **@MartinRossiter**
I remember [Blur frontman] Damon Albarn telling
me it was his favourite single of the year, but he
did that to all the boys.

✓ **@MusicMattJames**
Our first entry into the top 40 at number 36! We
were in a van when we found out and forged a
number 36 out of Edam cheese wax and stuck it
to the window. Lovely memory.

### 10. OLYMPIAN

✓ **MartinRossiter @MartinRossiter**
Probably the most well rounded track on the
album. We worked with a string arranger on this,
he based part of the arrangement on the quaver
piano line I wrote. I'd studied string arrangement
but wasn't confident enough to suggest I should
do it. I'm glad I didn't because he did a better job
than I would have done at the time.

✓ **@MusicMattJames**
Just love this song so much. Think it's timpani
drums at the beginning. We were afforded a real
string section which was a bloody good thing.
Another goosebump moment for me.

### 11. WE'LL FIND OUR OWN WAY

✓ **@MartinRossiter**
I really like this song, unpretentious, simple and
sweet.

✓ **@MusicMattJames**
You beauty!!! A golden bonus treat after the LP
kind of ends with Olympian. Think that was the
thinking anyway! Written last and in the studio,
possibly. I went hunting around the studio for
some different percussion that I didn't own and
found a bell tree. It's the last thing you hear on
the LP and it sounds smashing.

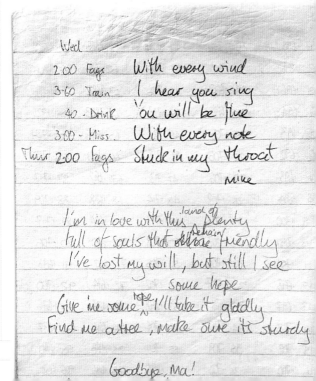

# The Specials
## The Specials
2 Tone, 1979

**SLEEVE DESIGN:**
David Storey

The Specials were more than just a band. Not only did the Coventry seven-piece establish their own 2 Tone label and kick-start their own music scene, they were also an expression of life itself. They offered an outlet for the ideas and influences that were beginning to permeate throughout British society as the country began to settle into its post-colonial place in the world. The band were a representation of the people who lived and worked together, the folk who made up modern, multicultural Britain. Crucially, The Specials were also an encapsulation of their own times – of youthful energy growing frustrated with a stagnant world, of young visionaries tired of being told "no". And, of course, with their blend of ska revival, prized Jamaican reggae 45s, post-punk attitude and their songwriting chops, The Specials were an expression of great music.

Part protest, part party, Terry Hall (vocals – tweeting from **@HoracePanterArt**), Neville Staple (vocals), Lynval Golding (guitar), Roddy Radiation (lead guitar), Jerry Dammers (keyboards), Horace Panter (bass – **@HoracePanterArt**) and drummer John Bradbury's debut album wore its Prince Buster and Toots & The Maytals influences proudly in the form of covers, yet brimmed with the Coventry crew's own distinct character and articulated their concerns. Aided during the sessions for the album by the talents of genuine ska trombone legend Rico Rodriguez, and by the non-prescriptive enthusiasm of fellow artist-turned-rookie producer Elvis Costello, The Specials' eponymous debut manages to be simultaneously generation-defining and timeless.

Too much too young? Remarkably with Terry Hall and Horace Panter – both still active members of the ever-relevant band – hosting the playback, the Listening Party demonstrated why the expression The Specials encapsulated on their debut has continued to resonate strongly down the ages.

## LISTENING PARTY
### 17 MAY 2020

## 1. A MESSAGE TO YOU, RUDY

🔵 @HoracePanterArt

Terry: This remains my fave song on the album; it's amazing how it lights up an audience wherever we play in the world. Still doing it 40 years on...

🔵 @HoracePanterArt

Horace: The difference the horns made to the song. We weren't used to horns before we recorded this...

## 2. DO THE DOG

🔵 @HoracePanterArt

Horace: Big reverb. The bass is double-tracked. Normal bass and one an octave lower... my idea! This song was our set opener when we reformed for the 2009 shows... storming!

## 3. IT'S UP TO YOU

🔵 @HoracePanterArt

Horace: You can hear Nev's original vocal take bleeding through the instrument mikes. I make a real blooper of a mistake just before the last chorus but it seemed to work in the track. Great drum sound!!

## 4. NITE KLUB

🔵 @HoracePanterArt

Terry: The party scene on Nite Klub was heavily staged until someone dropped their trousers! Day 2 of recording, Elvis [Costello who produced the album] leans back on his swivel chair and the whole thing collapsed... definitely an ice-breaker!

🔵 @HoracePanterArt

Horace: Elvis Costello bashes a tin tray in time with the snare drum and I get to do a solo!! Still love playing this live! [The Prentenders] Chrissy Hynde doubles up on 'girls are slags'!

## 5. DOESN'T MAKE IT ALRIGHT

🔵 @HoracePanterArt

Horace: Rock hard bass line especially in the chorus. What I consider to be Roddy's finest solo on any Specials recording. I consider this to be a really important song... never play it without meaning it!

## 6. CONCRETE JUNGLE

🔵 @HoracePanterArt

Horace: I never understood why Roddy sang this – I wasn't there when they did his vocal. Elvis Costello apparently took Jerry aside and said 'you need to get rid of that kid, he's trouble'! Pleased with my bass line on the verses. A bloke called Keith (friend of Lynval) broke the bottle before the solo... and then wanted paying for it! H. x

🔵 @HoracePanterArt

Terry: Roddy was always insistent on 'my song my voice' ... as in 'my football my game'. That was still his agenda when we reformed 30 years later... thankfully he was heavily outvoted.

## 7. TOO HOT

🔵 @HoracePanterArt

Horace: This was the first song we recorded in the session just to ease ourselves into the vibe. I push the bass a bit too much I think!

🔵 @HoracePanterArt

Terry: The first few days of making the record felt a little overwhelming... major label... album... London. I was very young and it became a real eye-opening... as things settled down it proved to be a great experience. Discovering kebab shops was a massive bonus!

Future Fun Boy. Terry Hall on stage with The Specials in 1979.

### 8. MONKEY MAN

✓ @HoracePanterArt

Horace: Groove wise it's my favourite song on the album. Neville's talk over is so ridiculously spontaneous. Still a high point of any Specials show. Brings the house down every time!

✓ @HoracePanterArt

Terry: Horace... remember Keith, as well as smashing bottles in the studio, also broke the toilet in the flat on the Kings Road. We nicknamed him Big Keith after that!

### 9. (DAWNING OF A) NEW ERA

✓ @HoracePanterArt

Horace: We used to play this when we first started out. Brad had never played it. We rehearsed it in the studio and took it. A very funny song. Jerry had a great sense of humour. Horace x The song's about Chelmsley Wood in Birmingham... a girl that Jerry met on holiday who came from there!

### 10. BLANK EXPRESSION

✓ @HoracePanterArt

Horace: My favourite mistake on the whole album the third chord in the second intro after the solo. Some of us are on the beat – some ain't! Listen out for it!

(↓)

Dawning Of A New Era. Co-vocalist Neville Staple and the rest of The Specials reflected the reality of contemporary British culture.

### 11. STUPID MARRIAGE

✓ @HoracePanterArt

Terry: Still conjures up lovely memories of Neville dressed up as a judge. The only judge ever to climb and successfully leap off a PA stack!

✓ @HoracePanterArt

Horace: Probably my least favourite song on the album... we performed it like a comedy number and I just didn't feel like I inhabited it! Chrissie Hynde heavy breathing just before the chorus! Jerry wrote it... he was, and still is, against marriage!

### 12. TOO MUCH TOO YOUNG

✓ @HoracePanterArt

Horace: This was the only song not recorded at TWStudios in Fulham. It was done at Ramport, The Who's studio in Battersea. Different drum sound, different vibe. Nowhere near as earthy as far as I'm concerned. I'm glad we sped it up for our live performance. The version that got to No.1 in February 1980 clocked in at 1m59s... the shortest No.1 EVER! Brad always wanted us to do a dub version of it... we never did! #RIPBrad This song got banned from radio play because of references to contraception!

### 13. LITTLE BITCH

✓ @HoracePanterArt

Terry: My least favourite song on the album. It felt like a horrible personal attack on someone I didn't know. We have dropped this from our live set; back in the day we dropped it quite quickly as well.

✓ @HoracePanterArt

Horace: My mate, Wayne Skate Deavers, a 2-Tone DJ in Washington DC, said that if his set was going badly all he had to do was play Little Bitch and it filled the floor.

### 14. YOU'RE WONDERING NOW

✓ @HoracePanterArt

Horace: The perfect end to album and the live show!

AKA... (clockwise from left) Roddy Radiation, Terry Hall, Jerry Dammers, Horace Panter, Neville Staple, John Bradbury and Lynval Golding.

# *University*
## Throwing Muses
4AD, 1995

To make their sixth album, *University*, Rhode Island alt-rockers Throwing Muses occupied a building in New Orleans' French Quarter. While the album is a compelling brew of choppy guitars, strung-out drums and frontwoman Kristin Hersh's powerfully pure vocals, the stories about the place where it was recorded that emerged during the LP's Listening Party feel more suited to Deep South drama rather than the background for creating one of America's finest alternative albums. Perhaps unsurprisingly then, the author of psychological thriller *Before I Go To Sleep*, SJ Watson (**@SJ_Watson**), is a fan of Throwing Muses and joined in the playback, although as things got underway Hersh (**@KristinHersh**) revealed not everything about their life in The Big Easy is gothic novel material. "I believe we have Dave [Narcizo, drums – **@DaveNarcizo**]," she confirmed of Throwing Muses' Listening Party participants, "but Bernie [Georges, bass] said he has to go to CostCo."

**SLEEVE DESIGN:**
Vaughan Oliver

Full faculty. Kristin Hersh onstage in London in 1995.

## 1. BRIGHT YELLOW GUN

### @KristinHersh

This was recorded here in New Orleans, at Kingsway Studios… a big old swampy mansion in the French Quarter. It was so very hot that summer that no one but dumbass us would work here.

## 2. START

### @KristinHersh

There was a room off our dining room full of amps made out of horns and old radios…nothing, nothing else ever sounded like that room.

## 3. HAZING

### @KristinHersh

Hazing is a song that sounds so tame here compared to the live version which is kinda… awful.

## 4. SHIMMER

### @KristinHersh

We'd hit an odd sweet spot if you can call it that. Straddling an industry we didn't like. I wasn't gonna be radio friendly or do fashion shoots and somehow we made the biggest record of our career.

## 5. CALM DOWN, COME DOWN

### @KristinHersh

We had brought back to life the cliché about bad bands' singles being their best songs and good bands' being their worst a few times, if we were a good band, that is…

## 6. CRABTOWN

### @KristinHersh

So many of our songs begin and end with me laughing. People who know me describe me variously as "sunny" and "annoyingly sunny." Never really heard another description.

## 7. NO WAY IN HELL

### @DaveNarcizo

I think this is my favorite track on this record its hardest for me to deconstruct so it feels more foreign… I think.

## 8. SURF COWBOY

### @KristinHersh

Surf Cowboy, the quintessential T Muses song. I have no idea how one is supposed to feel listening to this song… it gives you no hints. A Rorschach ink blot.

## 9. THAT'S ALL YOU WANTED

### @KristinHersh

Acoustic cello and glassy guitars… from outer space.

## 10. TELLER

### @KristinHersh

On the little island where we grew up, the bank is next door to a bar. When I tried to take too much money out of the bank, the teller read my backstory and sent me to the bar next door, told me not to run away. I didn't run

## 11. UNIVERSITY

### @KristinHersh

Little Ryder [the child's voice on the song] on my lap singing into the mic, with headphones on, listening to his brothers playing in the reverb. Ryder is our manager now.

## 12. SNAKEFACE

### @KristinHersh

Isn't the Snakeface intro what you can't stop playing, Dave? As a lifestyle? I don't blame you. It's… irresistible.

### @DaveNarcizo

Still playing it…

## 13. FLOOD

### @SJ_Watson

Flood breaks my heart. This album breaks my heart basically.

## 14. FEVER FEW

### @KristinHersh

A woman visiting us disappeared into her room for a week with only a blue light on. My bandmates made me go in to make sure she wasn't dead and there was a kind of wild eyed TB Sheets [Van Morrison album] thing goin' on In that crazy blue light. Anyway, I caught whatever she had and wrote this song. I opted for a regular lamp, though.

# *Primary Colours*
## The Horrors
XL Recordings, 2009

Despite the heart and commitment on show to anyone who saw them live, The Horrors were initially in danger of being dismissed as a novelty act. With a distinctive range of haircuts, eyeliner and nicknames, the band, hailing from Southend in Essex, wore their garage-rock influences proudly on debut album *Strange House*. Yet it was no pastiche, and whatever cartoony traits might have accompanied The Horrors' rise they meant every note. Keeping the band's rawer edge, Faris Badwan (vocals – **@HorrorsOfficial**), Joshua Hayward (guitars), Tom Furse (keyboards), Rhys Webb (bass) and Joe Spurgeon (drums) added an array of atmospheres and synths to their dark blueprint.

Produced by Portishead's Geoff Barrow, the much in-demand Craig Silvey and Chris Cunningham (who was previously better known for directing revolutionary videos for Aphex Twin), in parts *Primary Colours* is sense-dazzling, while in others it proves to be tender and expansive. It is a record that dispelled any notion The Horrors were just haircuts, displaying a stunning musical dexterity that builds towards the album's epic, emotive closer, Sea Within A Sea.

**ARTWORK:**
Ciarán O'Shea

Mirror's Image. (Front row) Tom Furse, Joshua Hayward and Faris Badwan; (back row) Joseph Spurgeon and Rhys Webb.

Buoyant. Sea Within A Sea early lyrics shared during the Listening Party by Faris Badwan.

## 1. MIRROR'S IMAGE

✅ **@HorrorsOfficial (Faris Badwan)**
This is weird I haven't listened to the album in ages ages ages.

## 2. THREE DECADES

✅ **@HorrorsOfficial**
Three Decades started with us trying to do an [Brian] Eno Here Come The Warm Jets [1974 album] kind of track. It ended up going somewhere else.

## 3. WHO CAN SAY

✅ **@HorrorsOfficial**
It more or less came together in a day – lyrics and everything. It was written about Hollie [Warren] from [band] Novella who I had been dating not long before.

## 4. DO YOU REMEMBER

✅ **@HorrorsOfficial**
One day in the writing room Tom was away for some reason and Rhys switched from organ to bass. I guess that was a big catalyst in writing a load of new songs because Mirror's Image, Do You Remember and Primary Colours all came together that week.

## 5. NEW ICE AGE

✅ **@HorrorsOfficial**
Josh came up with a great guitar sound on his pitch shifter pedal. The vocals were recorded in one take. Geoff Barrow [member of Portishead and album co-producer] was always going on about keeping things "rough" as he said and that's an approach we were fully on board with... most times.

## 6. SCARLET FIELDS

✅ **@HorrorsOfficial**
Always love playing Scarlet Fields live because the chorus is usually filled with strobes.

## 7. I ONLY THINK OF YOU

✅ **@HorrorsOfficial**
When we used to play this song at festivals it really separated the casual observers from the fans who wanted to stick around. Live it was a ten minute brutal drone. I love the phasing on the drums, one of my fave parts of the album.

## 8. I CAN'T CONTROL MYSELF

✅ **@HorrorsOfficial**
We were trying to do a song a bit like Rocknroll suicide by Bowie.

## 9. PRIMARY COLOURS

✅ **@HorrorsOfficial**
I love the balance of the synths. Something really celestial and dense about them.

## 10. SEA WITHIN A SEA

✅ **@HorrorsOfficial**
Sea Within a Sea is the song that we released first. My favourite song to play even if it's also the most difficult.

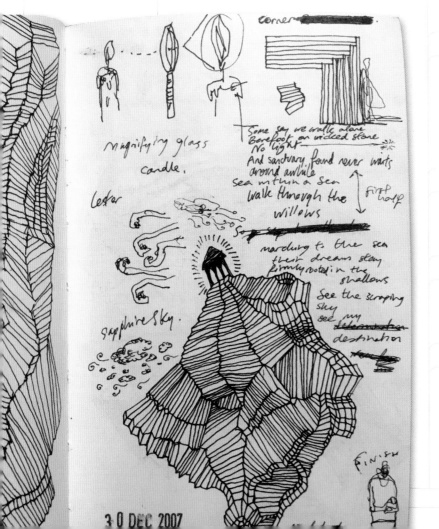

# No Regerts
## Chastity Belt
Help Yourself Records, 2013

The road to musical success is paved with the names of long-forgotten college and university bands. Flush with a first taste of freedom, idealistic about the world and full of energy, many is the group formed in the first week of the first term that never played a note. It is probable that more college groups have been "formed" and named, than band rehearsals have ever taken place. Yet every so often one band manages to successfully juggle songwriting and gigs with lectures and essays – or simply drops out because the music is that good – and invariably you know you're on to a good thing.

Remarkably, Chastity Belt are not just the college band that got away, but they actually made much of their stirring debut album while still studying. Hailing from Walla Walla in Washington State, the four-piece have been heavily championed by the Godfather Of Home Recording, R Stevie Moore. A lo-fi legend with over 400 albums to his name, he was raving about Julia Shapiro (guitar/vocals), Lydia Lund (guitars), Annie Truscott (bass) and Gretchen Grimm's (drums) (all tweeting from **@CHAST1TYBELT**) songwriting before their finals.

Moore was not wrong. Though simply recorded, the band's debut album, *No Regerts*, is full of dreamy atmospheres and luscious melodies, while Shapiro's raw yet haunting vocals manage to convey an artistic seriousness while also sending up stereotypes around her with a wry, quirky humour. A remarkably accomplished and moving record that will both stir and tickle the soul, *No Regerts* proves why Chastity Belt are top of the class.

ARTWORK:
Jacob Muilenburg

LISTENING
PARTY
**23 MAY
2020**

### 1. BLACK SAIL

**@CHAST1TYBELT**

Julia: This song was about a dream I had... wrote it in 2012 right after moving to Seattle. Lydia and I were living together at the time and the song really just came together naturally. Wow this song really holds up, not to brag.

### 2. SEATTLE PARTY

**@CHAST1TYBELT**

Julia & Annie: What a classic! We recorded this song in a cold basement before all the others on this album... our very first single!!!! After shooting this music video we played a show where we were all sitting on the couch.

### 3. JAMES DEAN

**@CHAST1TYBELT**

Julia: Wrote this song with Gretchen in a basement when we lived together in 2010... that drumbeat! So classic. One of the first songs I ever wrote.

**@CHAST1TYBELT**

Gretchen: We recorded the first version through computer speakers... Jules stood as close to the comp as possible so the vocals were audible. The mix was amazing.

**@CHAST1TYBELT**

Julia: The first version has a special *charm*.

## 4. HEALTHY PUNK

### ☑ @CHAST1TYBELT

Julia: I haven't listened to this song since the record came out? OMG this guitar solo. "Buy an eighth and light it up" lololol. In college we were at a house party and decided to break bottles in the back. Then the neighbour told us he had a cat and was worried about her stepping on the glass, so we swept up the pieces. #healthypunk

## 5. NIP SLIP

### ☑ @CHAST1TYBELT

Julia: Nip Slip's working title was "fake estate" cause we thought it sounded like [New Jersey band] Real Estate. I remember jamming on this in the college house I lived in senior year, the salty boot. Didn't have a mic stand for a while so we duct-taped the mic to the wall.

## 6. FULL

### ☑ @CHAST1TYBELT

Julia: Wow, I forgot about this one! So moody. This song is about a [American author] Ray Bradbury short story from The Illustrated Man ;)

Gretchen Grimm and Julia Shapiro onstage at The Roxy Theatre, West Hollywood, in May 2015.

### ☑ @CHAST1TYBELT

Annie: This song hits hard!! Lydia's lead line!! wowwwww

## 7. HAPPINESS

### ☑ @CHAST1TYBELT

Julia: Happiness is an overlooked song, honestly one of my fave songs of ours!! A hidden gem. I remember recording an un-amplified electric guitar, it adds a nice *texture*. This break down! So many "break downs" on this album.

### ☑ Lydia Lund @CHAST1TYBELT

Lydia: This is one of my favs, I was trying to channel [Atlanta band] Deerhunter.

## 8. GIANT (VAGINA)

### ☑ @CHAST1TYBELT

Julia: Is this the song where people stop listening? lol. I originally was singing "I'm a giant" but somehow we all thought it sounded like "giant vagina" so we changed the lyrics. OMG Lydia whispering "vagina" I'm dying. It came out of this drunk convo we had late one night. I remember looking down at my legs and thinking "I'm a giant!" but it's because I'm so much closer to my own legs than other people's…. it's all perspective. Usually played this towards the end of the set and I'd be totally out of tune by then.

## 9. PUSSY WEED BEER

### ☑ @CHAST1TYBELT

Julia: Another song we wrote in college… sooo college. I remember writing this song the summer before senior year in my parents' house, so angsty!

### ☑ @CHAST1TYBELT

Gretchen: I remember playing this at a party the Condemned House, people bouncing around, Prego sauce [a Portuguese barbecue condiment] spilling everywhere.

## 10. EVIL

### ☑ @CHAST1TYBELT

Annie: I just still write the same basslines.

### ☑ @CHAST1TYBELT

Julia: The last song we wrote for this album, a pop hit!

# *War Stories*
## UNKLE
Surrender All, 2007

While break-up albums might be a musical staple, there aren't many records that chart the break up of bands and even fewer that were actually made while its core creatives were in the process of severing ties. Having formed the collective in the early 1990s and working with DJ Shadow on their 1998 *Psyence Fiction* debut, UNKLE king-pin James Lavelle (**@UnkleOfficial**) had moved forward by forging a partnership with Rich File. However by mid-2000s the men from UNKLE were in disarray and despite starting *War Stories* together, the album could only be completed via working in separate studios. Remarkably *War Stories* was not only finished and released, but with contributions from the likes of Queens Of The Stone Age leader Josh Homme and The Cult's Ian Astbury it adds a sun-kissed, rock'n'roll edge to UNKLE's electronic sound without ever unravelling into acrimony.

**ARTWORK:**
3D (Robert Del Naja)

---

**LISTENING PARTY
23 MAY 2020**

### 1. INTRO

⊘ **@UnkleOfficial (James Lavelle)**
The intro is my answer back to Rich [File, UNKLE co-member] leaving the band at the time!

### 2. CHEMISTRY

⊘ **@UnkleOfficial**
Recorded at RX Studios, Burbank, LA. Josh's [Queens Of The Stone Age frontman Josh Homme] guitar playing that night was like nothing I'd seen before. This was one take. It was a pretty lit session, but something magic happened that night!

### 3. HOLD MY HAND

⊘ **@UnkleOfficial**
Chris Goss [producer] had been very encouraging about me singing on this record, and gave me the confidence to do that, for his sins! Lol. Also contains one of two samples from David Bowie on this album, God rest his soul.

### 4. RESTLESS (FEATURING JOSH HOMME)

⊘ **@UnkleOfficial**
The idea for Restless was to do something more like Beasties [Beastie Boys'] Check Your Head meets UNKLE. That album was a big ref doing this album.

### 5. KEYS TO THE KINGDOM (FEATURING GAVIN CLARK)

⊘ **@UnkleOfficial**
I'd heard some tracks of Gavin [Clark, Sunhouse/ Toydrum singer], and thought it would be a good idea to try him out at our studio on this and Broken. It was one of those incredible moments where the stars aligned, and I fell in love with him deeply that day.

### 6. PRICE YOU PAY

⊘ **@UnkleOfficial**
Started in the Rancho de la Luna sessions, and one of the last tracks to be finished and mixed on the album. Mine and Rich's relationship by that

point had become very fractured. On this track we went back and forth insanely. I think it was mixed and recorded 21 times!!

### 7. BURN MY SHADOW (FEATURING IAN ASTBURY)

☑ @UnkleOfficial

Firstly it's not about DJ Shadow! Lol. It was recorded in isolation before we embarked on the main recording of the album, and was the first track recorded with the amazing Chris Goss.

### 8. MAYDAY (FEATURING THE DUKE SPIRIT)

☑ @UnkleOfficial

I started listening to [London band] The Duke Spirit and fell in love with them and [lead singer] Liela Moss' voice. Eventually I got hold of them and we all met up in London. I asked if they'd collaborate on the track. They then ironically ended up going to LA touring, and recording with Chris at Rancho de la Luna, adding their parts to the track.

⊕

The man from UNKLE. James Lavelle onstage in Manchester in 2007.

### 9. PERSONS & MACHINERY

☑ @UnkleOfficial

One of my faves on the album. The track was reworked by Rick Smith for Danny Boyle's Trance, both of whom I'm a huge fan of, which was nice!

### 10. TWILIGHT (FEATURING MASSIVE ATTACK'S 3D)

☑ @UnkleOfficial

This track is really the bridge between the last album and this album to me. One of the main things I wanted on the album was harmonies, which Chris is the master of, so it's really beautiful to hear Massive Attack in such a Beach Boys moment.

### 11. MORNING RAGE

☑ @UnkleOfficial

I wrote the verse, and Rich wrote the chorus. I think the lyrics perfectly sum up our relationship at the time.

### 12. LAWLESS

☑ @UnkleOfficial

I love this track. The lyrics sum up our attitude at the time. We got out of London, moved to LA for three months. I'd just split up with my partner, Rich was single. We were definitely living the LA dream.

### 13. BROKEN (FEATURING GAVIN CLARK)

☑ @UnkleOfficial

[Broken] ended up being the only song to be featured in the ill-fated X-Files 2 movie. I was so excited to work on that film, after being a huge fan of the show and first movie. A major disappointment.

### 14. WHEN THINGS EXPLODE (FEATURING IAN ASTBURY)

☑ @UnkleOfficial

Last track. We'd really tried to stay away from doing the classic string-epic UNKLE on this album. But I wanted one moment on the album which felt like it had a foot in that world.

# Colour By Numbers
## Culture Club
Virgin, 1983

Nestling behind irresistible, golden pop, Boy George has always been a force for change. His androgynous appearance in the 1980s immediately triggered speculation about his sexuality, inviting fans to consider and celebrate their own identities. With *Colour By Numbers*, and notably its opening track – international mega hit Karma Chameleon – George's candid lyrics encouraged mainstream audiences to take stock and consider other sexualities and alternative lifestyles, often for the very first time (his later unlikely, yet famed cameo in an episode of '80s TV show *The A-Team* even saw him bring that spirit to tea-time American television). It's fitting then, that the Listening Party hosted by Boy George (**@BoyGeorge**) and album producer Steve Levine (**@MrSteveLevine**), was staged in honour of Broken Record, a campaign organised by Tom Gray from the indie band Gomez (**@MrTomGray** – see pages 90–91) and supported by the chair of the British songwriter's group Ivors Academy, Crispin Hunt (**@CrispinHunt** – better known to many as the frontman of influential Britpop band Longpigs ), to get fairer royalty payments for streaming. So this listening party helped raise awareness of the issue – and it created a fleeting '80s pop paradise too, naturally bathed in red, gold, and green…

PHOTOGRAPHY:
Jamie Morga

SLEEVE DESIGN:
Malcolm Garrett

⊕

Clubbers. Jon Moss, Boy George, Roy Hay and Mikey Craig.

**@CrispinHunt**

Boy George made the world a better place not just through music but so much more. My son will not bat an eyelid wearing make-up to school and one of his very best friends is free of gender. George did this, thank you, thank God you did.

## 1. KARMA CHAMELEON

### ✔ @BoyGeorge

Karma Chameleon, also known as 'I'm a comedian' was the camel that broke the straws back. The boys, the three straight ones, lol, all hated it, led by Roy who said it was the final nail in our credibility. I asked Steve Levine if Roy had recorded the intro guitar as a joke and in defiance but apparently the sound was what happened when Roy plugged in his guitar. Beautiful accident.

## 2. IT'S A MIRACLE

### ✔ @BoyGeorge

Once I was in Steve's car and he was playing me the latest Carly Simon track 'Why' on his brand new car CD which kept jumping. I think we were in an open top Porsche. Steve was a much better rock star.

### ✔ @MrSteveLevine

If you're old enough to remember the show 'Please Sir' this song features Deryck Guyler playing the washboard.

### ✔ @BoyGeorge

I loved interesting song titles. I still do. All the early T-Rex songs like Salamanda Palaganda, Bowie, The Width of a Circle. I think you can make sense of a lyric after the fact. In the early days the songs were my personal diary. It was all drama.

It's a miracle. Tim Burgess and Steve Levine (pic shared by @mrstevelevine during the Listening Party).

## 3. BLACK MONEY

### ✔ @MrSteveLevine

This song is one of George's finest vocal performances with @helenterry sublime BV's [backing vocals].

### ✔ @BoyGeorge

Wow, Helen Terry on Black Money. She does everything. Layered perfection then that belt on the bridge. OUR QUEEN! I met Helen Terry outside a nightclub. My friend told her to sing on the spot and she said "fuck off, I'm not a performing seal." One of my favourite Culture Club songs. It's better now. Fuck, Helen at the end.

### ✔ @MrSteveLevine

A personal fave of mine – Roy's superb Piano and @HelenTerry amazing BV's - the sound was achieved with a state of the art Reverb the QUANTEC QRS

### ✔ @BoyGeorge

There were so many new machines arriving at Red Bus Studios there was nowhere to sit. Steve loved his new gadgets and keyboards. What was your most favourite piece of technology?

### ✔ @MrSteveLevine

Has to be the Linn Drum and the Fairlight.

## 4. CHANGING EVERY DAY

### ✔ @BoyGeorge

Jon Moss [Culture Club drummer] totally influenced this. He loved his mambo and the Latin vibes. Probably the best production on this album. Well, my favourite!

## 5. THAT'S THE WAY (I'M ONLY TRYING TO HELP YOU)

### ✔ @BoyGeorge

It's the Helen Terry fan club here. I think we slowed it down for live but this was influenced by Madeline Bell who did Melting Pot. Helen at the end. It was about my mum and dad.

## 6. CHURCH OF THE POISON MIND

### ✔ @BoyGeorge

Take it to the church of the poisoned mind! When this played on Radio One Mike Read said "Aleister Crowley eat your heart out". I had no idea it was about the occult.

#### @MrSteveLevine
The opening of side two "Church of The Poisoned Mind" our collective love of Motown & Northern Soul. Note the distortion in the middle the mixing desk just went to 11.

## 7. MISS ME BLIND

#### @BoyGeorge
We were digging Shalamar and Mikey [Craig, Culture Club bassist] was close with Jermaine Stewart who sings on this. Such a great live song but soooo many words! Hello lovely people. Roy's [Hay, Culture Club guitars and keyboards] guitar solo! Legend! Hints of Prince. Nile Rodgers.

#### @MrSteveLevine
We loved Shalamar so we featured Jermaine Stewart on BVs – he actually did the high vocals on all their big hits.

## 8. MISTER MAN

#### @BoyGeorge
Mister Man was a song about the roughs who used to chase me when I was dressed as a nun! I loved them all!

#### @MrSteveLevine
This was the first track we recorded for the Colour By Number sessions. Focus on Helen's BVs – I used vari-speed (slowed the tape down whilst she recorded) in to get a different vocal sound from her.

## 9. STORMKEEPER

#### @MrSteveLevine
This took ages to mix! We had a problem with the two 24 multitrack machines and they would not run in SYNC so this mix was the only time they locked up.

#### @BoyGeorge
Love the music on this and those Phil Picket keyboards. Phil was once in the 70s pop group Sailor who I loved! I wanted this to be the single but...

#### @MrTomGray
[Phil Picket] That's the dad of my good friend Tom Marsh who drums for Lana Del Rey! POP FACT.

## 10. VICTIMS

#### @BoyGeorge
Victims is my fave song to sing live. It's much slower and more lived in but it's a proud moment!

#### @MrSteveLevine
The hardest track to record on the LP. Listen to the box set to hear the "Shirley Temple Moment" which highlights the slightly tense atmosphere behind the scenes!!!

#### @BoyGeorge
Yes. That string session got saucy, but shhh!

#### @MrSteveLevine
Such great orchestra parts arranged by Trevor Bastow strings recorded by Mike Ross at CBS studios. He taught me how to record when I was a tape op at 17.

## 11. BONUS TRACK: MAN-SHAKE

#### @MrTomGray
MAN-SHAKE. YES MAN-SHAKE. I'm a little inebriated. Love you all.

#### @MrSteveLevine
Tom, have the bonus track! Man-Shake was a 12" B Side!

#### @BoyGeorge
How good is Man-Shake!

"Let's Play!" The Spanish edition of Colour By Numbers shared by @MissCenizas during the Listening Party.

Changing Every Day.
Boy George, a pioneer
and trailblazer in so
many ways... often in
ways he didn't realise.

# Pale Green Ghosts
## John Grant
Bella Union, 2013

¶ John Grant enjoys a rare reputation among his fellow musicians. The former frontman of Denver shoegazers The Czars, turned solo artist, is regarded by many of his peers as the greatest swearer ever on record. Artists have refused to cuss on their records not to avoid obscenity but simply because they cannot do it as well as Grant. *Pale Green Ghosts*, with the stirring GMF, is where the singer-songwriter honed this ability. "I am the greatest mother fucker that you're ever gonna meet," he croons in the chorus, "from the top of my head down to the tips of the toes on my feet."

"Doing this on *David Letterman* was a highlight of my career thus far," Grant (**@johngrantmusic**) told Twitter as the *Pale Green Ghosts* Listening Party got underway. "He even let me say Greatest Mother Fucker on the first chorus and feigned horror."

The former talkshow host was just the latest in a long line to enjoy Grant's guided profanity. "I played this opposite Allen Toussaint a long time ago and he was making all sorts of good faces throughout the song," added Grant. "That was an honour. Very generous man, he was."

Of course the reason Grant's cusses are not just tolerated but celebrated, is their artistic context. Inspired by heartbreak and misery, soundtracked by synths and strings, *Pale Green Ghosts* is an emotionally raw, musically refined collection of songs that candidly lays it all on the line.

"[It's] that moment when after having access to all areas, your pass is revoked and it all never happened," Grant tweeted of the emotional tumult that informed tracks like It Doesn't Matter To Him and Why Don't You Love Me Anymore. "Sort like: horror. But part of the deal sometimes."

So naturally, in those circumstances, Grant is going to swear. However *Pale Green Ghosts* is not some foul-mouthed misery-fest, and Grant imbues this account of his crumbling life with a musical serenity which is stunningly beautiful, blending his vocals, contributions from Sinéad O'Connor and neat orchestrations with some moving electronic touches ("I put Juno-106 on my cornflakes. I also put vocoder on my cornflakes").

"It's really nice to remember making these FAT synth sounds with [producer] Biggi Veira. Biggi is an amazing sound designer as all you [influential Icelandic band] GusGus fans know," recalled Grant. "I'm luxuriating on my bed in Reykjavík currently. Thinking about all the piles of snow outside when we recorded this." This change of environment proves the subplot and hopeful redemption that underscores *Pale Green Ghosts*.

Songs Ernest Borgnine (about the American actor who's career stretched from *From Here to Eternity* to *Airwolf*) and I Hate This Town ("It was very cathartic to write and I always enjoy singing it. It's not Denver's fault, I could

**PHOTOGRAPHER:**
Hörður Sveinsson

| 1 | Pale Green Ghosts |
|---|---|
| 2 | Black Belt |
| 3 | GMF |
| 4 | Vietnam |
| 5 | It Doesn't Matter To Him |
| 6 | Why Don't You Love Me Anymore |
| 7 | You Don't Have To |
| 8 | Sensitive New Age Guy |
| 9 | Ernest Borgnine |
| 10 | I Hate This Town |
| 11 | Glacier |

● @Tim_Burgess

When it comes to songwriting, John Grant is ninja level 10.

be miserable anywhere. And probably have been") chart Grant's discombobulation in America. Before album closer, Glacier, revels in a soaring freedom and escape from doubt and derision (complete with some top-notch swearing!) that Grant achieved by making the country he recorded *Pale Green Ghosts* in his own.

"You can really tell I'd just moved to Iceland on this one," he told the Listening Party. "This was such an amazing time what with all the piles of snow and everything and being in Iceland for the first time. And eight years later, I'm still here."

I swear. "Anger. Check. Can't conceal. Check." The former Czars frontman John Grant gets candid and curse-happy on his second solo album.

LISTENING PARTY
24 MAY
2020

**@Tim_Burgess**
Ahhhhhh! *Pale Green Ghosts* are my therapist right now. Current anxiety levels were high but dropping as I listen to this amazing record with all you lovely people around the world – and we are all listening with actual John Grant. Amazing, eh???

**@JohnGrantMusic**
Sinéad [O'Connor] sounds so amazing, shimmering in the background.

**@JohnGrantMusic**
I was a little obsessed with EB [Ernest Borgnine] for a while and then I met him while waiting tables in New York.

**@JohnGrantMusic**
Can't believe I don't hate my vocals on this record.

**@JMusic77Fan [fan]**
Hearing John Grant belt out GMF full lyrics in Ast John's Shopping Centre Leeds on a busy May afternoon. How he was not cautioned for language…

# Deserter's Songs
## Mercury Rev
V2, 1998

Mercury Rev and The Flaming Lips are two bands who bear a remarkable bond. Not only was Rev's co-founder Jonathan Donahue a one-time member of The Flaming Lips, but bassist and producer Dave Fridmann has overseen most of both bands' records. Each group also flourished in an era when artists were not judged entirely on their debuts. Mercury Rev had existed for nearly ten years and had featured various line-ups before Donahue, Fridmann, Sean "Grasshopper" Mackowiak (guitar – **@mercuryrevvd**) and Jimy Chambers (drums) crafted *Deserter's Songs*, their fourth album. An evocative twilight of wonder, the record hurtles across America's vast badlands with angelic vocals, stirring guitars, eerie effects and snatches of Silent Night, as it explores a wilderness full of Edward Hooper figures breathed into life with a Disney-ish magic. Guiding us across this plain of musical imagination, Grasshopper presented a Listening Party that took us straight to *Deserter's Songs'* dark heart.

**PHOTOGRAPHY:**
Kate Hyman & Kevin Salem

Hudson Line… and then some. Mercury Rev performing Deserter's Songs in Antwerp, Belgium in 1999.

### 1. HOLES

✅ **@MercuryRevvd**

(Sean "Grasshopper" Mackowiak)
Recorded about halfway through the sessions (10 months of recording off and on). We dragged our rascal 8 track 1/2 inch up to Portland Maine to record the saw of Mr. Joel Eckhaus [owner of Earnest Instruments and member of Dos Eckies].

### 2. TONITE IT SHOWS

✅ **@MercuryRevvd**

Dave [Fridmann, producer] did most of the orchestrations on this one! I played a bunch of the percussion – castanets, tambourine, snare.

### 3. ENDLESSLY

✅ **@MercuryRevvd**

It was my idea to quote Silent Night in the bridges. Definitely a [composer, producer] Jack Nitzsche feel to this.

### 4. I COLLECT COINS

✅ **@MercuryRevvd**

I collect coins was a late late night dream we all recorded. We wanted it to sound like music from an old silent movie accompaniment.

### 5. OPUS 40

✅ **@MercuryRevvd**

Opus 40, Hudson Line and Funny Bird were the first three songs we wrote for *Deserter's Songs*, and they sort of set the mood for the whole shebang.

### 6. HUDSON LINE

✅ **@MercuryRevvd**

Hudson Line was one I brought in to be reworked. We got [The Band's] Garth Hudson to play sax on it. He would play a few notes at a time on different tracks and we were like "what is he doing?" But when you put it all together, it was genius!

### 7. THE HAPPY END (THE DRUNK ROOM)

✅ **@MercuryRevvd**

The Happy End was another late night recording. Me on one piano, Dave on another, Adam Snyder on Mellotron, Jonathan engineering.

### 8. GODDESS ON A HIWAY

✅ **@MercuryRevvd**

Goddess On A Hiway was one Jonathan wrote back during [1991 debut album] *Yerself Is Steam*. I begged him to record it for Deserter's, even as a b-side. But we all loved how it came out, so it made it onto Deserter's Songs!

### 9. THE FUNNY BIRD

✅ **@MercuryRevvd**

Funny Bird was originally the first song on the album. Abbo (Steven Abbott) [A&R man, manager and former member of the band UK Decay] at V2 said, let's swap those two songs, it adds more drama to the album. He was correct.

### 10. PICK UP IF YOU'RE THERE

✅ **@MercuryRevvd**

The third instrumental on *Deserter's* and another late night recording (those are always the best). At the end, that's Garth Hudson's voice mumbling something cryptic messages...

### 11. DELTA SUN BOTTLENECK STOMP

✅ **@MercuryRevvd**

Delta Sun! Jimy brought in this song and we rearranged it. Jonathan rewrote some of the lyrics. Check out the Chemical Brothers' remix of this one! "Sliding away in a washed out Delta Sun!" Ain't that the truth! "Waving goodbye, not saying hello..."

➡️

Rev-ellers. Jonathan Donahue and Sean "Grasshopper" Mackowiak.

# *Want One*
## Rufus Wainwright
Dreamworks, 2003

Referencing Richard Wagner, *The Wizard Of Oz* and crystal meth, Rufus Wainwright's third album is a brilliantly eccentric, but personal affair. Written in the aftermath of an addiction, the aforementioned drug that culminated with him temporarily losing his sight while staying at New York's Chelsea hotel, and being the son of folk-rock royalty Loudon Wainwright III and Kate McGarrigle, the singer-songwriter could easily have fallen into the depths of cliché when he came to make sense of his life in song. Instead, these utterly candid, yet magically illuminated piano-driven and orchestrated songs are at once raw and elaborate. As you would expect from the creator of such an album, Wainwright's (**@RufusWainwright**) Listening Party for *Want One* (a companion album *Want Two* was released a year later) proved suitably honesty, witty and wonderfully charming.

**ARTWORK:**
Rufus Wainwright

**PHOTOGRAPHY:**
Yelena Yemchuk

**SLEEVE DESIGN:**
Janet Wolsborn

Oh What A World. Rufus Wainwright photographed in October 2003.

## 1. OH WHAT A WORLD

✓ @RufusWainwright

I wrote this song on the Eurostar from London to Paris. It captures the glamorous voyage between possibly the two most luxurious cities in the world.

## 2. I DON'T KNOW WHAT IT IS

✓ @RufusWainwright

This is a very important song for me personally, since I am speaking of the internal voyage that I had to take in order to save my life battling my demons.

## 3. VICIOUS WORLD

✓ @RufusWainwright

Yet another number about unrequited love. I am particularly proud of my harmonies on this one!

## 4. MOVIES OF MYSELF

✓ @RufusWainwright

I like the lyrics on this one. It's about addiction, really, about knowing how it's all going to end up. In that sense, you're watching a movie of yourself all the time – and then you want out of that movie.

## 5. PRETTY THINGS

✓ @RufusWainwright

It is important on my albums to have simple piano/voice moments and this is one of them. Pretty Things is a song about being a universe apart even though you are right next to each other.

## 6. GO OR GO AHEAD

✓ @RufusWainwright

It starts noticeably quieter than other songs on the record, but this cathartic release that comes in brings the volume way up. Sometimes you have to scream so loud that heaven can hear you.

## 7. VIBRATE

✓ @RufusWainwright

Possibly my most beautiful vocal. I return to this song's themes a lot – how quickly the world changes and leaves those of us who can't keep up in the Dark Ages. The feeling of being out of the game...

## 8. 14TH STREET

✓ @RufusWainwright

So funny to listen to such a snarky break-up song in the company of my wonderful husband and our beautiful daughter and new puppy. I guess I really won that one!

## 9. NATASHA

✓ @RufusWainwright

Back to a more reserved sound for this one. I wrote this song about my friend [actress] Natasha Lyonne who was suffering a lot and all I could do really was to write a song about her.

## 10. HARVESTER OF HEARTS

✓ @RufusWainwright

The brushes are on the drums and the time has come to sway in your seats.

## 11. BEAUTIFUL CHILD

✓ @RufusWainwright

This song I wrote after 9/11 and I was hanging out on Yoko Ono's farm with Sean Lennon and Bijou Phillips. We were all being very naughty and I had a vision of the end of the world but it wasn't scary. It was more about becoming a child again.

## 12. WANT

✓ @RufusWainwright

It's a song about aspiring to love and having a family as wonderful as my own. Happy to say I've achieved this goal and more.

## 13. 11:11

✓ @RufusWainwright

11:11 is a love letter to New York City after 9/11 in which I am just trying to come to terms with that tragedy and the surreal life afterwards.

## 14. DINNER AT EIGHT

✓ @RufusWainwright

Dinner at Eight was at first an angry song directed at my father after we had a fight, but on relistening, it's really a love song about wanting to get closer together.

# I Love The New Sky
## Tim Burgess
Bella Union, 2020

Pop music as pop art… or pop art as pop music… There is a bright brilliance and a delicious immediacy to the songs of *I Love The New Sky,* which echoes the 1950s art movement's intention to make a deep connection through accessible culture. That is because this is an album (the fifth LP with the name "Tim Burgess" on the cover) that will make friends quickly, before moving in and setting up residence in your heart. It is filled with fizzy, chiming tunes that will instantly buzz around your brain, though the ideas that inspired those songs should last a lifetime. So get ready for a little rush of "pop art music", one that will hopefully remind anyone who listens that …*The New Sky* is not the limit, but a horizon full of possibilities.

**ARTWORK:**
Nik Void

LISTENING
PARTY
**27 MAY
2020**

→

Lucky Creatures. Tim and his band performing live for Paste Magazine in New York. Picture shared by **@CountessCameron** during the Listening Party.

### 1. EMPATHY FOR THE DEVIL

**@Tim_Burgess**
Struggled with calling it Empathy because Rose Keel Her [the project of Rose Keeler-Schaffeler] had a song called the same name. Homage to The Cure there ; ) There was a gap in the chorus where (for the devil) slipped in very easily. The Boys Don't Cry intro came at the very end of writing, when I realised that if I used the sequence of the two chords in the verse. Added first chord of the chorus then it sounds like Boys Don't Cry. I say 'sounds like' but actually isn't. It's like an illusion in a way before the song even starts (what do you call that ?????). Someone spilt a coffee on my friend while trying to help - they said "like all bad ideas it seemed a good one at the time" Nicked it for this song.

Sky squad. Tim
and band, shared by
**@WeirdoMusic4evr**
during the
listening party.

## 2. SWEETHEART MERCURY

**@Tim_Burgess**

"I love getting lost in your world, I'm too far gone to figure it out. Whoever called you Mercury could see, I named you after me." This song began with the title, I thought a lot about Prefab Sprout, yet it reminds me of The True Wheel by Brian Eno which would be understandable as my son, after hearing it once, demanded to listen about 1000 times everyday to school and back for week... then the whole of Taking Tiger Mountain. This happened also with Prefab Sprout's The Best Jewel Thief In The World. I am not complaining, both songs are genius and Littlest B can see that, plus the added

police sirens at the beginning of the PS one meant extra points. Nik Void and Daniel's vocals in the middle section are just incredible. Doctor Kiko's Cat 'Mercury' should also get a mention. Oh man. These songs!! I've not listened properly when working on them. I love them ; )

## 3. COMME D'HABITUDE

**@Tim_Burgess**

I wanted it to be as interesting as There Goes A Tenner by Kate Bush that over a year ago became my favourite Kate song. Surpassing Cloudbusting after a lot of thought because it was slightly a little more low key. Fun Fact: Comme D'Habitude is the title of the original song that was made into My Way, in English. Anyway I had been going through a few issues with a former manager and an ex mate both issues were escalating quite quickly and it became clear that there was some skulduggery. You can either let it wash over you or write a song about it. Guest vocal by The Littlest B. FRAMED!!

## 4. SWEET OLD SORRY ME

**@Tim_Burgess**

About life in LA. A past life with zero regret but in order to move forward I had to leave my old life behind.  It's a song though that has all the element of a song written in LA (well it was really, just LA from memory and only a few recent visits). I lived there for 12 years, have the best memories and can't wait to see my friends there again as soon. Alex Ward on soulful sax. We got to play the songs to an audience over four shows in New York. We had to catch the last flight home before lockdown. So glad we got to play them. Recording the strings at jet studios in Brussels was a highlight

## 5. THE WARHOL ME

**@Tim_Burgess**

Life is about variety and travel so a quick flight to New York (metaphorically speaking) and we're at [punk venue] Max's Kansas City watching Suicide or the Velvets even. With all the songs there was never a chat about which way they were going to go I just knew that the people involved in making this record understood me aesthetically and where it was going. Dan on (john Cale (style) Piano and drums  Thighpaulsandra and Nik Void on synths smashed this one. My little three chord bubblegum track that I wrote in five minutes at the big mushroom (now with extended outro provided by well... Grumbling Fur (Alex Tucker joined us on processed cello) and Nik Void's grumbling electronics

## 6. LUCKY CREATURES

**@Tim_Burgess**

Written mostly in LA while on tour with The Charlatans and finished in Norfolk. Recorded at Rockfield in the quadrangle. "Feeling lost and found, Tacos on the underground" lots of the time this song is my favourite on the album – just because of the dramatic intro and the soulful Young Americans feeling. Quite Steely Dan too and ThighpaulSandra likened it to Andrew Gold. "Don't you recall San Francisco at all/I was inspired by the look in your eye"  beautifully sung by Nik Void. Shots been fired, brain rewired effects

 Empathy For The Devil. Tim and a misunderstood friend.

 I Got This. Recording the strings at Jet Studios in Brussels was a highlight.

 Sweet... Tim's handwritten original lyric sheets for the recording of Sweet Old Sorry Me. Shared by the man himself during the Listening Party.

156

↑
@Tim_Burgess
So sleepy at Eve Studios. Seems like a while ago still sleepy now – I do love this album it was a real joy.

by Thighpaulsandra who for a while thought this song was his favourite on the record too. Gorgeous strings by Echo Collective and "we were lucky creatures all the while" beautifully sung by Ivy O'Sullivan. I feel like a lucky creature right now. Thanks x x x

## 7. THE MALL

☑ **@Tim_Burgess**

My favourite lyrics on the album – its definitely about someone, but that will be a mystery. Sunlit vision of a mackerel sky ;) Dan's arrangement on this and the string playing by Echo Collective is amazing Recorded in the Quadrangle at Rockfield and Jet Studios in Brussels. The Doors moment at 2.09 followed by a Roxy moment. I dedicate this song to one of my best friends Susan Lynch x she made the video for me and is ....well......just amazing x here is a pic of us F Christmas ????

"They say that you can't win them all/But you can if you're at the mall" Was hoping for a big tie in deal with a shopping centre

## 8. TIMOTHY

☑ **@Tim_Burgess**

"Dreaming Is Free (the second time I reference Debbie Harry/Blondie)/Oh! Those songs make us strong" Maybe my second favourite lyrics on the record Timothy – We gotta get out of this place. I guess I was singing this to me. "I can count all my friends on one hand, two of them are in punk bands/I can count all my friends on one hand, one of them lives in Japan" Nice guitar solo, Tim.

## 9. ONLY TOOK A YEAR

☑ **@Tim_Burgess**

Dan thought this song had a Kevin Ayers feeling about it – Eno, Nico, Kevin Ayres live 1974 is one of my favourite albums. Walking round on this movie set not having learned all of my lines yet was reference to the short film I made with Susan Lynch. Ivy O'Sullivan's second vocal on the album. "What's your favourite Cure LP? I Like Pornography, but it could be any one of three!" Came from one of the ridiculous conversations me and my mate Nick Fraser have many times, on many days of the week.

## 10. I GOT THIS

☑ **@Tim_Burgess**

Recorded in the coach house in Rockfield Studio – I think this is spectacular. Vince Guaraldi meets Crosby, Stills and Nash. My stadium song. "There is treasure beneath all the dirt" Amazing rhythm track by Dan, ace backing vocals by Keel Her In the main bulk of the song, then at the end Nik Void goes gospel. "I'll be the one who walks you through the darkness." Was trying to think of a big message for our six year-old.

## 11. UNDERTOW

☑ **@Tim_Burgess**

I wanted to write a song called undertow for as long as I can remember – this was the time. It's a different mood entirely and is a song about a grudge. Things aren't getting worse but things are getting meta. Amazing strings by Echo Collective. Beautiful Backing Vocals by Daniel O'Sullivan.

Only Took A Year. Tim outside Brussels' Jet Studios.

## 12. LAURIE

@Tim_Burgess

I always thought the backing track reminded me of The Fall. Nice backing vocals by Nik "Other dimensions, as a state of being/A perceived reality, a plane of consciousness/All things made possible oblique strategies" Peter Broderick played violin again bookending the album. I Love the New Sky came from a text by Nick Fraser asking if I had heard the new Sky Ferreira track Downhill Lullaby? I responded "I LOVE The new Sky". I looked at what I had written and it ended up in the song Laurie which I originally titled. "I Love The New Sky, Laurie."

# Original Pirate Material
## The Streets
679, 2002

⚲ "This reminds me of being about to go onstage," tweeted Mike Skinner (**@MikeSkinnerLtd**) moments before pressing play on the *Original Pirate Material* Listening Party. With a nervous energy underpinning the tingling charge that fizzes through The Streets' lyrics, it's understandable – whether rapping or writing – why the pioneering MC and producer might get a little edgy before hitting us with his words. And with Skinner it isn't just what he says, but how he says it too. *Original Pirate Material* didn't just connect with post-millennium counter culture, charting chemically-enhanced escapades and fractured relationships. Skinner also unlocked something special when he rapped in his own accent, with his own voice, and inspired the next generation of artists around the globe who confidently followed in his wake, establishing new genres in the process. Fittingly then that Skinner's Listening Party was part tweet, part performance. A flow of consciousness that shone new light on his debut album, it also proved to be a fascinating public reassessment of *Original Pirate Material* by the man who made it.

**LISTENING PARTY**
**29 MAY 2020**

### 1. TURN THE PAGE

**@MikeSkinnerLtd**
The words have become noise to me now. I could sing it backwards. I remember it took ages to make an orchestra out of samples, not quite Hans Zimmer.

### 2. HAS IT COME TO THIS?

**@MikeSkinnerLtd**
This reminds me of being in a nightclub DJing with the lights coming on. Was trying to sound like DJ Premiere with the scratches.

### 3. LET'S PUSH THINGS FORWARD

**@MikeSkinnerLtd**
Kevin Mark Trail [Reggae artist and songwriter]. I think this might have been the first time we met. He recorded this in my wardrobe in Brixton. CULT CLASSIC, NOT BEST SELLER. Hmmm.

### 4. SHARP DARTS

**@MikeSkinnerLtd**
I can't drive by the way [Mike raps he's the driver]. I am always the passenger.

### 5. SAME OLD THING

**@MikeSkinnerLtd**
Just noticed I've said peel the label off a beer in 3 songs. Please psychoanalyse.

### 6. GEEZERS NEED EXCITEMENT

**@MikeSkinnerLtd**
"Lock stock and two stroking guts." "Superman eye lasers"… I might use that. "Runnings. we've all got our runnins." No one says that anymore.

I'm forty-fifth generation Roman. "Obviously, I had been to see Gladiator with my sister..." Mike Skinner, the Caesar of British rap, made a triumphant entry with his debut album *Original Pirate Material*.

### 7. IT'S TOO LATE

**@MikeSkinnerLtd**
Laura Vane, the lovely lady who did [A Grand Don't Come For Free track] Blinded By The Lights, [on vocals]. She was so lovely. She used to bring candles, I think.

### 8. TOO MUCH BRANDY

**@MikeSkinnerLtd**
Marlon Brando = brandy. The cocaine thing really happened in Too Much Brandy. Most of this song is true.

### 9. DON'T MUG YOURSELF

**@MikeSkinnerLtd**
That video was insane. They were building a set just before we moved to shoot in it while they dismantled the other one. I remember the first time someone told me every one said ROAD now instead of street.

### 10. WHO GOT THE FUNK?

**@MikeSkinnerLtd**
Inspired, obviously, by Daft Punk. All these samples sound bait now, sample packs have got a lot better.

### 11. THE IRONY OF IT ALL

**@MikeSkinnerLtd**
Irony of it all, lets be clear, I have always been more like terry ["the law abider" who likes drinking as opposed to Tim the weed smoker].

### 12. WEAK BECOME HEROES

**@MikeSkinnerLtd**
Radio said it wasn't commercial enough, so we did a studio session to make it more playable. Super weird. Didn't use it, obviously.

### 13. WHO DARES WINS

**@MikeSkinnerLtd**
"Kronenburg." Fun fact, if you are in Europe then you need to order SEIZE as the 1664 bit is important.

### 14. STAY POSITIVE

**@MikeSkinnerLtd**
This goes on too long at the end. Can we edit it? I think that string might be a sample you know. I've just realised...

# *Searching For The Young Soul Rebels*
## Dexys Midnight Runners
EMI, 1980

Sometimes you need to look backwards to move forward. The future might belong to the next generation, but they need to figure out what they want to do with it. Dexys Midnight Runners' debut album is just such a call to arms. Fuelled by punk's ambition and heralding Irish writers on Burn It Down (a re-recording of debut single Dance Stance), R&B hero Geno Washington on the ubiquitous Geno, and possessing brass and organ arrangements inspired by Mowtown and Stax recordings, Dexys were set on their own vision. That even extended to stealing and holding to ransom their own master tapes in order to get a better deal out of their record label. At the time of recording, the band's line-up was Kevin Rowland (vocals – **@DexysOfficial**), Kevin "Al" Archer (guitar/vocals – **@Kevin_Archer1**), "Big" Jim Paterson (trombone – **@JamesMPaterson1**), Pete Williams (bass – **@PeteWilliamsMus**), Geoffrey "Jeff" Blythe (saxophone – **@saxofficer**), Steve "Babyface" Spooner (alto saxophone), Pete Saunders (organ), Andy "Stoker" Growcott (drums) and Andy Leek (organ), and they made a formidable negotiating team. Part manifesto, part romance, *Searching For The Young Soul Rebels* might not be a record that wanted to smash it all down and start again like some of its punk forebears, but Dexys Midnight Runners' debut is clearly a glimpse of the future.

SLEEVE DESIGN:
Fly By Night

@Mr_Dave_Haslam
"Teams That Meet In Caffs". 1970s meet friends in a greasy spoon cafe, make a milky coffee last hours, make plans, change the world.

New Soul Rebels. Kevin Rowland and co on the streets in Birmingham, March 1980.

@Mr_Dave_Haslam
I first saw Dexys in August 1979. Support act of Joy Division.

## 1. BURN IT DOWN

✓ **@DexysOfficial (Kevin Rowland)**
I feel like I'm hearing it fresh – without the usual critical ear! I'm starting to hear what others might hear. Sounds good! Jim's trombone leading the way.

✓ **@saxofficer (Geoff Blythe)**
A top 20 hit rework. A few seconds too long. Came up with a middle 8 edit while on a bathroom break during rehearsal.

## 2. TELL ME WHEN MY LIGHT TURNS GREEN

✓ **@PeteWilliamsMus**
Chose to underpin this great melody sung in two part harmony, except for the brass riffs where I attempt a Calypso feel. Stoker rock solid and powerful, with his usual killer swing. No Timbale but a Metal Rogers Snare tuned up high, no bottom skin, Rim Shott!! Avanti. Beautiful Trombone Solo from James Paterson, first take I think.

✓ **@JamesMPaterson1**
Tell Me When My Light Turns Green always confused me for some reason, I always wanted to start the solo much earlier.

✓ **@DexysOfficial**
Tell Me When My Light Turns Green sounds great! I'm hearing this one in a different light too. Full of passion. I'd forgotten.

## 3. THE TEAMS THAT MEET IN CAFFS

✓ **@saxofficer**
Great tune by Kev Archer. It was surprisingly hard solo to do. Pete's bass on this excellent

✓ **@DexysOfficial**
Teams That Meet in Caffs sounds great and shows the genius of Kevin Archer.

## 4. I'M JUST LOOKING

✓ **@DexysOfficial**
Sounds great. The album tonight sounds completely different to me tonight as opposed to when I listened alone last weekend – the power of all listening together!

✓ **@PeteWilliamsMus**
A blues, almost lazy feel – and B side to our first single, glad we got a chance to do a different (better) version. Plectrum style, keep it subtle, dynamic, simple. Great vocal from Kev.

✓ **@JamesMPaterson1**
My favourite instrumental of all time and the most physically demanding piece of music I've ever played. Breathing and tuning were the problem for me. I loved it so much though, I was quite prepared to render myself unconscious.

### 5. GENO

**@saxofficer**

I had just finished playing with Geno Washington and was attracted to this project as he was quoted as main influence. Look how it all turned out.

**@PeteWilliamsMus**

Originally a poem from KR, worked on the music in Kevin Archer's bedroom. Bass on is informed by Coz I luv You and Happy Together, Give it groove and movement in the chorus, tough and tight with Stoker. Blocks of Brass Breezeblock. Vibraslap..

**@DexysOfficial**

It's hard to comment on Geno – its so well known. Except that my vocal sounds a bit too shrill. The playing is amazing!!

**@Kevin_Archer1**

[producer] Pete Wingfield rearranged the intro, Kevin had the lyric, Geoff arranged the brass. Rhythm sounds tight solid.

### 6. SEVEN DAYS TOO LONG

**@saxofficer**

Great cover and superb piano by our producer Pete Wingfield.

**@PeteWilliamsMus**

Used to love playing this live, Pete Wingfield suggested the intro party ambience, that's us and him in the live room. Himself on Glockenspiel, four beaters! Stoker putting his broad Bloxwich back into it. In the Pocket!

**TIM'S THOUGHTS**

Of the bands that have changed my life the most, Dexys Midnight Runners would be somewhere near to the top of my list. While lots of my favourites found a groove that they liked and remained in, Dexys were a different thing completely. At times held together, and at other times pulled apart by their shamanic leader Kevin Rowland.

*Searching For The Young Soul Rebels, Too-Rye-Aye* and *Don't Stand Me Down* came out when I was 13, 15 and 18 respectively, so they were markers throughout my teenage years. Born of destruction, redemption and battles with record labels they were everything I could have hoped them to be.

Kevin would eventually become a prominent voice in telling the world about the restorative powers of the Listening Parties but at first they, maybe rightfully, didn't appeal to him. He was about looking forwards, and his relationship with his own songs and past band members was a difficult one, but we opened up a dialogue and via phone calls and voice memos the

idea started to appeal to him – instead of being on his own listening to potential flaws in the music he'd recorded, he changed his tack. If he was just one of the many thousands who were listening maybe he could enjoy the music as much as everyone else – to not have to worry about the level of the bass, to ignore the drum sound that had always niggled him, and to hear the albums as we hear them. As soon as the final notes of the last track on *Searching For The Young Soul Rebels* faded Kevin got in touch to say the experience had been all he could have hoped for and much more, and could I please send him potential dates for *Too-Rye-Aye* and Don't Stand Me Down.

**@Kevin_Archer1**

Stoker's drumming, Pete's bass is good on this, that with a great vocal from Kev, it lifts the intensity and of course Pete Wingfield's piano. Brass is good too.

## 7. I COULDN'T HELP IF I TRIED

**@PeteWilliamsMus**

Sometimes when we played, the sheer focus, intensity, whatever, turned into a kind of transcendence, the band became an engine, beyond our control almost, I'll never forget that feeling. It often happened on this song.

**@saxofficer**

Love the trombone and Kev Rowland's voice on this.

**@DexysOfficial**

Jim wrote the music – for ages it was, Jim's song {didn't have a title}. Jim brought the song to us in typical understated Jim style. Amazing song. Well done Jimmy - the greatest. Pete Williams and Stoker totally in charge!

**@JamesMPaterson1**

Another confession, I think I said I'd come up with the chords for Couldn't Help when I was at college but I actually made them up on the spot. I'm quite proud of that though.

**@DexysOfficial**

You know what? I wondered if that was the case!

## 8. THANKFULLY NOT LIVING IN YORKSHIRE IT DOESN'T APPLY

**@PeteWilliamsMus**

Yorkie as we called it. This rolling bass line always cramped my hand. James Paterson on falsetto Beep Beeps.

**@JamesMPaterson1**

Kevin said "Wear your tightest underpants Hamish, you're going high."

**@saxofficer**

Different approach. Motown sound as opposed to Stax.

## 9. KEEP IT

**@DexysOfficial**

Genius arrangement by Kevin Archer. Great playing and performance from everyone. Really good words from Geoff Blythe. We should have released this version as a single. I shouldn't have tried to rewrite lyrics, but that's another story. Great sax at the end, Geoff.

**@PeteWilliamsMus**

Simple, fluid, forward moving, slightly menacing, some sweet BVs and added keys from Pete Wingfield. Steve Spooners Alto tone, the Glue. Favourite vocal harmony on the whole album.

**@saxofficer**

I wrote the lyric to this brilliant Kev Archer song after original lyric was declined by producer. Best horns on the album IMO.

## 10. LOVE PART ONE

**@PeteWilliamsMus**

Beat poetry? Ginsberg... Howl... original lyric to the previous track. Bit of triple tonguing in the upper register eh Geoff?

**@saxofficer**

Came up with the idea of spoken word for Kev R using original Keep It lyrics against my improv. Love the result. A writing credit would have been welcome.

## 11. THERE, THERE, MY DEAR

**@PeteWilliamsMus**

My favourite track from this period, the power I mentioned earlier would happen on this track also. Band flying in full force. Rolling R explosive vocal intro, like the Temps, "I'll be there."

**@DexysOfficial**

It's criminal how under acknowledged Kevin Archer is. The media picked me out and I needed no encouragement. Without Kevin Archer's music, we wouldn't have made a 10th of the impact.

# FIBS
## Anna Meredith
Black Prince Fury, 2019

⚲ Anna Meredith was the Listening Party's first fully fledged composer. The Scot who was trained at the Royal College of Music, has composed for the Proms and the BBC Scottish Symphony Orchestra and has received an MBE for her work. She is also a shape-shifter. Experiencing her version of a Bob-Dylan-going-electric moment – or in her case going electronic – a few years ago Anna decided to smash through traditional, purist musical boundaries and start making synth-saturated works alongside her orchestral commitments. *FIBS* was her second album exploring this bleep-filled environment, but as she kicked off her Listening Party Anna revealed for the record she's not just a shape-shifter when it comes to genres, it's how she writes her music too.

Inspired by a teacher, the composer plans out many of her works by drawing connected angular shapes that represents the changing energy within her music, and having rediscovered the diagrams that helped her make *FIBS* she posted the blueprint for each track.

Sculpting awe-inspiring melodies out of individual and intricate keyboard pulses, the album's sweeping electronics combine to form enveloping sonic landscapes. Creating these glacial-like musical moments not only requires a lot of musical energy, as demonstrated by the shapes, but they need physical energy too – as the thumb of Meredith's cellist attests.

"I must show you all the most immense "jelly baby" [blister] on my left-hand thumb from the many octave chromatic scales in Sawbones," Maddie Cutter (**@MaddieCutter**) offered the Party, demonstrating the impact of her work on the opening track, not that she is the only one to revel in *FIBS'* exertions.

"When we do this live I get to play this synth solo and I feel like some kind of evil space emperor," tweeted Meredith (**@AnnaHMeredith**) herself of Calion, a track formed from a constellation of soaring notes, flickering scales and pulsing bleeps. "It's probably one of the few tracks I've done that could potentially be called 'cool'," she added. "I wrote it straight after writing the soundtrack for [film] Eighth Grade

**ARTWORK:**
Eleanor Meredith

**PHOTOGRAPHY:**
Martina Lang

| 1 | Sawbones |
|---|---|
| 2 | Inhale Exhale |
| 3 | Calion |
| 4 | Killjoy |
| 5 | Bump |
| 6 | Moonmoons |
| 7 | Divining |
| 8 | Limpet |
| 9 | Ribbons |
| 10 | Paramour |
| 11 | Unfurl |

**@AnnaHMeredith**
So I do this thing where I draw out the graphic shape for each track as part of the composing process.

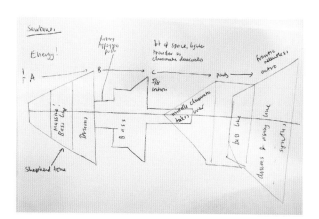

and think all those synths I used there were sitting in my head."

That is part of *FIBS'* true appeal: while its instrumental passages are thought out and carefully plotted, there's a real heart to the album too, particularly when Anna embeds her vocals into the synth-formed landscapes. The skipping Inhale Exhale finds Meredith singing about "being a bit of a cautious person and watching others doing their crazy zany bonkers living while I watch on like an evil Edwardian gnome from the sidelines." Ribbons captures "distance and depression" ("Even though I have a really small voice I love singing this."), while on Killjoy, the Talking Heads-like vocals are sung by Meredith's percussionist Sam Wilson (**@SamWilson323**) on a rare trip away from the kit. "The lyrics here are not directed at a jilted lover, etc," he wrote, joining in the Listening Party. "All looking inward; how we self-criticise, get in our own way, and block out light when it's there all along."

From intense moments like the organic strings on Moonmoons (who's song-shape diagram Anna suggests "looks like a beetle") via the rocky Divining, to the blissful positivity of closing track Unfurl, *FIBS* proves an impressively diverse yet accessibly coherent work, both intellectually challenging and emotionally welcoming. Still heralded by the classical establishment while carving out this electronic voice of her own, Meredith's compositions really are the shape of things to come.

*Unfurl. Composer Anna Meredith embraced an electronic edge while creating FIBS.*

**LISTENING PARTY**
**31 MAY 2020**

**@AnnaHMeredith**
So I do this thing where I draw out the graphic shape for each track as part of the composing process. I've found the sketches & I'll post them as we go.

**@AnnaHMeredith**
Genuinely think INHALE EXHALE is the best "pop" song I've written.

**@MaddieCutter**
Moonmoons trivia. Anna Meredith and I met the day before recording to finish writing the cello part & she suggested me taking a turn around TK Maxx whilst she finished it off, an hour later I came back and it was totally perfect and complete.

**@AnnaHMeredith**
My fun fact [for Moonmoons] is that these big stabs (we call them confetti stabs) are the rest of the audio compressed and slowing down.

**@AnnaHMeredith**
Whilst making Divining there was an unfortunate moment where a loop of "rivers of blood" played for hours which drove us all a bit nuts.

**@SamWilson323**
LIMPET the sort of music I thought all the cool people played when I was 12.

**@MaddieCutter**
Unfurl makes me want to close my eyes into half-moons of happy-sad and stare into a sunset over the Atlantic.

167

# Transangelic Exodus
## Ezra Furman
Bella Union, 2018

The concept album has taken some beating over the years. Heavily associated with prog rock, for some listeners the idea of an overarching narrative sets off alarm bells that sound suspiciously like long, noodlely, self-indulgent instrumental sections. Well not only is Ezra Furman's *Transangelic Exodus* a concept album, it is also an album without an inch of fat on it. Direct, gloriously harmonic, candid yet bold, Furman's record has a theme worthy of a multi-season TV series, let alone one record. In fact, "concept album" is too small a term for *Transangelic Exodus*, as Furman explained on the record's release in 2018. "Not a concept record, but almost a novel, or a cluster of stories on a theme, a combination of fiction and a half-true memoir", Furman (**@EzraFurman**) explained. "A personal companion for a paranoid road trip. A queer outlaw saga." Here we not only discovered the album's concept, we also uncovered the concept's concept.

**ARTWORK:**
Luke Jarvis
Ezra Furman

Transangelic! Ezra onstage in Berlin in 2018.

### 1. SUCK THE BLOOD FROM MY WOUND

**@EzraFurman**
I like that the album starts with me with a pillow held over my face trying to call for help, like I'm being kidnapped into the album against my will. It did feel a bit like that.

### 2. DRIVING DOWN TO L.A.

**@EzraFurman**
Written under the influence of Sparklehorse and The Beach Boys. Specifically, Piano Fire and Let Him Run Wild. That shuffling percussion sound at the top of and throughout the track is from a YouTube clip of a demo of a money-counting machine. Used without permission. Shh don't tell.

### 3. GOD LIFTS UP THE LOWLY

**@EzraFurman**
I do think this song is some of my best writing. Or most ME writing. This, somehow despite the fictions of it, is where I was actually at as a human being. Still am. Points for anyone who knows where the Hebrew at the end comes from…

### 4. NO PLACE

**@EzraFurman**
Written after first hearing Life During Wartime by Talking Heads. Did you know the Greek root of the word "utopia" mean "no place".

## 5. THE GREAT UNKNOWN

**@EzraFurman**

I couldn't sing this song. I was doing terribly. Then Tim [Sandusky, producer and member of former backing band The Visions] said something like, "You have to think of who would sing this song who's not you, and just keep that person in mind while you sing." I chose Ariel from the Little Mermaid. That got me in the right mood somehow.

## 6. COMPULSIVE LIAR

**@EzraFurman**

Wrote this in London at my manager's house the night before a tour started. May 2015 it was. Highly confessional. Those rumbly sounds at the top of the track (and periodically throughout) are this thing that happens on the old organ at Tim's studio when you hold down multiple foot pedals at once.

## 7. MARASCHINO-RED DRESS $8.99 AT GOODWILL

**@EzraFurman**

I wrote this on the same day as Amateur [which featured on Furman's 2020 soundtrack for TV series Sex Education] and Love You So Bad. Well, I had started So Bad a few days before. Still, pretty good songwriting day.

## 8. FROM A BEACH HOUSE

**@EzraFurman**

Getting PROPERLY weird now. I like how we made a lot of these odd sounds rather inventively. This track starts with drumming with pencils on the strings of a distorted bass guitar. I think we put some video of us doing it on Instagram.

## 9. LOVE YOU SO BAD

**@EzraFurman**

I figured this was a guitar-drums-bass type of deal. In fact Sam [Durkes, backing band member] and I recorded a version like that (See "To Them We'll Always Be Freaks"). Wasn't that exciting. But then Ben [Joseph, backing band member/producer] made a demo version on keyboards, influenced by Alex Cameron who we'd just gotten into. Ben wrote that backup vocal hook "So bad, s-so bad." I was overjoyed. I could suddenly hear what the song was supposed to be.

## 10. COME HERE GET AWAY FROM ME

**@EzraFurman**

How I feel about meeting new people and gaining new fans! It makes me really happy that Tim counting this song in comes from the first demo we made on the first day we tried out recording anything at all. I came over one day and me and Tim made the version that's on the ALWAYS BE FREAKS comp, listen for that count-in at the top of the demo. No one cares I know but it warms my heart.

## 11. PEEL MY ORANGE EVERY MORNING

**@EzraFurman**

I had the titles "Peel My Orange Every Morning" and "Transition From Nowhere to Nowhere" written in a single note on my phone for about a year before I wrote this. Got around to "Transition" a little later.

## 12. PSALM 151

**@EzraFurman**

Another song count-in lifted from a very early demo version. Also available on TO THEM WE'LL ALWAYS BE FREAKS. The sound of this song was directly influenced by Moonchild by King Crimson. Listen you'll hear it. That was Tim's idea, I don't listen to prog rock OBVIOUSLY. Good idea tho. I love the drums on this song, how they sound and how Sam played them, so so much.

## 13. I LOST MY INNOCENCE

**@EzraFurman**

Is this the most underrated song of the 2010s? Joking. Or am I? I really thought this was going to be a kind of Beach Boys or soul song. But my band is full of surprises. This song as the closer just makes me feel strong. Like there's hope for the queers.

# *True*
## Spandau Ballet
Chrysalis, 1983

Drawn together by a shared love of Tony Bennett and Frank Sinatra found in parental record collections, Tony Hadley (vocals), Gary Kemp (guitars/keys – **@GaryJKemp**), Martin Kemp (bass), John Keeble (drums) and Steve Norman (percussion/saxophone) launched onto the New Romantic scene with their unique combination of fast tunes, passionate pop and full-blown pageantry. Their third album *True* represents the moment where Spandau Ballet truly enthralled the world with an artistic dance of their own. Led by global smash hit Gold, the whole album proves an adventurous meld of irrefutable pop hooks, 1980s production at its best (before their sound was much copied) and sophisticated music – well Gary Kemp would end up playing in Nick Mason's post-Pink Floyd band after all (see pages 270–273) so he knew what he was doing. And it was Kemp senior who hosted a Listening Party for *True* that really joined the dots of this unique musical evolution, explaining how a bunch of teenage Pistols fans ended up recording this record in Nassau. Still, never mind the Bahamas, here comes Spandau Ballet....

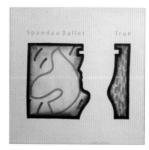

ARTWORK:
David Band

Complicated shadows.
Spandau Ballet posing
in 1983.

Hat trick. Gary Kemp outside his London home in 1982. The band soon moved recording sessions to the Bahamas for musical – and sunbathing – reasons.

## 1. PLEASURE

### @GaryJKemp

Most of the songs for the True album were written by me during the Spring/Summer of 1982 at my parent's council house in Islington. I'd finish a song in my bedroom then call Martin in to have a listen. We were still living at home. I was just 23 he was 21 and we'd had seven hit singles and two hit albums. And STILL living at home! Originally the record was going to be produced by Trevor Horn and was called the Pleasure Project. We rehearsed this track with him at Nomis Studios and started recording it at Air Studios Oxford St. Horn had produced Instinction for us which had been our last hit before this. Unfortunately he wanted to lose John our drummer for some reason and we refused to do so so Trevor and us parted company. The only section of Trevor's arrangement ideas we kept was the single 7/8 bar that ends the song. Look out for it. We'd bought a Rhodes Chroma synth which was polyphonic. This sound came straight out of it. I'd originally written it on guitar as a rockabilly thing.

## 2. COMMUNICATION

### @GaryJKemp

We then found Tony Swain and Steve Jolley who'd produced Bananarama and Imagination. We got on and they came to watch us routine the album at Nomis studios in Shepherds Bush. They didn't think Pleasure was the first single  they preferred Lifeline. Video for Communication, the second single from the album, was shot 27th - 28th January 1983, directed by Chris Springle, and features actress Leslie Ash and only Tony Hadley from the band. No other members appeared in it. John Conte the boxer was also in. We appeared on TOTPs on 24th Feb 1983 performing Communication.

## 3. CODE OF LOVE

### @GaryJKemp

Code of Love was the first thing we recorded at Compass Point [Nassau, The Bahamas]. We went there cos Robert Palmer and Talking Heads recorded there. And we wanted to get away from London. And we could sunbathe! Two songs were demoed at Pathway Studios, Islington, on 17th July. These were Code of Love and Heaven Is a Secret. They're on the True 40th anniversary edition. This really was a Nassau vibe. Hard to get most of the band out of the pool though. Steve has really just discovered the congas and sax. He's a genius musician. That's me on backing vocals. It became a sound we discovered them of tracking up my voice. It complemented Tony.

## 4. GOLD

### @GaryJKemp

I remember wanting to write a Bond theme. This was my homage. I remember playing it to Martin in my bedroom. He went and got his bass out and we played that riff till Dad went to bed! Big thanks to Jess Bailey on Keyboards. I was in his band at school and later and then I asked him to play keys on this album. Fantastic player. Vid was shot directed by legendary 60s photographer, Duffy. While in Seville with shooting Duffy walked off the shoot. I was being too bossy.

PLATES L

-24 18 12 6 0 6 +12 ovld dB

300MA: 308P: R

lexicon

| 1 | 2 | 3 | 4 | 5 |

PROG   REG

| 6 | 7 | 8 | 9 | 0 |

BANK  SETUP  STO  CTRL  MACH  MUTE  ENTER  PAGE
      VAR

RTM  SHP  SPR  SIZ  HFC  POLY

Fader invader. The Lexicon reverb unit was a much coveted piece of studio kit in the 1980s.

(Clockwise from top left) Ace of bass: Martin Kemp onstage at the Market Cellar Club; Tony Hadley emotes onstage in Chicago; the 'Ballet photographed in Munich.

directed the Durrells. We performed Lifeline for the first time on TV on Noel Edmund's The Late Late Breakfast Show on 25th September 1982, which I also wrote the bloody theme tune for. The rest of the album was recorded and mixed back in London at Redbus Studios from 22nd November and finished by 7th January 1983. I remember mixing Gold all night and Boy George waiting cross outside to get in to do one of his!

## 6. HEAVEN IS A SECRET

### @GaryJKemp

The record company wanted this as a 5th single and we said no, too much. So much of this album was influenced by my trips to Glasgow to hang with Altered Images. They loved Marvin Gaye and Al Green. And that's where I met David Band. David and I went on a climbing trip to the Lake District and sitting in a pub one night he sketched out the cover idea for me. I loved his mad naive work. David RIP. This was also important.

## 7. FOUNDATION

### @GaryJKemp

I always wanted to write Nile Rodgers guitar parts. Foundation was our opening song on the True tour. Props to Hadley!!! Steve Norman hadn't picked up a Sax till the year before. Mental.

## 8. TRUE

### @GaryJKemp

So I admit Clare Grogan [Altered Image singer/actress] was an influence in my writing this. I had a mad crush and we hung out. She played Marvin [Gaye] and we just remained friends. She gave me [Vladimir Nabokov's novel] Lolita and I nicked a few lines. There. I hid behind that question. Tony didn't think it was a single but Simon Bates in Radio 1 played all 6 mins twice. Back to back. I said "cause it's a fucking single!" I loved Ed Norton singing it in Modern Family. And Steve Buschemi's version. And Maggie from the Simpsons! Everybody crammed in the control room in Nassau when we first played this back after I'd done the guitar. All of us singing along. Great memories.

## 5. LIFELINE

### @GaryJKemp

The first single from the album, Lifeline, was recorded at Redbus Studios, London, 16th-20th August 1982. It went top ten as we flew to Nassau. As I said this was Swain and Jolley's choice after listening to all the songs at Nomis rehearsal studios. This album doesn't have sadness!!! The video for Lifeline was shot on 7th September in London at a warehouse in Docklands and directed by Steve Barron who recently

# Let's Get Out Of This Country
## Camera Obscura
Elefant/Merge, 2006

✣ Full of truly heartfelt lyrics ("A song about my breaking heart" was a memorable refrain throughout this Listening Party), shuffling percussion and Kodak-coloured melodies, Camera Obscura's third album *Let's Get Out Of This Country* is a heady cocktail of romance and escapism. A departure from its self-produced predecessors, the Glasgow band literally did get out of the country to make this record as Tracyanne Campbell (vocals – **@Juniortcampbell**), Carey Lander (keyboards) Gavin Dunbar (bass – **@kingofpartick**), Kenny McKeeve (guitar – **@KennyMcKeeve**), Lee Thomson (drums) and Nigel Baillie (trumpet/percission) decamped to Sweden to record the record with help from much of the country's indie-rock royalty (it seems). Having paused their activities in 2015 following the death of Lander who had been treated for a rare type of bone cancer, the group reunited in 2018 and were working on a new record when the Covid-19 pandemic struck. Happily their Listening Party allowed Camera Obscura to pay tribute to Lander and gave us all a chance to *Get Out Of This Country*, musically at least.

PHOTOGRAPHY:
Fredik Ottosson

---

LISTENING
PARTY
**6 JUNE
2020**

### 1. LLOYD, I'M READY TO BE HEARTBROKEN

✅ **@Juniortcampbell (Tracyanne Campbell)**
Apparently Lloyd used to come on to this. I hope so. Thanks Lloyd Cole and thanks to Dion for writing Abraham, Martin And John. We sort of 'borrowed' the structure. Lots of choruses. Lloyd Cole you've been a massive influence on me. Thank you sir x

✅ **@Lloyd_Cole**
Which makes me very happy.

### 2. TEARS FOR AFFAIRS

✅ **@Juniortcampbell**
A song about my breaking heart. Someone told me after the fact the boy I loved had cheated on me.

### 3. COME BACK MARGARET

✅ **@kingofpartick (Gavin Dunbar)**
This was played on the One Show when Maggie Thatcher died. We weren't consulted.

### 4. DORY PREVIN

✅ **@KennyMcKeeve**
I had a nice, neat 'country-lite' solo prepared for Dory Previn. Producer Jari thought it was too 'Christian'. He got me to down a laaaarge whisky, told me to improvise, and (with a glint in his eye) "play it clumsy, like a big drunk idiot".

### 5. THE FALSE CONTENDER

✅ **@KennyMcKeeve**
If anybody pinched a setlist from the stage saying "The Great Soprendo", think yourself lucky; that was our nickname for The False Contender. Worth MILLIONS now.

### 6. LET'S GET OUT OF THIS COUNTRY

✅ **@Juniortcampbell**
I wrote this on the streets of Dundee and Arbroath sticking posters up, fantasising about running away with a frenchman François [Marry, frontman of Frános & the Atlas Mountains, touring member of Camera Obscura]. He didn't know that until now.

I Need All The Friends I Can Get. Nigel Baillie, Carey Lander, Gavin Dunbar, Tracyanne Campbell, Kenny McKeeve and Lee Tomson in 2006.

↓

"RIP Carey. What a band!" During the Listening Party @tomorybristol shared this picture of keyboard player Carey Lander, who passed away in 2015.

## 7. COUNTRY MILE

✅ @Juniortcampbell
I fell in love after playing a show in Sweden, or was it infatuation? I wrote this in the taxi on the way to the airport. Stockholm has very pretty trees.

## 8. IF LOOKS COULD KILL

✅ @Juniortcampbell
Half of Stockholm's artists are singing on this. Such fun – we got them all drunk and had a dance party. At the time I thought it sounded like a bag of spanners. It sort of does.

## 9. I NEED ALL THE FRIENDS I CAN GET

✅ @Juniortcampbell
I remember this being one we almost didn't make work. Jari was running round from the control room to the live room to play percussion. It was chaos.

## 10. RAZZLE DAZZLE ROSE

✅ @KennyMcKeeve
Razzle Dazzle Rose is usually our live grand finale. A bloody racket. I'll never tire of playing it, even on a "bad" night, because it always feels like we've made it, whatever that is, for everybody, crowd and band, together, for better or worse.

# Hardcore Will Never Die, But You Will
## Mogwai
Rock Action, 2011

**PHOTOGRAPHY:**
Antony Crook

**SLEEVE DESIGN:**
DLT

⚲ With a title like *Hardcore Will Never Die, But You Will* you might imagine a Mogwai Listening Party might be more listening, less party (they also did one for their album *Come On Die Young…*). However, despite the Glasgow post-rock band's fearsome live reputation for all-enveloping volumes and relentless strobes, there is also a sardonic humour behind Dominic Aitchison (bass), Stuart Braithwaite (guitar – **@plasmatron**), Martin Bulloch (drums – **@mogwaiband**), Barry Burns (guitar/keyboards) and then guitarist John Cummings' work. So much so the Listening Party for this, their seventh album, was punctuated by a series of laugh-out-loud moments including one confusing the cinematic origins of their band name (*Jungle Book* rather than *Gremlins*). With former touring musicians – Error's James Hamilton – and fans including the author Ian Rankin also swinging by to make their contributions, what Braithwaite and Bulloch's tour around their 2011 album revealed was not just the comedy behind their creations, but also demonstrated the enduring power of the band's textured, intricate and immersive landscapes.

→
Grand Prix. Fan @moggieboy attended five Mogwai gigs on the trot as the band warmed up to tour *Hardcore Will Never Die…* and shared some of the setlist retrieved after the shows.

1 WHITE NOISE
2 ITHICA
3 LETTERS TO THE METRO
4 I KNOW YOU ARE
5 MEX GRAND PRIX
6 JIM MORRISON
7 WEREWOLF
8 HUNTED
9 RANO PANO
10 LONG WAY
11 SAN PEDRO
12 LIKE HEROD

THATCHER
JESUS
BATCAT

MOGWAI
JANUARY TOUR OF SCOTLAND
SEASON TICKET
STIRLING TOLBOOTH WED 26 JANUARY
PAISLEY TOWN HALL THUR 27 JANUARY
PERTH THEATRE FRI 28 JANUARY
ABERDEEN MUSIC HALL SAT 29 JANUARY
GLASGOW GRAND OLE OPRY SUN 30 JANUARY

1 WHITE NOISE
2 MEXICAN GRAND PRIX
3 FLIES
4 JIM MORRISON
5 WEREWOLF
6 FRIEND
7 METRO
8 JESUS
9 THATCHER
10 RANO PANO
11 HELICON 1
12 LIONEL RICHIE

CODY
SATAN

Hello! Mogwai
frontman and
(apparently) awestruck
Lionel Richie fan
Stuart Braithwaite.

### 1. WHITE NOISE

**@plasmatron (Stuart Braithwaite)**

White Noise is one of my favourites. I think this song sets the tone for the whole record. It sounds like us but not like anything we'd done before.

### 2. MEXICAN GRAND PRIX

**@plasmatron**

We played a festival on the site of the actual Mexican Grand Prix in Mexico City which was pretty cool. I don't think I've listened to this since we made it. I'd forgotten how good it sounds.

### 3. RANO PANO

**@plasmatron**

Rano Pano is bananas. Barry wrote it and always said the riff was like something the Muppets would sing. The title came from Barry walking in while a football game was on and reading the score as RANO PANO. It was Rangers 0 - Panathanaikos 0.

### 4. DEATH RAYS

**@plasmatron**

We almost called the album Death Rays. Our good pal Albert who sells our merch on US tours named his company after it. Martin is going some hard sounding drums there!

**@mogwaiband (Martin Bulloch)**

It's all about the drums. Obviously.

### 5. SAN PEDRO

**@plasmatron**

San Pedro is a banger. We got on real telly to play this on Jimmy Fallon which was incredibly surreal. It was like 30 Rock but a lot less funny.

### 6. LETTERS TO THE METRO

**@plasmatron**

This song is named after the letter page in The Metro newspaper which we were totally obsessed with for some reason. The song is really pretty.

### 7. GEORGE SQUARE THATCHER DEATH PARTY

**@plasmatron**

The title comes from the party that had been prepared in anticipation of Thatcher's death. When she died we got a few mentions in the right-wing press. I was proud as fuck.

### 8. HOW TO BE A WEREWOLF

**@plasmatron**

Named after an instructional video on the BBC website to show kids how to dress up as a werewolf.

### 9. TOO RAGING TO CHEERS

**@mogwaiband**

Jesus, where do any of them [the titles] come from? Drunken nonsense probably.

### 10. YOU'RE LIONEL RICHIE

**@plasmatron**

Ok. I was DJing in Barcelona with Arthur Baker and had ....quite a good night. At the airport on the way home I randomly saw Lionel Ritchie and all I could think of to say to him was You're Lionel Richie. He just smiled at me like I was daft.

# The Hour Of Bewilderbeast
## Badly Drawn Boy
Twisted Nerve/XL, 2000

⚑ Many musicians have a penchant for hats. Stetsons, Fezzes, trilbies and cowboy hats have all adorned album covers and defined scenes. Few however have the immediate iconic status – or the creative inspiration – of the simple, knitted black-and-white beanie hat worn by Damon Gough. Now synonymous with the Bolton singer-songster, better known to the world as Badly Drawn Boy, that headwear proved something of a lucky charm as he made his debut album – so much so a reward was paid for the hat's successful return after it was pinched after a gig. Whether it was the hat, or, more likely, the brains under it, *The Hour Of Bewilderbeast* proved to be a charming, rolling work that enchanted audiences with its heartfelt melodies, playful innocence and irresistible tunes. It also won Gough the Mercury Prize in 2000.

Bad Drawn Boy's Listening Party revealed the care and thought that Gough (**@badly_drawn_boy**) had put in to capturing his homespun, lo-fi soul on record. A point underlined by his producer, label boss and pal Twisted Nerve's Andy Votel (**@AndyVotel**), who not only released the album, performed on it, toured it and designed its artwork, but also joined in the Listening Party, sharing stories and many different versions of his work for the record's sleeve. "Andy's artwork played a huge part in the journey this album went on, amazing!" Badly Dawn Boy tweeted as the playback got underway, so enjoy a vivid picture of *The Hour Of Bewilderbeast*'s time.

**SLEEVE DESIGN:**
Andy Votel

(Below left)
@badly_drawn_boy
How I might have looked whilst writing this song [Camping Next To Water]; (middle) A draft unused version of the type for Andy Votel's "original proposed artwork" for 2000 single Another Pearl; (below) @badly_drawn_boy Outtake from the video to Disillusion! Shot in New York.

## 1. THE SHINING

🔘 **@badly_drawn_boy**

This was always going to be the opening song on the album. However this intro wasn't always there. I asked the producer Ken Nelson to solo the cello and French horn one day and realised I wanted this to start the album.

## 2. EVERYBODY'S STALKING

🔘 **@badly_drawn_boy**

A play on the title Everybody's Talkin'. Ian Smith played drums, not his first instrument but a fantastic 'feel' drummer. As with all the Ken Nelson tracks, this was mostly recorded at my studio in New Mount Street, Manchester. Then finished and mixed at Parr Street, Liverpool.

## 3. BEWILDER

🔘 **@badly_drawn_boy**

I'd refer to this as a little 'palate cleanser' between songs. I played it on a harmonium. It also serves as a taster for the title track Bewilderbeast.

## 4. FALL IN A RIVER

🔘 **@AndyVotel**

And so begins the WATER SUITE.

🔘 **@badly_drawn_boy**

Recorded in [Producer Joe Robinson's] bedroom on a tiny desktop microphone. If I had a pound for every person that said 'why is this song not longer?'...on tour it became the show opener, sometimes 15 minutes long.

## 5. CAMPING NEXT TO WATER

🔘 **@badly_drawn_boy**

A song about going camping to get away and sort your head out and re-appreciate a relationship. This actually never happened though!

🔘 **@AndyVotel**

I remember listening to River by Terry Reid a lot at the time, so really loved how this triptych turned out.

## 6. STONE ON THE WATER

🔘 **@badly_drawn_boy**

I had an interview down the pub with Select Magazine. It took 2 hours... when I got back Andy had more or less put the intro together. With other samples. Then we put the vocal down in 1 take using a bass drum mic as it was the only one available.

## 7. ANOTHER PEARL

🔘 **@badly_drawn_boy**

Can't imagine anyone other than Andy to help me achieve this song. His approach was exciting, using my guitar parts like samples, cello parts too. The drum programming in particular is unique to Andy and gives the song its character. They sound real but you kind of also know they aren't.

🔘 **@AndyVotel**

I actually played that piano!!!?! Must have been possessed?!? The track has some lovely samples of my favourite Polish singer, we also sampled strings of an Iranian Googoosh record, but they got lost in the mix.

## 8. BODY RAP

🔘 **@badly_drawn_boy**

Another palate cleanser if you will! There were more sections to this song, could have been epic but we just looped a small section.

🔘 **@AndyVotel**

Touring Japan with a Hasbro Body Rap attached to your chest is no joke!

## 9. ONCE AROUND THE BLOCK

🔘 **@badly_drawn_boy**

I honestly wasn't sure about the auto-wah effects on the guitar. But what do I know?! I'm glad I went with it!

## 10. THIS SONG

🔘 **@badly_drawn_boy**

I sang the song roughly 10 times and we stacked up all the takes, ignoring rules of harmony. Then put the whole song through a tremelo.

## 11. BEWILDERBEAST

🔘 **@badly_drawn_boy**

All of the band Alfie played on this song. I liked the idea that the title track was an instrumental, that the music meant more than the words perhaps. The success of this album enabled me to meet some of my heroes too.. !! With Joe Strummer at Q awards.

### 12. MAGIC IN THE AIR

○ @badly_drawn_boy

"Shep n Ando" Explained.. Shep was Ken Nelson's nickname. @ChrisMartin of Coldplay said he looked like a shepherd. Ando was Andrea our assistant in the studio. This song was my take on a Bacharach style song. Like [Bacharach and David's] This Guys In Love With You.

### 13. CAUSE A ROCKSLIDE

○ @badly_drawn_boy

This was supposed to evoke me being lost at a fairground as a kid, my voice sped up.

○ @AndyVotel

Always loved Damon's felchy falsetto! Soul Attitude being a fave. The sign of an artist not taking himself too seriously... not many Mancs would have dared doing this at the time.

### 14.    PISSING IN THE WIND

○ @badly_drawn_boy

Doves were my backing band on this song. Joan Collins was in the video but had to re-record it for radio to Spitting In The Wind.

### 15. BLISTERED HEART

○ @badly_drawn_boy

Another Palate cleanser for a bit of respite and reflection before the final push to the end!

### 16. DISILLUSION

○ @badly_drawn_boy

The band Doves played on this one as well. As a title Disillusion is a reference to Stevie Wonder's Superstition and the beat was inspired by that song too.

### 17. SAY IT AGAIN

○ @badly_drawn_boy

I was going for a New Orleans thing. A student brass band came in to play the parts. I seem to remember them watching the clock, dying to leave!

○ @AndyVotel

My cousin Spencer Birtwhistle plays drums on this track, he was also in The Fall and was a founding member of Intastella.

### 18. EPITAPH

○ @badly_drawn_boy

I very rarely use open tunings. Erland [Øye] from the band Kings Of Convenience showed me a simple tuning. I only ever wrote this one song with it. My ex partner Clare sings the final verse. She'd never sang before and needed a bottle of wine for courage!

@badly_drawn_boy
I think this is the only photo of me in the studio while making the album.

←
@AndyVotel
First Twisted Nerve press shots, downstairs in Piccadilly Station.

**@AndyVotel**
A very early gig, organised with @stan_chow and Rakhi Kumar, truly amazing time.

Badly Drawn Boy performing at the launch of the 2000 Q Awards wearing his (possibly) magic hat.

# *MTV Unplugged (Live at Hull City Hall)*
## Liam Gallagher
Warner, 2020

PHOTOGRAPHY:
Jake Green

⚓ Liam Gallagher tweets like he fronts a band: direct and straight from the heart. While there is often a brevity to the former Oasis man's posts, a unique charisma peppers his observations of the world. Just like when he is behind a microphone. Liam does not dance. Instead he floats stoically, loose-limbed like a boxer sizing up his opponent, but then when he opens his mouth and sings, hands clasped firmly behind his back, his voice invokes the emotions of the masses – whether that's on record or in person at a gig. Fittingly the album he chose for his Listening Party captured both those environments.

Following in the footsteps of the likes of Nirvana, Liam had just released a live *MTV Unplugged* album so he turned his laser-like Twitter focus to talking us through that record. Like many other sets recorded for the music network, Gallagher's performance at Hull City Hall made a bit of musical history too, as it saw the frontman perform live with Oasis bandmate Paul "Bonehead" Arthurs (**@BoneheadsPage**), who had quit the group in 1999. So we did not just get the unique Liam Gallagher (**@LiamGallagher**) Twitter experience channelled into a Listening Party, but we also got a mini Oasis reunion, of sorts, as Bonehead joined in too. Tweet fer it…

➡

**@BoneheadsPage**
Had a wander round
Hull day of the gig.

LISTENING
PARTY
12 JUNE
2020

↓

All my people right
here right now.
Liam G onstage and
unplugged in Hull.

### 1. WALL OF GLASS

**@LiamGallagher**
This is the first time I'm listening to it. Sounds good.

**@BoneheadsPage**
First time back in Hull since Oasis played the Adelphi back in '94 I think.

### 2. SOME MIGHT SAY

**@BoneheadsPage**
Some might say it's sounding good.

**@LiamGallagher**
I gotta say you lot sound absolutely CELESTIAL.

### 3. NOW THAT I'VE FOUND YOU

**@LiamGallagher**
Was a bit nervous about this one as was the first time I sang it with Molly [Moorish, Liam's daughter who the song is about] there.

**@BoneheadsPage**
Written for Molly, I was watching side of stage, love the lyrics. The future's yours and mine, now and forever more. My first time hearing this song, think I'd only heard about 5 or 6 six from the album as demos.

### 4. ONE OF US

🗸 **@LiamGallagher**

It was all very nerve wracking as I'm a bit shitbag when it comes to acoustic gigs.

🗸 **@BoneheadsPage**

I'm a sucker for strings, how good do they sound?

### 5. STAND BY ME

🗸 **@BoneheadsPage**

Stand by me. Liam introduces it "without the seagulls" someone recorded the soundcheck the day before from outside the venue, complete with seagull noises and posted it online. Sounded cool. Strings, backing vocals and seagulls.

🗸 **@LiamGallagher**

This ones going out to NG.

### 6. SAD SONG

🗸 **@BoneheadsPage**

Standing up there with Liam playing this song was up there as one of my best moments next to him. First time I'd ever played this song live, Liam's too. Worked didn't it?

🗸 **@LiamGallagher**

I'm not one to blow my own trumpet but I sound half decent. This is a shoutout to all my mates who I went to school with you know who you are it's been lovely getting to know you again.

### 7. CAST NO SHADOW

🗸 **@LiamGallagher**

This ones going out to the mighty Richard Ashcroft. I'm feeling very emotional now brothers and sisters as far as I'm concerned there was two bands in the 90s and it was Oasis and The Verve.

🗸 **@BoneheadsPage**

One of my favourite Oasis songs. Liam sounding as good as he ever did. Strings, backing vocals and what a top band. Was like being back for 5 minutes.

### 8. ONCE

🗸 **@BoneheadsPage**

Dedicated to Bonehead who gets to do MTV unplugged twice. Think there's only me and REM ever played it twice. One for the pub quiz.

🗸 **@LiamGallagher**
YOU GREEDY BASTARD

🗸 **@BoneheadsPage**

This song has touched me like no song has for a long long time. What a song, kills me every listen.

⊕

The frontmen's union out in force, Tim and Liam.

### 9. GONE

🔘 **@BoneheadsPage**
First time I'd heard this. I posted a clip from sound check earlier. Walking into the venue while the band and singers were playing it, was like walking into a James Bond film. Love it.

🔘 **@LiamGallagher**
Lost the plot here. We're having some technical difficulties, maybe it's the tequila. What track is everyone on? Listening to music and typing at the same time is like tapping your head and rubbing your belly.

🔘 **@Tim_Burgess**
Liam is playing a blinder here. Got a vision of Bonehead as Mr Miyagi and LG as the karate kid learning about #TimsTwitterListeningParty. Wax on. Wax off. Our kid.

🔘 **@BoneheadsPage**
You should have heard the phone call 10 mins before we started.

### 10. CHAMPAGNE SUPERNOVA

🔘 **@LiamGallagher**
As far as I'm concerned Rkid's [Noel Gallagher] best tune thanks for listening and being patient with this old parka monkey. I love you and I'll see you at the next gig. That's just spun me rite out need a big line down I mean lie…

**TIM'S THOUGHTS**

A couple of years after The Charlatans hit their stride, a few people I knew told me there was this kid who fronted this band who I really ought to go and see. As the months passed the mentions got more and in 1992 I ended up watching said kid and his band at the Boardwalk in Manchester – you might be ahead of me here but the kid was Liam and the band was Oasis, and to cut a long story short they were on their way to a fairly busy 15 years.

Our paths crossed many times in the intervening decade and a half, and at our Night For Jon Brookes at the Royal Albert Hall the young whippersnapper even replaced me as the frontman of The Charlatans for a few songs giving me the surreal experience of watching my own band from a box.

In 2020 Liam released a live album and word came through that he was up for doing a Listening Party. On a couple of occasions he'd been due to join Bonehead for the celebration of Oasis albums but it just didn't happen. People spoke to people and a time and day was arranged and here we were 20 years after I'd first seen him and we'd both embraced communication via Twitter. It was a match made in heaven.

# *Bebey*
## Theophilus London
My Bebey Records/Independent, 2020

There is one word that seems to encapsulate Theophilus London's third album: tropical. Boasting an array of superstar collaborators – including members of the Wu-Tang Clan and Tame Impala – languid beats and unexpected samples, the whole record coalesces around London's bright, pitch-shifting vocals that give each song a rich, exotic atmosphere. This record is exotic and hot… truly tropical. With the album's creative spirit being nourished by a disco pioneer, an avant-garde composer and a weekend in the desert, while taking its title from Cameroonian author and composer Francis Bebey, *Bebey* is an album you can dive into deeply. Fortunately London (**@TheophilusL**) was on hand to take charge of a Listening Party that floated us around the record's musical caves and coves.

ARTWORK:
Isabelle Calin

@WeirdoMusic4evr
Theophilus in L.A. earlier this week.
Photo:
@CountessCameron

---

**LISTENING PARTY**
**13 JUNE 2020**

### 1. LEON

✅ **@TheophilusL**
First song Leon is a tribute to my guy and mentor [producer, songwriter and artist] Leon Ware. He left me a bit of the sample before he passed. It was his dying wish!

### 2. MARCHIN'

✅ **@TheophilusL**
I felt like Wyclef [Jean, Fugees] recording this one. Also do note I give Bert and Ernie [from Sesame Street] a shoutout on Marchin. Cuz thy came out as gay and it was beautiful!

### 3. BEBEY

✅ **@TheophilusL**
The album title! Yeah, it's the whole ethos for all my brands. BIG UP [Cameroonian writer and composer] Francis Bebey. His song Lily inspired this song.

### 4. ONLY YOU

✅ **@TheophilusL**
We hit the lottery aka the jackpot! With Bebey and Only You! Kevin Parker [Tame Impala frontman and collaborator on this track] I love ya.

### 5. CUBA

✅ **@TheophilusL**
Is about me not being so popular in elementary. And my dancehall days. Black is beautiful. Never forget that!

### 6. GIVE YOU

✅ **@TheophilusL**
This is that soul train line record while yo mama eating a wing at the bbq. I'm in my boxers about to drink mint. And dancing to GIVE U !

### 7. SEALS

⊘ **@TheophilusL**

I produced this one. U ready for it? I produced this by listening to [composer] John Maus NAVY SEALS off [2007 album] Love Is Real. Me and John share the same bday.

### 8. WHIPLASH

⊘ **@TheophilusL**

I'm dancing with my girl to WHIPLASH rn. She wearing my Navy Seals hoody.

### 9. WHOOP TANG FLOW

⊘ **@TheophilusL**

My boy Teddy [Fantum, Canadian rapper] came back from the desert after a wknd mushroom trip. And he brought back "WHOOP TANG FLOW" I finished the song that day. And I knew I wanted a Wu Tang member on it! So I called in a favor and boooom the CHEF [Wu-Tang Clan rapper Raekwon]. We did it the Covid way. Over email!

### 10. PRETTY

⊘ **@TheophilusL**

Most notable lines: "INTERNATIONAL PLY BOY SHIT! LOVE WOMEN GET BITCOINS" period. This one feats IAN ISIAH ! Produced by me.

### 11. BEBEY

⊘ **@TheophilusL**

Fun fact! My dad appears on Bebey feat my favorite UK rapper of all time Giggs. There is no one better in sorry! Caribbean men unite.

### 12. SEALS (SOLO)

⊘ **@TheophilusL**

Again if it wasn't for John Maus there would be no Seals (Solo) that's a factory finnact fact tho! This song is my solace ! It's my being. It's my algorithm. That song is like being on a motherfuckin boat.

### 13. REVENGE

⊘ **@TheophilusL**

Do note I peaked on mushrooms the whole time I recorded Revenge vocals! Everything was perfect and as is! That's weird! It's a perfect cover ! But Ariel [Pink] plays some original They All Come To The Carving Knife, I think it's called. [the track covers New Musik's 1981 song They All Run After The Carving Knife (See How They Run)]

**TIM'S THOUGHTS**

Celebrating classic albums has been a big part of the Listening Parties, but it's brilliant to be able to introduce new artists too. For oh so long I have wanted to work with a member of the Wu-Tang Clan so always kept a little eye on what the various members were up to, then this guy Theophilus London goes and does a track with Raekwon The Chef. "What did he have that I didn't have?" I asked myself. As it turned out, quite a lot. Theophilus London became one of my favourite artists so back in May 2020 I sent him a message and we were really excited to work on the Listening Party together.

# What Did You Expect From The Vaccines?
## The Vaccines
Columbia, 2011

Fast, breathless and exhilarating… and that was just the buzz that surrounded The Vaccines' early gigs at the start of the 2010s, quickly earning the band NME covers and a record deal. Fronted by Justin Young, formerly known as Jay Jay Pistolet and part of the same new folk scene which spawned Mumford & Sons and Laura Marling in the 2000s, the singer didn't need to be asked twice to join The Vaccines when the band's demos started being played on national radio. *What Did You Expect From The Vaccines?* is a fast, breathless and exhilarating rock'n'roll debut that ensured Young (**@TheVaccines**), together with bandmates Freddie Cowan (guitar), Árni Árnason (bass) and then drummer Pete Robertson, lived up to the hype. Full of short, sharp but totally tuneful songs, Young offered his own, suitably punchy, take on The Vaccines' debut.

PHOTOGRAPHY:
Jonay P. Matos

LISTENING
PARTY
13 JUNE
2020

### 1. WRECKIN' BAR (RA RA RA)

**@TheVaccines (Justin Young)**
This is still 'that song from FIFA' [football video game] for a lot of people. We played it on Later… with Jools Holland before we'd released any music. They let us have three songs because they were all so short. Sandwiched between MIA and Kings Of Leon which was very scary.

### 2. IF YOU WANNA

**@TheVaccines**
[DJ] Zane Lowe played the demo on Radio 1 with no warning and made it his hottest record. Everything changed after that. I was on holiday in Greece. Spat my tzatziki out when I heard. Still cry sometimes when we play this song, thinking where we'd be without it.

### 3. A LACK OF UNDERSTANDING

**@TheVaccines**
Everyone said we sounded like The Strokes. This was the one song that I thought maybe sounded like The Strokes. It doesn't sound like The Strokes at all.

### 4. BLOW IT UP

**@TheVaccines**
Oh yeh, I remember we wanted to write a song that sounded like [lo-fi American band] Times New Viking, who we all loved. Had a prototype of this riff at school too. Opened all our early gigs with this, been hibernating for a while now though.

### 5. WETSUIT

**@TheVaccines**
I started writing the verses about a friend that drowned. Completely shifted meaning by the time it was finished though. A lot less heavy now.

### 6. NØRGAARD

**@TheVaccines**
This feels increasingly creepy, but I was 21 when we wrote it. It was supposed to be a nod and a wink to The Beatles' I Saw Her Standing There. I've just googled 'creepiest lyrics in rock' and we're not on any of the lists yet.

Double dose. The Vaccines' Pete Robertson, Justin Young, Árni Árnason and Freddie Cowan.

## 7. POST BREAK-UP SEX

● **@TheVaccines**

Wrote this sat on my childhood bed with my dad's weird/ugly 80s bass when I was back home studying for my finals. Didn't actually own a guitar while we were saving guitar music.

## 8. UNDER YOUR THUMB

● **@TheVaccines**

Always forget about this song. Thought it was called European Sun.

## 9. ALL IN WHITE

● **@TheVaccines**

Always an outlier on the album I thought. Definitely wasn't my favourite song, but I've grown to love it.

## 10. WOLF PACK

● **@TheVaccines**

This is about my best friends. Dedicated it to them at Isle Of Wight Festival in 2011 but they'd all had a big Friday night and left before we played so they didn't hear their five seconds of fame.

## 11. FAMILY FRIEND

● **@TheVaccines**

Wrote this the day of the first Zane Lowe play. Really put the wind in my sails and I was on a boat too. Wow this ending is quite tame – but it ain't lame.

## 12. SOMEBODY ELSE'S CHILD

● **@TheVaccines**

Wanted to put a secret song on an album since hearing Endless Nameless on [Nirvana's] Nevermind. My vocal polyps were so bad at this point [Young had surgery on his vocal chords in 2012]. You can really hear me struggling to sing across the whole record actually. Maybe a good time to shut up and go back on voice rest now.

# Made Of Bricks
## Kate Nash
Fiction, 2007

Loud guitars, acclaimed acting roles, campaigns to help girls pick up instruments and form bands, being open about mental-health issues… Kate Nash (**@KateNash**) covers much within her artistic sweep. A powerful songwriter, confidently vocal in the name of the causes she supports, Nash has succeeded despite doing much of her personal and artistic growth in the glare of the spotlight. Signed aged just 20 after some songs she posted to 2000s social media platform MySpace caught the attention of the music industry A&R departments, the Brit School graduate was already evolving when she released her full debut album, *Made Of Bricks*, on a major label. She has since taken control of her music by releasing it herself, while her music as moved away from the piano-driven songs of her first full album – and she has also starred in Netflix wrestling drama Glow. However, *Made Of Bricks* remains the important starting point for Nash's journey. While forged by the prevailing indie-pop sounds of the day, there is a character and attitude in every track that not only makes it clear this album is the direct result of Nash's own personality, but it also heavily hints at the artist who would emerge. *Made Of Bricks* is also packed with really good songs.

ARTWORK:
Laura Dockrill

**@KateNash**
Thank you for the journey that I'm lucky enough to still be on. Not a lot of ppl in the industry had my back. But you guys always have.

## 1. PLAY

🔘 @KateNash

This song is literally made up of GarageBand loops. I wanted to do a fun little intro to the album, I was really inspired by lo fi records. When we do this live now Linda [Buratto, guitarist in Kate Nash's live band] wanks up the guitar a bit obvs.

## 2. FOUNDATIONS

🔘 @KateNash

I really remember a couple coming up to me after a gig and telling me this was their song. Couples with this as their anthem gotta be DOOMED.

## 3. MOUTHWASH

🔘 @KateNash

I wrote this song when I worked at Nando's. I was well late to work cause I got inspo from the streets of Harrow.

## 4. DICKHEAD

🔘 @KateNash

I was told by someone close to her that MADGE. yes MADONNA would sing this around the house before her divorce!! ICONIC

## 5. BIRDS

🔘 @KateNash

I wrote this when I had my broken foot! Why did I agree to go to the shopping centre with my parents and sit in the boot of the car with my guitar whilst they went shopping? Who knows, but thank god I did cause we love this song and that's how it was born.

## 6. WE GET ON

🔘 @KateNash

How many parties did you go to where you saw your crush gettin' off with someone else?! The horror.

## 7. MARIELLA

🔘 @KateNash

Mariella was inspired by Tim Burton's short film Vincent. I thought if Marbella and Vincent ever met they would fall in love and be happy being morbid together!

## 8. SHIT SONG

🔘 @KateNash

I was so into wastemen back then. Thank god you can grow out of that! Fuck anyone who doesn't treat you like the queens and kings and unicorns you all are.

## 9. PUMPKIN SOUP

🔘 @KateNash

I'm such a rebel with this nonsense title. Lolll. Honestly, about another wasteman. I cried in the studio recording this cause I felt so much pressure to make the most poppy song on the record.

## 10. SKELETON SONG

🔘 @KateNash

Remember the kids books about the family of skeletons?! Stanley is a real skeleton that lives in my mum's living room. Dresses up like a sexy Santa every year.

## 11. NICEST THING

🔘 @KateNash

The saddest, sweetest part of this song is that it's not about anyone in particular, was just so desperate to be loved! Too deep.

## 12. MERRY HAPPY

🔘 @KateNash

My bff/complicated not boyfriend relationship!!! You know the one.

## 13. LITTLE RED [INTERNATIONAL BONUS TRACK]

🔘 @KateNash

If you had the original record Little Red was the secret track. I'm emo, I wish we were in a dirty venue somewhere with crappy monitors and sweat dripping off the ceiling.

# Aladdin Sane
## David Bowie
RCA, 1973

When it came to technology, David Bowie was usually an adopter before "early adopters" knew what was going on. From the sci-fi infused lyrics early in his career and his taking a lead role in the forward-looking film *The Man Who Fell To Earth* (which seemed to both prefigure environmental concerns *and* the psychological pitfalls of celebrity), to being one of the first artists to embrace the internet, offering an album via download before anyone else, the boy from Bromley was always switched on. Listening Parties, where people could gather all over the world to communally enjoy a record together at the same time, is a use of technology that would have no doubt appealed to him, which is why many of Bowie's collaborators have signed up to take fans through a variety of his records.

The summit of the Ziggy Stardust era, featuring The Spiders From Mars backing band – Mick Ronson (guitars), Trevor Bolder (bass), Mick Woodmansey (drums) and, from this record, Mike Garson (**@MikeGarson**) on piano – this is an album that both contributed to and deconstructed Bowie's own international stardom. It also saw the innovator moving outside the glam bubble with a rawer rock sound that would prepare the ground for a generation of musicians who would soon follow his lead. Hosting the Listening Party for this most pivotal and iconic of records – and for once the word iconic is truly earned, Bowie's appearance on the album's artwork defined an era – pianist Garson's lamp truly illuminated the creation of *Aladdin Sane* – and even got Bowie's son Duncan (**@ManMadeMoon**) to join in from the other side of the world. It's a technical innovation you suspect Bowie would have approved of.

PHOTOGRAPHY:
Brian Duffy

**@MikeGarson:** My friend Billy Corgan sang The Jean Genie with David at his 50th birthday concert at Madison Square Garden in 97. So many greats with us at that one including Robert Smith, Lou Reed, Dave Grohl and Foo Fighters, Sonic Youth and Black Francis among others. Here's a photo of many of us backstage that night in 1997.

Let's Spend The Night Together. David Bowie in London during the 1973 *Ziggy Stardust/ Aladdin Sane* tour.

## 1. WATCH THAT MAN

### ⊘ @MikeGarson

This was an unusual piece for me to play on. My training was in classical and this is just straight up rock n roll with me banging away on 8th notes on the upper register of the piano. It was a lot of fun for me. Initially I was a bit of a snobby classical musician with jazz training looking down on simple rock like this to my detriment and quickly realized / embraced the community joy of playing with other musicians. I've loved playing this kind of music since. I played the UK a few years ago on an Aladdin Sane tour with an amazing vocalist [Guatemalan singer/songwriter/producer] Gaby Moreno and fellow Bowie alum [guitarist] Kevin Armstrong. We had a lot of fun playing the album in order much like this listening party tonight.

## 2. ALADDIN SANE (1913–1938–197?)

### ⊘ @MikeGarson

Most every track on this album, like this one, was done in one take. For years after we recorded it I never heard this song. It's only history, for me, that's told me it was substantial but at the time of recording it I didn't have that reality. So here's the solo. I think you have to be in your 20s to play so maniacal and with so much energy. I haven't been able to play this solo better since then. I did it with David dozens of times live and quite a bit on my @bowietour alumni shows over the years. Never did it better than this particular take. I think some sort of maniacal surge of energy came through me and I was just channeling. I was getting so much admiration and respect from David in the booth and [producer] Ken Scott – a wonderful producer along with Trevor [Bolder, bass], Mick and [drummer] Woody Woodmansey. I don't think I could have played a wrong note that day and there's thousands of notes on this particular solo! Davids' son, Duncan Jones has told me that this solo gave him nightmares for years as a child. Sorry about that, Duncan!

### ⊘ @ManMadeMoon (Duncan Jones)

Keep in mind I was a little kid on my own in the back stage area playing with crash cases, with no one but annoyed roadies watching me move their kit around…

## 3. DRIVE-IN SATURDAY

### ⊘ @MikeGarson

I love this song. It's just brilliant writing by David. It's a catchy song with great chord progressions and it evokes rock music I heard in the 50s but with a modern 70s twist. David was great at embracing the entirety of rock n roll. He understood it better than the rest of us with similar understandings of jazz and some classical. I didn't know much about rock at the time. It was always an education being around him.

## 4. PANIC IN DETROIT

### ⊘ @MikeGarson

This one uses a Bo Diddley kind of vibe. DUN du DUN du DUN - baDUM bum. Then in a very David-like way he switches and goes into something else in the verses. Then comes back to the catchy hook. When David was traveling through America I was with him in the limousine for much of the time. He really took in this country better than anyone. He just absorbed it like a sponge and found a way to make this album based on those amazing experiences. This is such a timely song, even nearly 50 years later. Much of this is also inspired by David's good friend Iggy Pop and stories of the race riots. Detroit was a pretty whacked out city at the time. He just had to write this song – it was inevitable.

## 5. CRACKED ACTOR

✔ **@MikeGarson**

I love this one. David grasped what was going on in society. Sadly much of the same is going on today. He seems to have had an intuitive insight even way back then, of what was still to come. That's David for you. Playing with David in 70s was different from later in his career when we played to a click track with everything exact. In days of the Spiders we played without a metronome. Much looser. Speeding up and down but had a great feel so it hardly mattered. David was the ultimate chameleon. He could sing to any style and had great support from Mick on backing vocals.

## 6. TIME

✔ **@MikeGarson**

This is truly one of my favorite songs ever. Only David could figure out how to mine every style of piano playing I had learned the prior twenty years and find a place for each style in his vast library of

songs. This is a style of playing called stride piano which came from a 20s ragtime technique with that old corny rinky-dink sound. He even altered the piano to sound old. But then BOOM he brings in the pop elements and changes things. Mick played the most beautiful lines. Both David & Mick were masters at musical hooks. They gave me all the freedom to play stride style and in some places very avant-garde with some outside touches. Middle section and chorus I'm playing straight pop.

## 7. THE PRETTIEST STAR

✔ **@MikeGarson**

This is a really catchy song with a very 70s sound. I'm not as connected to this one as others but it makes me smile listening to it. If David had released this album this week it's just as timely as it was then. Agree? As I listen to this with you all I still can't realize it's actually me playing that piano. Just enjoying it today like you are. This is really special.

## 8. LET'S SPEND THE NIGHT TOGETHER

✔ **@MikeGarson**

The original version of this song was released by The Rolling Stones back in 1967. A lot of people have enjoyed my crazy piano introduction on this song over the years. I don't quite know how that came about. I think I must have been infused when I came to these recording dates at the great

⬇

(Below left)
David and Mick Ronson (in the background on left) in 1973.

(Below right)
**@MikeGarson**
Here's a great photo by Michael Ochs from 1973 of me on tour with David.

Trident Studios and their great Bechstein piano. That was the very same piano the Beatles recorded Hey Jude on, Elton John recorded Your Song with and so many more great recordings from amazing artists over the years...

## 9. THE JEAN GENIE

### @MikeGarson

What really can be said about this? It's just become an anthem. People really love this one. I know much of that has something to do with the great Iggy Pop on this one. It's just very, very catchy. So bluesy. Right here you'll hear a mistake that we made as a band when we recorded this - an extra bar! Leave it to David to leave it in. So when we played this on my alumni @bowietour shows we'd have to remember the extra bar because it's just not natural. I'm hearing Mick's incredible solo with single notes so fast! He's one of the top rock guitarists.

## 10. LADY GRINNING SOUL

### @MikeGarson

This is also high on my list of favourite songs he wrote. He knew I could play this classical, romantic Spanish piano and gave me the opportunity to give a great intro, letting loose on his beautiful song. His use of space is incredible. Think about it at this spot where he left such a long gap of silence before he comes in with his first lyric. And Mick's amazing Spanish guitar solo in the middle of this is so great. We join each other with some of the same melodies. I'm using all these little tremolos on the piano. You sort of shake the chords as you're playing back and forth holding the chords down. It gives a particular vibe. This song has a very interesting, sophisticated set of chord changes with a beautiful bridge. This is genius songwriting. David never sang this one live. Perhaps because it was too high - which doesn't make a whole lot of sense because he successfully took a lot of chances. Regardless, he was just going with his vibe and how he felt. I love playing this one. My piano playing sits on the support my fellow amazing musicians. I was, of sorts, the whip cream on the cake. If they weren't laying down such a great foundation, my playing wouldn't mean shit. Nice guy, an old friend of mine Ken Fordham on saxophone. Every musician David ever chose was amazing. David had a knack as the ultimate casting director. I miss David every day. Thank you, David.

195

# *Kitchen Sink*
## Nadine Shah
Infectious, 2020

⚲ Nadine Shah (**@NadineShah**) is a hard artist to pin down, but really there's no point trying because it is her cascading, creative energy that makes her so vital. While recording several jazz-leaning records at the start of her career the singer formed a strong bond with Blur and Elbow producer Ben Hillier, who has been a constant creative presence ever since, enabling Shah's music to evolve. *Kitchen Sink* is Shah's fourth album, it is also her most complete. "I have never felt so properly represented by an album I have made like I have with this one," the South Tyneside native explained when introducing it to the world via this Listening Party, just after its release. "My mate texted me today saying 'this sounds like YOU'… This album was inspired by so many great women. One being my good friend [former Fall guitarist] Brix Smith who taught me to be bolder and braver." As Shah's commentary for the record showed – with help from Hillier (**@BenHillier**) and guitarist/engineer Daniel Crook (**@CrookSoundTech**) – *Kitchen Sink* is not just bolder and braver, it is brilliant too.

PHOTOGRAPHY:
Fraser Taylor

→
Nadine Shah toasting the launch of *Kitchen Sink* in her own kitchen. "I REALLY LIKE WINE," she told the Listening Party of the beverage's appearances in her lyrics.

### 1. CLUB COUGAR

@NadineShah

The second verse in Club Cougar is made up of responses to properly misogynistic lyrics in songs like Baby it's cold outside and Wives and Lovers. And yes, those are my cat calls too!

### 2. LADIES FOR BABIES (GOATS FOR LOVE)

@BenHillier

The sample at the start of this comes from my kids CD skipping (probably had jam or snot on it).

### 3. BUCKFAST

@NadineShah

This song is about a toxic relationship and gaslighting.

### 4. DILLYDALLY

@NadineShah

I'm constantly reminded that my time is running out when it comes to having children. "I am aware of the passing of time". I'm happy and I don't need reminding, cheers.

### 5. TRAD

@NadineShah

"Shave my legs, Freeze my eggs, Will you want me when I am old?" This was the first lyric I had for the whole album. This song scares the shit out of my boyfriend when I play it live.

### 6. KITCHEN SINK

@CrookSoundTech (Daniel Crook)

The sound on the intro is... this bass, just playing all the muted harmonics on fret 12. Live I play it on guitar pitched down a la White Stripes, but THIS is the authentic way.

### 7. KITE

@NadineShah

This one's hard for me to listen to as it was a very dark time. I'm off to pour a glass of wine...

@BenHillier

Nadine's demo for this was beautiful and really sparse. I sat with it for a whole day trying to think of how to do it justice, almost gave up on it then played that one not guitar thing and recorded the whole backing tracks in about an hour.

### 8. UKRAINIAN WINE

@NadineShah

Ukranian Wine was written when I was particularly destructive. I've swapped my vices for gardening. It's alright you know!

### 9. WASPS NEST

@NadineShah

Ah bloody hell, another hard to hear one for me. Just in time for me to fill up my wine glass though.

### 10. WALK

@NadineShah

This song's about my walk from my house in Tottenham to the tube station Seven Sisters. It was literally like running the fucking gauntlet at times. Can you tell Ben and I were listening to American marching bands?

### 11. PRAYER MAT

@BenHillier

Drums recorded in a shipping container, just the loudest thing.

@NadineShah

Prayer Mat. This is a really important song to me and my family. It's for someone we love dearly who is very unwell. She is such an inspiration and fighter! This is her song.

G.O.A.T. Along with creating her most successful record yet, Nadine Shah has hosted the Q Awards and given evidence to parliament in the last few years.

# *Any Human Friend*
## Marika Hackman
AMF/Virgin EMI/Sub Pop, 2019

The album cover – complete with strategically placed guinea pig – should leave you in no doubt: *Any Human Friend* is a candid record. The third long-player from Marika Hackman is full of impulses and emotions, confessions and hopes, fears and feelings. It is also a record that is as colourful musically as it is about sexuality, with the London singer-songwriter's soothing vocals and twitching guitars gliding across an unexpectedly expansive musical landscape created in close collaboration with producer David Wrench. "It just felt like a natural shift and a growth in confidence," suggested Hackman of the album's open heart at the start of the Listening Party. And though this record is both frank and personal, it is also wonderfully accessible and relatable too. So allow Hackman (**@MarikaHackman**), with some observations from Wrench (**@DavidWrench**) too, to properly introduce you to her *Any Human Friend*.

**PHOTOGRAPHY:**
Joost Vandebrug

@MarikaHackman

Out of sheer laziness/ writers block, I set myself the challenge to write a song around four repeated chords and I'm Not Where You Are is what happened. It was nice to start with such a simple bedrock and then have so much room to play with different riffs and harmonies. Lol I actually did a guitar solo.

## 1. WANDERLUST

@MarikaHackman

I actually wrote this song before I even started making I'm Not Your Man, but decided it didn't gel with the record so I just waited for the right time to release it. I recorded it on my Apple headphones microphone into Garageband at my kitchen table in east London. I had only just finished writing it so it felt very raw and exciting. I remember finishing it and then plugging it into my big speakers and bursting into tears when the harmonies came in. I think I knew then that I would never record another version of it. I love the way it sits against 'the one' on this record. It feels to me like the part of the journey where you're on dry land and then the trippy theramin outro/intro comes in and sucks you up into a brash, trippy wormhole for the next 40 minutes…

## 2. THE ONE

@MarikaHackman

Making the video for this was so much fun, I was so worried that I wouldn't be able to physically smash up a photocopier but when it came to crunch time [the director] put The Prodigy on full blast and I really got rid of a lot of pent up rage. I wanted to do something brave and raw and unabashedly natural to reflect some of the themes on the record. 'I've got BDE, I think it's a venereal disease' is a strong contender for my favourite lyric on the record.

## 3. ALL NIGHT

@MarikaHackman

I had the first incarnation of the pre-chorus lyrics on my phone notes for about six months before I wrote the song. I think I was drunk on a bus heading home at the end of a night out when I came up with them. WE GO DOWN ON ONE ANOTHER. I think I felt empowered to use such direct sexual language from reading Blood and Guts in Highschool by Kathy Acker. She's so visceral with the words she uses to describe sexual encounters and it was very refreshing and absorbing to get lost in her world for a bit whilst writing this album.

## 4. BLOW

@MarikaHackman

First time I've faded in the drum beat and my god it brings me so much joy. I remember we used

David Wrench's massive beast of a synth (David what was it called?) to double the bass in the riffy bit to pant dropping levels.

@DavidWrench

The ARP2600. My pride and joy!!

@MarikaHackman

For the last 'we won't go back's, David and I stood across the room and recorded ourselves shouting it at each other in different vocal styles and then layered it all up so it sounded like a mini crowd.

@alexxabooth [fan]

Are there any instruments that you used in the studio that you wish you owned?

@MarikaHackman

Wouldn't mind getting my mitts on @DavidWrench's theramin

@DavidWrench

Ironically it doesn't work if you actually touch it. You hover your mitts in its vicinity!

## 5. I'M NOT WHERE YOU ARE

@MarikaHackman

Being repeatedly slapped in the video was actually much easier than I thought it would be, except for one particularly vicious take . The hard part was having tomato juice poured all over me whilst standing in the street. That stuff really stings the eyes.

## 6. SEND MY LOVE

@MarikaHackman

This is my favourite drum beat on the record, when the high hats shift emphasis on the chorus oooooooooh baby. We had a little wigout sesh at Konk Studios, where David Wrench, @jessica_batour and I improvised over the looped bass riff at the end. I'm too much of a control freak to enjoy improvisation but we had some fun chopping up bits that we'd recorded and building them up back at David's studio - it really came alive when we added the shrieky violins courtesy of Gillian Maguire.

@DavidWrench

We recorded the record in lots of small sessions. I'd often text Marika at the start of a week to see if she had any new songs finished. If she did, she'd come over and we'd record them.

### 7. HAND SOLO

**@MarikaHackman**

Yes, that is a cowbell. I like the little ear break this outro gives to the record, that harmonised bass riff bringing that horizontal warpaint vibe with some airy vocal samples. Quick breath before being thrown right back in with Conventional Ride.

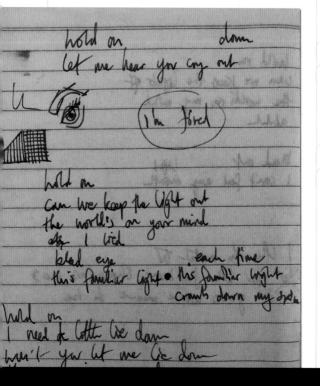

### 8. CONVENTIONAL RIDE

**@MarikaHackman**

So I actually fully intended for this to be an instrumental. I had the intro and verse guitars/ drums written for ages but just couldn't get beyond it I think it was one of those late night moments of inspiration and I found it hard to try and capture it again. Anyway @DavidWrench told me to stop being a lazy shit and go and write a melody for it hahaha.

### 9. COME UNDONE

**@MarikaHackman**

Oooh that bassline, she's a naughty giiirl. So much fun to play, especially alongside those sassy little mellotron string chords.

### 10. HOLD ON

**@MarikaHackman**

This song is about feeling overwhelmed and suffocated by depression, I got into a bit of an emotional rut towards the end of the year I was writing Any Human Friend it felt incredibly cathartic to sit down and channel all my fears and frustrations into a piece of music.

**@MarikaHackman**

The lyrics are quite hard to make out on this one but 'hold on, I want to be newborn, reprise of the child, I'm tired' really connect with that feeling of wanting the simplicity of being young. Sometimes being an adult can feel so incredibly oppressive.

**@DavidWrench**

Here are some studio pics I took of @MarikaHackman.

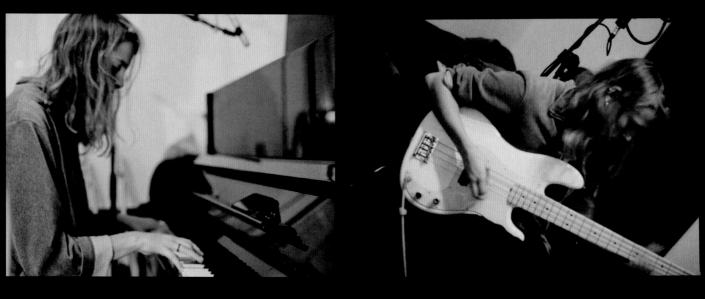

**@DavidWrench**
And here are pics of @MarikaHackman on drums.

◉ **@MarikaHackman**
The lyrics are quite hard to make out on this one but 'hold on, I want to be newborn, reprise of the child, I'm tired' really connect with that feeling of wanting the simplicity of being young. Sometimes being an adult can feel so incredibly oppressive.

## 11. ANY HUMAN FRIEND

◉ **@MarikaHackman**
Happy Pride everyone. This song is all about being true to who you are and accepting yourself and other people without judgement. We're golden babyyyyyyy.

◉ **@MarikaHackman**
This song always felt like the last song. It conjures an image of pushing a paper boat out into the sea on a warm sunny evening, and at the end you can just see it in the distance before it disappears behind a wave.

# One Step Beyond
## Madness
Stiff, 1979

PHOTOGRAPHY:
Cameron McVey

Cool and fun are rarely bedfellows, yet Madness always seemed to get them to bunk up. At the forefront of the ska revival at the end of the 1970s, the London six-piece managed to boast both an irrepressible spirit and the ability to wear dark glasses indoors. Capable of creating complicated songs and arrangements, they also possessed a considerable sense of humour which peppered their lyrics and a series of music videos (among the first to be made) that charmed serious ska-heads and Saturday morning children's TV audiences alike. This blend of these seemingly incompatible qualities fizzes through their debut album *One Step Beyond*. Featuring some very credible reggae and ska standards – at a time when even knowing about the existence of the originals was a badge of cool – the record also boasts gleeful adaptations of a Tarzan TV theme and Tchaikovsky's Swan Lake and, most notably of all, a series of new, original songs inspired by the grim realities of Mike Barson (keyboards), Chris "Chrissy Boy" Foreman (guitars – **@CBoyForeman**), Lee Thompson (sax), Cathal "Chas Smash" Smyth (bass), Dan "Woody" Woodgate (drums) and Graham "Suggs" McPherson's (vocals) lives in the capital.

Several steps beyond. Dan Woodgate, Chas Smash, Suggs, Chris Foreman, Mark Bedford and Mike Barson.

## 1. ONE STEP BEYOND

✓ @CBoyForeman

There's a story that this was 30 seconds long, but hey the intro is 30 seconds long.

## 2. MY GIRL

✓ @CBoyForeman

When Mike wrote this I thought, game over. One of his best ever.

## 3. NIGHT BOAT TO CAIRO

✓ @CBoyForeman

Clive Langer said I should play a sitar, I was like WTF I ain't playing one of them, so much to my relief this was the sitar in question...

## 4. BELIEVE ME

✓ @CBoyForeman

The old Roland Jazz Chorus strikes again! By the way the sax was out of tune the whole album. Thommo wasn't to sure how to tune it. You move the mouthpiece and he sort of went too far as it were.

## 5. LAND OF HOPE AND GLORY

✓ @CBoyForeman

All about Thommos time in an approved school [a court boarding school, one down from borstal]. Bridges and Sharkey and Jackson were real kids there so this song is pretty true to life.

## 6. THE PRINCE

✓ @CBoyForeman

Sax solo, haha. We thought what a genius, he nicked it from an old song [Prince Buster's Texas Hold-Up]. Not the first time Thommo nicked anything.

## 7. TARZAN'S NUTS

✓ @CBoyForeman

Tarzans Nuts, from the TV series with Tarzan as Played by Ron Ely. There's a few versions, my fave is Lawrence Welk & His Orchestra doing Tarzan (Tarzan's March).

## 8. IN THE MIDDLE OF THE NIGHT

✓ @CBoyForeman

First song Suggs and I ever wrote. I had an amp in my son Matthew's room. I had a few chords and played them to Suggs. Suddenly we could write songs!

## 9. BED AND BREAKFAST MAN

✓ @CBoyForeman

Mark Bedford told me they called our mate John Hasler [early Madness drummer/singer] the Bed And Breakfast Man because he'd turn up for B and B.

## 10. RAZOR BLADE ALLEY

✓ @CBoyForeman

Thommo classic. He saw a film called Boys From Company C and the guy had the clap said he was "pissing razors".

## 11. SWAN LAKE

✓ @CBoyForeman

Nicked [Dutch rock band] The Cats' arrangement. Another instrumental lolz

## 12. ROCKIN' IN Ab

✓ @CBoyForeman

This is a Bazooka Joe [pub rock band named after a comic character given away with bubble gum] cover. Mike's brother Danny was in a band called Bazooka Joe. Adam Ant too.

## 13. MUMMY'S BOY

✓ Chris Foreman

This has got the lot! Starts off the Steptoe and Son theme, which was a great influence on the band, goes reggae now, now goes punk, Tommy Gun drums at ending.

## 14. MADNESS

✓ @CBoyForeman

Woody said how about naming ourselves after a song? I said "yeah, like Madness"... BOOM

## 15. CHIPMUNKS ARE GO!

✓ @CBoyForeman

The Marine chant is Chas and Brenno [Brendan Smyth, Chas' brother]. That's all folks.

# Demolished Thoughts
## Thurston Moore
Matador, 2011

As a driving force in Sonic Youth, Thurston Moore is a key player in helping to define alternative American music over the last four decades. Able to switch from a melody to a static storm to a Madonna cover, the New York-based band – led by Moore, his former wife Kim Gordon and Lee Renaldo – connected the fledgling indie scene in the US with artists, poets and writers, subsequently inspiring the generations who followed. Yet in contrast to the loud, often artistically uncompromising sounds Sonic Youth excelled in, for his third solo album Moore created a fragile folkish affair, spurred on by swooning strings, simple guitars and gentle harps. The sound is in part down to the album's producer, Beck. Not only did Moore make the most of the musical outlaw's mind and melodic wizardry, but also the same Malibu beach environment that inspired Beck's own soft, sun-drenched album *Sea Change* – AKA Beck's home studio. Equally conjured from raw, vintage studio equipment and nights around the campfire, listening to surf hit the shore, Moore (**@nowjazznow**) recreated the beach party feel for a listening party that gently shared the truths behind *Demolished Thoughts*.

ARTWORK:
Steven Parrino

LISTENING
PARTY
6 JULY
2020

### 1. BENEDICTION

✓ **@nowjazznow (Thurston Moore)**
A lot of these songs were played on a very old Gibson acoustic Beck had at his place in Malibu. During the recording sessions we would take hikes over Malibu dunes to the beach to record the sounds of waves.

### 2. ILLUMININE

✓ **@nowjazznow**
A lot of the weird ambient howling sounds were Beck's vocal takes. Some sounds were all of us (me, Beck, Samara [Lubelski, violin], Mary [Lattimore, harp] and Eva [Prinz, Moore's partner]) howling in the middle of the night on the dark beachfront.

### 3. CIRCULATION

✓ **@nowjazznow**
The original concept [for the record] was just the guitar/vocals with violin and harp. Beck added flourishes bringing in friends to play some percussion and contrabass.

### 4. BLOOD NEVER LIES

✓ **@nowjazznow**
I actually haven't heard this since we stopped touring the music. I decided to go back to electric guitar action soon after, which meant no more harp as it would become obliterated, and we morphed into [band, named after Philip Glass' between-composition-jobs moving firm] Chelsea Light Moving. Think it stands to reason that anything could very well sound like Sonic Youth – it is/was/always will be there. Sonic Life, it's written on my body.

Thurston Moore onstage at The Pearl concert theater at the Palms Casino Resort in October 2010.

### 5. ORCHARD STREET

✅ @nowjazznow

Orchard Street is on the lower east side of New York City - an old stomping ground of inspiration (and love).

### 6. IN SILVER RAIN WITH A PAPER KEY

✅ @nowjazznow

The first song I wrote for the LP – defining the rest of the tunes.

### 7. MINA LOY

✅ @nowjazznow

Mina Loy, poet and painter, was a charter member of the generation that – beginning in 1912 with the founding of Poetry magazine – launched the modernist revolution in poetry in the United States. I've heard of those who'd wake from a dream and hear their voice in this tune (true story).

### 8. SPACE

✅ @nowjazznow

Heavy emotional transitions in play. It was recorded a decade past. Today I find myself in the welcome of England – thank you for your kindness and spirit majesty.

### 9. JANUARY

✅ @nowjazznow

This is the final song on the LP proper. Beck's vocals in the haunted distance are most apparent here.

# *Reverence*
## Faithless
Cheeky/BMG, 1996

The impact of Faithless' debut album on the shape of modern music should not be understated. After the sister of one of the band's members helped out on vocals, she found she had enough recording experience and exposure to sign her own record deal, creating a song that found its way into an Eminem track, turning Dido into a global star in the process. Additionally, then Faithless member Jamie Catto completed this record before leaving to form 1 Giant Leap – a project that would boast musical collaborations with the likes of Dennis Hopper, Kurt Vonnegut, Michael Stipe, Susan Sarandon, Stephen Fry and Brian Eno – before directing a series of films. And, perhaps most notable of all, *Reverence* also catapulted Faithless' own genre-defying career to greatness, as Maxi Jazz (vocals), Sister Bliss (keyboards – **@theSisterBliss**) and Rollo (production/Dido's brother) came to not only dominate international club culture, but were *the* dance band who were routinely picked to headline rock festivals – thanks in no small part to a live reputation founded on the anthems Salva Mea and Insomnia they crafted for this record. In fact, it is a good job the latter was included on the album, because, as Sister Bliss revealed during this Listening Party, Faithless did not always have reverence for their Insomnia, meaning musical history – and dancing – could have been quite different.

PHOTOGRAPHY:
Simon Chaudoir

Sister Bliss tweeted that her classical piano training came in surprisingly handy in Faithless.

## 1. REVERENCE

✓ @theSisterBliss

Maxi's lyrics are a blueprint/manifesto for living. The first we really learned about his Buddhist perspective.

## 2. DON'T LEAVE

✓ @theSisterBliss

Jamie Catto wanted to perform this naked. We said no. He sung it topless. Still so vulnerable.

## 3. SALVA MEA

✓ @theSisterBliss

First tune as Faithless, we were totally free, no expectations. This is the sound of musical freedom. No wonder it sat on a shelf at Island Records for six months, they didn't know what the f*** to do with it.

## 4. IF LOVIN' YOU IS WRONG

✓ @theSisterBliss

Love how lairy this is, people maybe forget we have sense of humour.

## 5. ANGELINE

✓ @theSisterBliss

Rollo asked me to write in waltz time 3/4, complete with smoker's cough and Oliver Reed menace from Jamie. Dido on recorder and BVs – recorder on an electronic record? Risky stuff.

## 6. INSOMNIA

✓ @theSisterBliss

And there it is. The start of our international career. Insane. Had no idea at the time how far this song would carry us. Insomnia was also only on the album to balance Salva Mea – a B side to our A side, and as a more accessible dance track as Salva Mea so uncompromising and probably impossible to dance to.

## 7. DIRTY OL' MAN

✓ @theSisterBliss

Lots of texture in there. A love letter to London, all the grime and all the glory.

## 8. FLOWERSTAND MAN

✓ @theSisterBliss

He was behind Highbury Station I think, a small obsession obliterating all worldly concerns. We've all had them…

## 9. BASEBALL CAP

✓ @theSisterBliss

Spent hours talking about Karma with Maxi. What happens if you do something in a past life and punished in the present, he explained it with this lyric.

## 10. DRIFTING AWAY

✓ @theSisterBliss

Penny Shaw singing a tragic opera intro about woman whose baby dies. A French guy chopped up the Break 4 Luv beat for us – we were too stoned to bother – can't recall his name.

Rollo, Sister Bliss and Maxi Jazz with Jamie Catto, who provided backing vocals on *Reverence*, in 1996.

# *Black Up*
## Shabazz Palaces
Sub Pop, 2011

❚ Taking inspiration from strange record discoveries and Kenyan-American artist Wangechi Mutu as much as from rap history, Shabazz Palaces' (**@ShabazzPalaces**) minimalistic hip hop is stark yet swelling with a range of unexpected flavours. Jazz breaks, podcast snippets and handclaps interweave with idiosyncratic beats and laconic flows. Debut album *Black Up* set the pattern. Intricate and enthralling, the then duo Tendai Maraire (the multi-instrumentalist who left the group after 2017 album *Quazarz Vs. The Jealous Machines*) and Ishmael Butler created a record full of sonic innovation and smouldering emotions. Butler – who has been something of a constant at hip-hop's cutting edge having previously been a member of the jazz-infused, highly influential trio Digable Planets – hosted a Listening Party for Shabazz Palaces' debut, which, like the record itself, provoked as many questions as it answered. Which is what such a bold and uncompromising album deserves.

**ARTWORK:**
Dumb Eyes

(Below left)
Palace dwellers.
Ishmael Butler and
Tendai Maraire.

(Below)
**@ShabazzPalaces**
Stellular @maikoiyo
far right tho leans left.

## 1. FREE PRESS AND CURL

✔ @ShabazzPalaces

I thought this one was a smooth lead off hitter for forecasting the approach on prod and arrangement styles to come on the album: freeeeeee!!!

## 2. AN ECHO FROM THE HOSTS THAT PROFESS INFINITUM

✔ @ShabazzPalaces

I copped these vocal riffs from an old recording of spiritual music morphed em up good and replayed them adding the drums. Tedai goes fantastic mode on the mbira. Diamond dust special.

## 3. ARE YOU... CAN YOU... WERE YOU? (FELT)

✔ @ShabazzPalaces

Without question the most influential artist to my production style at this time was (is) Wangechi Mutu [Kenyan-American artist]. I saw her once at Afropunk [festival], the dopest.

## 4. A TREATEASE DEDICATED TO THE AVIAN AIRESS FROM NORTH EAST NUBIS (1000 QUESTIONS, 1 ANSWER)

✔ @ShabazzPalaces

Fun fact Maikoiyo [Alley-Barnes, artist and member of the Black Constellation, which also includes Butler] came up with all of the song titles on this album. Had a korg vocoder keyboard I used for this joint (hey where is that?). This was a song I'd written for my lady at the time. We broke up but I liked the lyrics still soooooo...

## 5. YOULOGY

✔ @ShabazzPalaces

Unknown fact: This song had my kids Dee, Khaila and Jazz doing vocals on this. Pretty sure this first time Lil Tracy voice was committed to tape.

## 6. ENDEAVORS FOR NEVER (THE LAST TIME WE SPOKE YOU SAID YOU WERE NOT HERE. I SAW YOU THOUGH.)

✔ @ShabazzPalaces

Smoked out joint, feat SassyBlack [Cat Harris-White] on vox, [from the vocal duo] TheeSatisfaction was still rocking as a group at this time and they were always at the crib often when I was recording.

## 7. RECOLLECTIONS OF THE WRAITH

✔ @ShabazzPalaces

There is a cold reason the identity of the voice on this sample must remain a secret. It's an iPhone recording from a concert at the Paramount in Seattle. Hint: she had to forget in order to be good, who can guess??????? I wrote this on a tonight like this.

## 8. THE KING'S NEW CLOTHES WERE MADE BY HIS OWN HANDS

✔ @ShabazzPalaces

I had just lost my favourite "beat" in a "hard drive fiasco"...

## 9. YEAH YOU

✔ @ShabazzPalaces

My hand so flush you'll have to fold the played out riddles that you told for all the priceless things you sold you corny... self explanatory.

## 10. SWERVE... THE REEPING OF ALL THAT IS WORTHWHILE (NOIR NOT WITHSTANDING)

✔ @ShabazzPalaces

TheeSatisfaction tears the joint up. One of my favourite songs to perform from this album especially when the whole Stellies crew [Black Constellation] was all together. Thaddillac guitar break fascinates. [TheeStatisfaction singer] Stas THEE Boss kill shit.

# *Swim*
## Caribou
City Slang/Merge, 2010

⚓ Inspired in part by his own travels (hence some of the place names used as track titles), Caribou's *Swim* is an album that takes its listeners on a journey, too. A mix of conventionally structured songs, thoughtful club bangers and evocative tapestries of sound, this is a record to truly immerse your ears in, thanks to the joyful, blissed-out spirit that effervescently fizzes across its nine tracks. Plunging straight in at the album's deep end, Caribou – AKA Canadian, producer, DJ and composer Dan Snaith (**@CaribouBand**) – used his Listening Party to present a series of thoughtful notes for each of his breakthrough album's exhilarating tracks. Full of detail and illumination, Snaith's observations also contain the same wide-eyed wonder that makes *Swim* such a euphoric and hopeful experience.

ARTWORK:
Matthew Cooper

Dan onstage at Field Day
Festival in Victoria Park,
London in 2010.

## 1. ODESSA

✅ **@CaribouBand** (Dan Snaith)

This track was written for a member of my family trapped in a controlling, toxic marriage. It imagines her 'taking the kids, driving away'... At the time that I wrote it, it was hypothetical – a wish of what could happen. Ten years later, because of her immense bravery, she did free herself from this marriage. The song 'New Jade' on my new album is about her finally being liberated. In that way, these two songs are a pair.

## 2. SUN

✅ **@CaribouBand**

Lots of music on this album was inspired by club music in London at the time/going to Plastic People lots, but not this one. I was taken totally by surprise when this took on a life of its own in clubs, Ibiza, etc.

## 3. KAILI

✅ **@CaribouBand**

Kaili, Guizhou, China – This is where I was when the melody for the chorus of this song popped into my head. I mean, what if [avant-garde jazz saxophonist] Albert Ayler HAD played a solo on a trance anthem?

## 4. FOUND OUT

✅ **@CaribouBand**

There's a 10 minute long version of Found Out somewhere that I used to play out in my DJ sets. It wasn't very good – better as a short pop song, I think.

## 5. BOWLS

✅ **@CaribouBand**

When this riff came on that first time at Plastic People, people started cheering and shouting even though I knew for a fact they'd never heard it before. I was in the bathroom afterwards and heard two guys 'What the fuck was that track?' I took that as a good sign.

## 6. LEAVE HOUSE

✅ **@CaribouBand**

We played 180 shows in 8 months from Apr to Dec 2010. There were only 27 days in those 8 months that we were not either doing a gig or travelling to the next one. We started the tour in small clubs, quite often they were half empty, and finished the tour for that album a couple years later playing to [festival] crowds and opening for Radiohead around the world. It still seems crazy to me that this was the album that changed things like that... I thought I'd made a super weird record!

## 7. HANNIBAL

✅ **@CaribouBand**

I spent a lot of time practicing swimming while I was making this record and a lot of the sound of the record came out of that – the sounds sloshing back and forth from one ear to the other etc... You hear it here in Hannibal and Kaili and Jamelia.

## 8. LALIBELA

✅ **@CaribouBand**

There's the melody from Kaili again. I'm a sucker for a reprise to tie the different parts of an album together.

## 9. JAMELIA

✅ **@CaribouBand**

I've not always totally 'got' classical music but I read Alex Ross's [book] The Rest Is Noise while making this album and was excited by lots of the ideas and music I encountered therein – this is one of a few places that influence crops up in the album.

⊕

Dan Snaith, Ryan Smith, Brad Weber and John Schmersal backstage at Channel 4 in 2010.

# Closer (plus 12-inch singles)
## Joy Division
Factory, 1980

Whether or not the dark shadow that is cast across Joy Division's story had occurred, *Closer* would always have been an historic record. With its taut atmospheres, brutal yet emotional playing and those stark, mesmerising lyrics, Ian Curtis (vocals), Bernard "Barney" Sumner (guitar/keyboards), Peter "Hooky" Hook (bass – **@PeterHook**) and Stephen Morris' (drums – **@StephenPDMorris**) second album was not just a post-punk masterpiece, but a classic album full stop. Yet before the Manchester-based band could release the record Curtis had taken his own life. With *Closer* finally out two months later, its significance – from its cover image of a funeral monument to Curtis' introspective words – would always be framed by the loss of this towering yet fragile talent.

Revisiting the album more than four decades later would naturally prove an emotional affair, not least because following their career together in New Order, Hook has become estranged from Sumner and Morris and is no longer making music with them. However, such is the communal, celebratory atmosphere that the Listening Parties can inspire, the playback did not just offer an insight in *Closer*, but also added humour to the Joy Division story – and hinted at a slight thawing between former bandmates. Peter Hook led the commentary while Stephen Morris tweeted along and icon-making Manchester photographer Kevin Cummins shared pictures of Joy Division recording *Closer*. Hooky was even able to take us through each of the band's 12-inch singles as an encore, and what an encore it was.

**PHOTOGRAPHY:**
Bernard Pierre Wolff

**SLEEVE DESIGN:**
Peter Saville

(Below left)
**@PeterHook**
I got the chance to visit Staglieno cemetery in Genoa, Italy before The Light's 2015 gig. Two tombs there are featured on the sleeves of *Closer* and Love Will Tear Us Apart Again.
(Below middle) Ian leaving the stage at the Russell Club in April 1980.
(Below right) Ian Curtis' autograph from October 1979 shared by @Birmingham_81.

Colony. Stephen
Morris, Ian Curtis,
Bernard Sumner
and Peter Hook
in Manchester,
January 1979

### 1. ATROCITY EXHIBITION

**@PeterHook**

A wild opener, with a startling production. Very unusual song built around Steve's great drum riff. Name comes from the J G Ballard novel that Ian had read. A very different kind of opener to Unknown Pleasures. Only a year on and yet our songwriting is a lot more mature. Ian really let rip live, that doesn't really translate to the studio version.

**@StephenPDMorris**

It's not bad is it? I did some of weird noises too. Synare 3 through a fuzz box sounded evil.

### 2. ISOLATION

**@PeterHook**

One of my best riffs and probably the closest we get to my actual live bass sound on either album. Contrast to the previous track in that we now have an effect on Ian's vocals. Great chorus – this should definitely have been a single. Isolation has a very futuristic, almost robotic vibe – it reminds me of Blade Runner for some reason.

### 3. PASSOVER

**@PeterHook**

Important for me, my first use of the Shergold Marathon 6 string bass. Great drum intro – lots of reverb on the snare, but the bass drum sounds very dry and up front. Nice bass riff – only happens at the start! Threw away a great riff there.

### 4. COLONY

**@PeterHook**

More of a traditional Joy Division rock song – probably the straightest on the LP. We never asked him [Ian] what he was singing about – it just sounded right so we never bothered. Of course, after Ian's death everybody looked at the lyrics & they almost read like the story of his life. But it really didn't feel like that at the time.

Peter Hook and Ian Curtis performing with Joy Division at Leigh Open Air Festival, Lancashire, August 1979.

**@PeterHook**

I'm playing a barre chord on the bass while dampening the E string, a new technique [on Passover]. It almost sounds like poetry – it's very American Prayer by Jim Morrison. We loved The Doors. Great, intricate guitar playing – I love how the riff is different after the third verse. The bass is quite dry and the guitar is very effected: clever contrast. A very gothic vibe, quite distant sounding.

**@StephenPDMorris**

Colony is the one drum riff I was really proud of. It's "inspired" by a Captain Beefheart tune. Can't say for sure. Something off Trout Mask Replica probably. Ella Guru? Possibly…

## 5. A MEANS TO AN END

**@PeterHook**

This is a bit more poppy than Colony. Musically weird as it has major and minor chords at the same time. I didn't even know what that meant at this point. A great example of the chemistry between the three of us as players.

## 6. HEART AND SOUL

**@PeterHook**

This still sounds fresh 40 years on. The live version of Heart And Soul was very different as we couldn't have guitar and keys playing together.

## 7. TWENTY FOUR HOURS

**@PeterHook**

Amazing song if I do say so myself. One of the last tracks we wrote. The feeling of what could have been is heartbreaking. It sounds to me like the vocals were done after the music - the music is very frantic & has a couple of mistakes in it, but the vocal is very confident and strong. Fast, slow, fast, slow – it's almost like two songs put together. Some of Ian's best words.

## 8. THE ETERNAL

**@PeterHook**

This features the grand piano that was in the studio at Britannia Row. We were reluctant as it went against our punk ethos but Martin insisted that it would work for this track and he was right. The bass does have a very funereal feel.

## 9. DECADES

**@PeterHook**

I always think that this song is about Joy Division – the story of the band – and this is a perfect ending. Ian has found his true voice – Tony was forever trying to get him to sound like Frank Sinatra but this is Ian Curtis. It really does sound like an end point.

## 10. ATMOSPHERE

**@PeterHook**

It's such a fantastic, beautiful song. Atmosphere was voted the UK's #1 funeral song, while Robbie William's Angels was voted #1 for weddings. When I heard this at [Factory Records boss] Tony Wilson's funeral I really did wish I'd written Angels. My wife is threatening to play Russ Abbott's Atmosphere when I go.

## 11. SHE'S LOST CONTROL (12-INCH VERSION)

**@PeterHook**

Martin was adamant that we do a longer version of this. So the 12" has an extra verse and brilliant keyboards at the end from Barney. We recorded each bass string separately in order to get that really dry bass sound.

## 12. TRANSMISSION

**@PeterHook**

We did a charity gig at Belle Vue [in Manchester] with 12 other bands – chaos. We played the new one – don't think it had a name – as soon as we started everybody stopped dead still and listened. That was the first time I thought we're onto something here. Ian was being a bit sarcastic with the chorus - at the time getting on the radio was the highest accolade, power of radio was huge. So here we have him literally singing about dancing to the radio. We did get on the radio with this one!

## 13. LOVE WILL TEAR US APART

**@PeterHook**

This was written at TJ Davidson's rehearsal rooms. We got the main riffs in about an hour. None of the words in Ian's bag suited, so he went off to write more. It's an odd song in that everybody listens to it like it's a great pop song but really it has quite twisted lyrics. I wouldn't like this song to have been written about me, put it that way. It's quite a bitter song well disguised as a pop tune.

# Fear Of Music
## Talking Heads
Sire, 1979

¶ "Talking Heads. A great little band," tweeted the band's drummer Chris Frantz (**@ChrisFrantzTTC**) during the Listening Party for his band's album *Fear Of Music*. All modesty aside, that is perhaps the understatement of a lifetime. By blending the most dexterous rhythms – which took the best drums from Afrobeat, disco and rock'n'roll – with precision post-punk guitars, the most addictive basslines and some searing vocals, Frantz, his wife Tina Weymouth (bass), Jerry Harrison (guitars) and singer David Byrne were a band who not only made some of the most forward thinking and original music, but much of what has followed in their wake was immeasurably better due to Talking Heads' influence.

The group's third album, *Fear of Music* is a great example of Talking Heads' power. Co-produced by Brian Eno, the record was put together in a truly innovative manner, yet the band's organic characters shine through. "This album was recorded in the loft where Tina and I lived, and the band rehearsed and wrote songs together," Frantz told the Listening Party, "9-01 44th drive Long Island City, NY. It was HEAVEN." And of course there is the swooning, ghostly melodic track Heaven to prove it.

Quoting the lyrics from Paper, Frantz encouraged fans to settle back and let Fear Of Music gently envelop them for the Listening Party. "Take a little time off and let the rays pass through," he wrote. "Please!"

It was a worthwhile experience. As you'd expect from a record made in collaboration with the archbishop of ambience, Eno, the record possesses a series of evocative atmospheres, which Talking Heads cleverly inhabit. Frantz's drums spin from gentle brushes to polyrhythmic rolls depending on the energy required; Byrne's seemingly disengaged vocals subtly exude a burning passion that commands attention; Harrison's guitar playing conjures touching melodies out of austere chords; while Weymouth's bass (deservedly) came in for special praise from the playback's host. "Tina's bass is amazing," declared Frantz. "Like a TUBA."

From opening track I Zimbra ("Aint that simply magic!" suggested Frantz of the chiming first salvo), via the moody Memories Can't Wait ("This may have been our most HEAVY tune. What do you think?" asked the drummer) to the ambient world of closer Drugs ("DRUGS? That would be a yes," joked the Talking Heads founding member), *Fear Of Music* captures one of the most influential bands ever in imperious form.

Joined by Lee Brackstone (**@LeeBrackstone**), publisher of Frantz's memoir *Remain In Love*, Chris Frantz took us though an album that would change the musical landscape for ever.

**SLEEVE DESIGN:**
Jerry Harrison

| 1 | I Zimbra |
|---|---|
| 2 | Mind |
| 3 | Paper |
| 4 | Cities |
| 5 | Life During Wartime |
| 6 | Memories Can't Wait |
| 7 | Air |
| 8 | Heaven |
| 9 | Animals |
| 10 | Electric Guitar |
| 11 | Drugs |

**@ChrisFrantzTTC**

Fear Of Music was recorded in the loft where Tina and I lived, and the band rehearsed and wrote songs together. 9-01 44th drive Long Island City, NY. It was HEAVEN.

**@LeeBrackstone**

Think I bought this album age 15 and it was an epiphany. It remains a thorough classic of the ages.

**@LeeBrackstone**

Track #2 MIND may be the defining genius of Talking Heads.

**@ChrisFrantzTTC**

Memories Can't Wait. This may have been our most HEAVY tune.

**@LeeBrackstone**

Absolute melancholic pop classic Heaven but it has that eccentric twist that makes it feel so otherworldly. Music as magic.

**@ChrisFrantzTTC**

Please don't play Heaven at my funeral tho.

**@LeeBrackstone**

Better choice than Psycho Killer, mate.

Remain In Love. Talking Heads' rhythm section and resident couple, Chris Frantz and Tina Weymouth.

# Soul Mining
## The The
Some Bizarre/Epic, 1983

New York or London bedsit? It is strange the places that can truly prove inspirational. Initially Matt Johnson (@TheThe) began work on his first album formally to be released as The The in the Big Apple. Having released first album *Burning Blue Soul* under his own name, a label bidding war saw the singer-songwriter was given the resources to make his next record in the US. However, those sessions proved unsatisfactory, resulting in Johnson ending up back in his Highbury flat, spending hours writing, re-writing and demoing tracks. Whatever that tiny space had over Manhattan creatively, many of the resulting songs made it on to the gloriously vivid *Soul Mining*. Synths, guitars and an exotic range of instruments created a bright musical backing for Johnson's breathy, sometimes whispered, sometimes shouted vocals as *Soul Mining* proved the fledgling post-punk sound could be as colourful and wide as it was direct.

**ARTWORK:**
Andrew Johnson

(Top row) @TheThe (Matt Johnson): My co-producer Paul Hardiman was fun to work with. Great sense of humour.

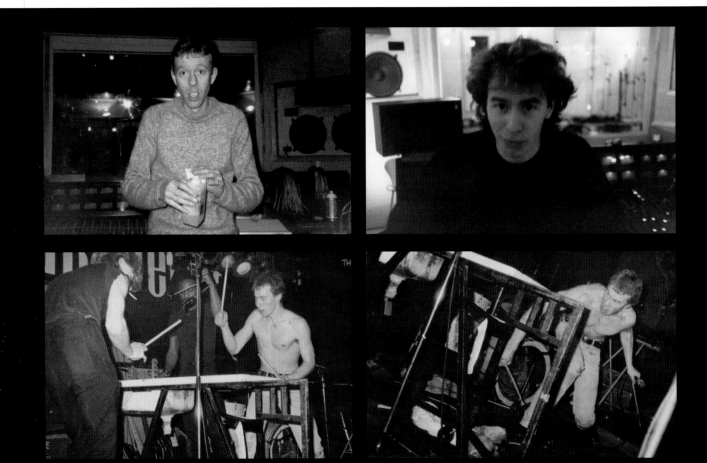

## 1. I'VE BEEN WAITIN' FOR TOMORROW (ALL OF MY LIFE)

✅ **@TheThe (Matt Johnson)**
Countdown [at the start of the track] misses the number 7. Why is this number special? Wonders of the world? Days of the week? Colours of the rainbow? The Book of Revelation = 7 churches, 7 angels, 7 seals, 7 trumpets, + 7 stars?

## 2. THIS IS THE DAY

✅ **@TheThe**
Doesn't seem too long ago I was lying on the floor writing these lyrics. I always used to lie on the floor writing lyrics when I was younger for some reason. Gently weeping on occasion too.

## 3. THE SINKING FEELING

✅ **@TheThe**
"I'm just a symptom of the moral decay/That's gnawing at the heart of the country". I think you can tell this song was written during the height of Thatcherism!

## 4. UNCERTAIN SMILE

✅ **@TheThe**
I was really blocked on lyrics for the second verse. Recording session was booked for the morning. But that night I saw this poor old fellow on the street. "A broken soul stares from a pair of watering eyes/Uncertain emotions force an uncertain smile" So, Jools Holland shows up on his motorbike – full leather – sweltering hot day – and nailed this piano solo first take. Paul and I looked at each other knowingly. We had a feeling we now had a classic on our hands. The rest as they say...

## 5. THE TWILIGHT HOUR

✅ **@TheThe**
One of my most underrated tracks. Rarely hear anyone mentioning it but I was really proud of it sonically as I tried to create something very cinematic, with a feeling of unbearable, claustrophobic heat to go with the lyrics.

## 6. SOUL MINING

✅ **@TheThe**
The atmospheric sound at the start of the track was the first time I'd used an Emulator. It was a sample of a boat horn that we then processed and manipulated. I used to love playing Marimbas. This album featured quite a lot of tuned percussion, including on this track. I think I need to get them out again.

## 7. GIANT

✅ **@TheThe**
I didn't own a sequencer when I made this album so I played all my repetitive, sequenced synth parts manually. My hands soon grew numb! We then mixed by playing the mute buttons on the mixing console. No computers or automation for us back then. My old mate Jim Thirlwell rustled up a great percussion track from pots & pans he found in the studio kitchen.

(Bottom row)
**@TheThe:**
My old mate Jim Thirlwell rustled up a great percussion track from pots and pans he found in the studio kitchen. A few months earlier he and I were literally playing the kitchen sink onstage at the old Marquee club in Soho.

**@TheThe:** The lyrics go through endless revisions. Often lyrics intended for one song end up in completely different songs. Here words intended for "Giant" ended up in *Soul Mining* and Twilight Of A Champion (*Infected*).

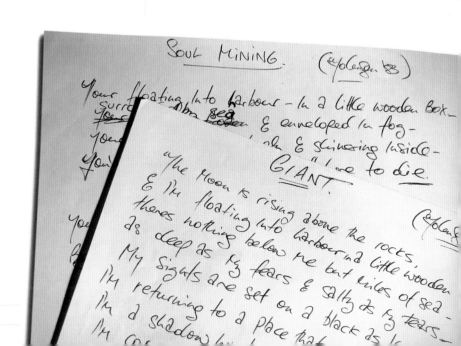

# *The Last Broadcast*
## Doves
Heavenly Recordings, 2002

⚓ Manchester trio Doves (**@DovesMusicBlog**) give hope that the good will out when it comes to music. Beginning their collaborations together as a dance act called Sub Sub for much of the 1990s, Jimi Goodwin and twins Andy and Jez Williams changed direction when a fire burnt their studio to the ground. Doves not only rose from the wreckage, but flew with their debut album, the brilliant *Lost Souls*. With their second, *The Last Broadcast*, they soared. The album not only topped the UK album charts on release, but Doves has since become beloved of fans and British bands alike. So it came as little surprise that when Andy and Jez took us through the record that cemented the trio's rebirth, it would be a poignant affair, not least because their Listening Party came hot on the heels of Doves' second renaissance. Having re-formed after a extended period apart (at the time of the Party they were set to release long-awaited fourth album *The Universal Want*, which duly went to Number 1, too), the track-by-track story of *The Last Broadcast* seemed to both chart the band's past and point to a happier future.

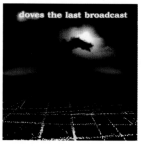

**PHOTOGRAPHY:**
Rich Mulhearn

**SLEEVE DESIGN:**
Rick Myers

---

**LISTENING PARTY**
**26 JULY 2020**

### 1. INTRO

✔ **@DovesMusicBlog**
Jez Williams: I wanted to capture that out-of-your-head isolated feeling in the Hacienda when you've done too much.

### 2. WORDS

✔ **@DovesMusicBlog**
Andy Williams: This track has a nice flavour of country music. Lyrically I wrote the verses, Jez the chorus. It's got a bit of me and you versus the world vibe.

### 3. THERE GOES THE FEAR

✔ **@DovesMusicBlog**
Andy: I have a very clear memory of writing the lyrics in my front room in Chorlton. I had no proper recording gear at home at the time. I used a tape recorder, rewinding the instrumental version all weekend and jotting down and correcting the lyrics.

### 4. M62 SONG

✔ **@DovesMusicBlog**
Andy: My vocal (and traffic noise) recorded under the motorway flyover bridge in Northenden, Manchester. Jez and Jimi lived there at the time, as well as our manager Dave.

✔ **@DovesMusicBlog**
Jez: We named the track after the wrong motorway! In fact we were under the M63 bridge.

### 5. WHERE WE'RE CALLING FROM

✔ **@DovesMusicBlog**
Jez: I always wanted to capture the feeling of having hot rushes crossed with a David Lynch soundscape. The album really needed an intense sonic (a no song) at this point.

## 6. N.Y.

 **@DovesMusicBlog**

Jez Williams: Nice bit of sonic chaos! We wrote this and a few others (including the song Valley) on the Isle Of Mull in a converted church.

## 7. SATELLITES

 **@DovesMusicBlog**

Andy Williams: The lyrics are about one of my first girlfriends. Our long time friend, and Manchester singing legend, Yvonne Shelton helped with the backing vocals. (Incidentally she also sings backing vocals on our 2020 album The Universal Want.)

## 8. FRIDAY'S DUST

 **@DovesMusicBlog**

Andy: A lovely lullaby with a darkness to it. Like M62 Song this track really shows a different side to the band and also helps with the flow of the album.

## 9. POUNDING

 **@DovesMusicBlog**

Andy: New Order were a bit of an inspiration on this one. We're still very happy to hear this getting played during the build-up Man City home games.

## 10. LAST BROADCAST

 **@DovesMusicBlog**

Jez: Can you hear it all going wonky? Took ages to get that effect. Lyrics are influenced by that 70s film called Network [starring Faye Dunaway and William Holden].

## 11. THE SULPHUR MAN

 **@DovesMusicBlog**

Jez: Listening back to this the intro sounds like Game of Thrones. But still works as a song set up. I actually think this is one of our best songs.

## 12. CAUGHT BY THE RIVER

 **@DovesMusicBlog**

Andy: The lyrics are about one of my best friends, who at the time moved to London but his life was spiralling out of control, drinking way too much, waking up on park benches, etc. I was genuinely worried about him. This is like a note to him to make him come to his senses.

➡

**@DovesMusicBlog**
(Andy) After *Lost Souls* did much better than we had expected it to – including to our surprise touring around the world – it gave us a lot of confidence as a band/songwriters. [We thought] we had a potential future in this, if we just applied ourselves.

# A Bath Full Of Ecstasy
## Hot Chip
Domino, 2019

Melancholic disco is the genre we didn't know we needed. However, the emergence of London band Hot Chip over the last decade has proven that emotional dancing is truly infectious. A swirl of understated beats, subtle electronics, live band organics and tender vocals has been the launch pad for some truly affecting bangers. What is more, is the group – Joe Goddard, Al Doyle (**@AlDoyleTweets**), Owen Clarke and Felix Martin and vocalist Alexis Taylor (**@Hot_Chip**) who swap creative roles more often than most people change their socks – has proven that introspective dance music can be as life-affirming, floor-filling and euphoric as any club classic.

Their seventh album, *A Bath Full Of Ecstasy*, makes this point by easily living up to the joyful interpretation of its name, although the Listening Party for the record was tinged with some sadness. Just over a year before, its Parisian producer Philippe Zdar (who created pioneering records with the likes of the Beastie Boys, Phoenix and Franz Ferdinand, plus for his own group Cassius) was killed in an accident. As Taylor and Doyle took us through the record he helped to create, they not only offered us a brilliant dive into *A Bath Full Of Ecstasy*, but a celebration of one of electronic music's true greats.

**ARTWORK:**
Jeremy Deller

**SLEEVE DESIGN:**
Fraser Muggeridge

**@AlDoyleTweets:**
Joe's bit [on *Postive*] reminds me of good old friends, like these guys...

LISTENING
PARTY
26 JULY
2020

## 1. MELODY OF LOVE

#### ✓ @AlDoyleTweets

Big long intro. Kinda two intros. Like you thought that was the intro, but haha! No! There's another intro! Now this is it. Love Felix's cut up vocal stuff on this one. So massive.

## 2. SPELL

#### ✓ @Hot_Chip (Alexis Taylor)

Written with Katy Perry in mind, but made Philippe Zdar move more than Katy did... "A memory in reverse", something you can't undo, but which plays over and over again, backwards, in the hope that it could be undone? The long breakdown section was a major change to the track instigated by Philippe. Nice repeating piano motif that Owen put in.

#### ✓ @AlDoyleTweets

This one has Zdar all over it. What a man. Jesus what a fucking human being. I remember all of us thinking the breakdown was a bit long... but you know what? Philippe was right cos it's AWESOME xxx So crazy sounding. Loads of weird ass shit going on. Really setting out the stall.

## 3. BATH FULL OF ECSTASY

#### ✓ @Hot_Chip

Title track up next. Made this with producer Rodaidh McDonald. Lots of discussion in RAK studios about the right direction for this one. We wanted the choruses and verses to feel like they were from different sound worlds. Also recorded some parts at Hackney Road Studios with Shuta Shinoda engineering. Big up Mike Horner who worked with us on this whole record, engineering along with Rodaidh as well as Philippe.

#### ✓ @AlDoyleTweets

I had a rap all ready for this one, but the other guys weren't sure about it. Went a bit like this:

I will wash away your fears

I will wash them up

I will wash them up with a bucket and a mop

I will wash them up

I will wash them away

You're not gonna have any fears today...

Come on guys! What's wrong with that? Big fag-hanging-out-the-mouth guitar solo here, me playing under Alexis's direction. Nice.

## 4. ECHO

#### ✓ @AlDoyleTweets

This is a dark horse. Haven't played this one live yet but we should. Kinda like an earlier Hot Chip song. Super fun and choppy and funky. Echo!

#### ✓ @Hot_Chip

We made a lof of these tracks – or the demos of them which we added to later – at Joe's Pitfield St studio. This one was very much built around the CS80 mega synth. I can picture Philippe dancing to this one as he mixed, a joyful sight. Sneaking some vocoder in at the end there... in case people didn't realise we were recording in Paris :)

#### ✓ @AlDoyleTweets

We were drinking a fair amount of whiskey sours at this point in Paris. The secret ingredient is this Nardini Acqua Di Cedro stuff, and decent cane sugar syrup. Sweet sequencing on the synths there. So many cool toys in Philippe's studio, here's a selection of coloured switches from different expensive things.

@AlDoyleTweets: Here's a few of us with the man [producer Philippe Zdar] himself celebrating a rare loading screen on the SSL desk.

←

**@AlDoyleTweets:**
So many cool toys in Philippe's studio, here's a selection of coloured switches from different expensive things.

### 5. HUNGRY CHILD

##### ✔ @Hot_Chip (Alexis Taylor)

Hungry Child was very much Joe's composition initially, and features his collaborator from solo records Valentina [Pappalardo, vocalist] joining us on vocals. Recorded at his studio then at RAK with Rodaidh producing too. Finished with Philippe at Motorbass. Featuring Ray Davies' [from The Kinks] mellotron, from the Konk studio recording sessions. Was nice playing this one live and seeing such a huge reaction to it.

##### ✔ @AlDoyleTweets (Al Doyle)

Oh shit this is a big one, Hungry Child! Absolutely massive. Drums on this one were distorted through a Culture Vulture unit. Sounds like a good friend slapping you in the face to bring you round. Oof what a landing on that drop! Valentina delivering some classy vocals here.

### 6. POSITIVE

##### ✔ @AlDoyleTweets

This might be my favourite, Positive. Really sounds like jetting off into another galaxy. Bass is an Arp. What a wonderful instrument. Just happiness in a big tolex box. This is a little interlude I played on the Korg PS3200, based on something Alexis had written on a song that wasn't used on the record.

##### ✔ @Hot_Chip

One of the first ones we recorded together. Little bit of car boot xylophone there at the start. A song about people suffering, but needing help and support to survive. Joe has a wonderful way with synthesizer melodies, interweaving with each other. Prudence, my daughter, is on backing vocals in the choruses. She came in to see us at RAK and Joe encouraged her to get on the track.

### 7. WHY DOES MY MIND

##### ◎ @Hot_Chip
A Beatles/Macca-like melody... maybe? This one written on [Big Star frontman] Alex Chilton's guitar, which a friend kindly lent me. This song was done without Philippe or Rodaidh producing, at Joe's studio. Maybe gives it a slightly different sound.

##### ◎ @AlDoyleTweets
Here's the board that was up on the wall at Zdar's studio to keep us on track kinda. He used to call me his "little Choux Fleur". No YOU'RE crying...

### 8. CLEAR BLUE SKIES

##### ◎ @AlDoyleTweets
Big feels coming up on Clear Blue Skies. Insane textures. Gates of heaven stuff. My notes on this one, apparently, were that it "should sound real sweet (epic)" so I think that was acted upon...

##### ◎ @Hot_Chip
A beautiful one. Strings at the start by Emma Smith, sampled from a song from my solo record which came out a year before. Philippe really loved this track. One of Joe's best, I think. Tom Waits lyrical ref at the start but the song goes somewhere completely different from that, and quite unlike other Hot Chip tunes. Great lyrics by Joe on this one. We had many other tracks we worked on during these sessions, which I feel are part of the whole experience. Some may see the light of day soon I reckon, was a great and productive period of writing, recording and making music all together.

### 9. NO GOD

##### ◎ @AlDoyleTweets
Weird little party vibes on this one huh? Philippe is using his Grammy award as a percussion instrument on this one cos he was that kind of laissez faire crazy cat. Here's a bit of his outboard gear signed by the beastie boys:

##### ◎ @Hot_Chip
I wrote this one thinking of my mother-in-law as the singer for it, imagining her and just a piano, for a reality TV show like The Voice. But then turned it into a Hot Chip song. It changed a bit! We got stuck on this song, but found a new way in right at the end of the album's production. Borrowed a middle 8 from another song we were working on; added these slightly baggy piano chords and then Philippe recorded himself doing all the beautiful percussion. Philippe helped bring it to life, as did Joe's positivity about it, and everyone's group playing.

---

@AlDoyleTweets:
Here's the board that was up on the wall at Zdar's [Philippe Zdar was Hot Chip's producer, who sadly died in 2019] studio to keep us on track, kinda. He used to call me his "little Choux Fleur". No YOU'RE crying.

# *Technique*
## New Order
Factory Records, 1989

⚲   The band are recording the album in Ibiza. There's a private pool at the studio. And a bar. What could go wrong? That was the set-up for at least some of the sessions for New Order's *Technique*. Installed at Mediterranean Studios early in the summer of 1988, the potential for the band's fifth studio album to become an expensive exercise in self-indulgence was high, yet Bernard Sumner (vocals, guitars), Peter Hook (bass), Stephen Morris (drums – **@StephenPDMorris**) and Gillian Gilbert (synths – **@Gillian_Gilbert**) managed to avoid at least half of those pitfalls (this LP was ultimately not cheap to make!). If anything, New Order were actually in the right place at the right time as the summer of 1988 coincided with the island's emergence as a dance-music pilgrimage point, with fans and cutting-edge DJs taking up residence in its clubs. Following their work afloat the wine-dark sea (and inside its nightclubs), *Technique* was finished at the equally inspirational, yet slightly more sedate, Real World Studios in Wiltshire, but those Balearic days had left their mark. Musically the finished album was imbued with a shimmering sunshine and vapours of the dance music revolution that was expressing itself on Ibiza, something the band personally *embraced* and *experienced*, as the *Technique* Listening Party revealed…

**SLEEVE DESIGN:**
Peter Saville Associates

↓

Gillian Gilbert shared some photos of New Order playing The Haçienda. The Manchester club became a crucible for British music and the emergent rave culture.

(Top)
**@Gillian_Gilbert:**
Stephen sampling
Speak And Spell
Holiday destinations
into the Akai, at home
in the cellar early 88.
(Bottom)
**@Gillian_Gilbert:**
A tipsy Stephen trying
his hand at scratching
on the studio Hi-Fi.

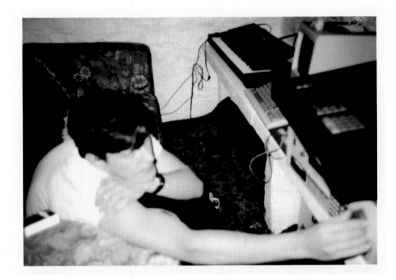

## 1. FINE TIME

**@StephenPDMorris**

And We're OFF!!!! 909. Great synth bass intro. Fine Time was a song that fell victim to computer malfunctions. The disk with a long night's work of arranging and editing got mysteriously wiped. It wasn't me honest. We just had to do it all again… again. We went overboard with the 909. Written entirely in the studio and inspired by the Ibiza club scene and the break from Funky Nassau. Bernard spent a lot of time fiddling with the synth sounds and programming on this. The title came about as a result of a parking incident in Bath. My car got towed and I wrote "Fine Time" on a notice board to remind me to go and bail it out from the Bath Police car prison. I was only ten minutes over.

**@Gillian_Gilbert**

You can tell we'd been listening to a bit of Acid House on Fine Time, Theme from S'Express was a big studio favourite.

## 2. ALL THE WAY

**@StephenPDMorris**

I love All The Way! Absolutely brilliant. Another fantastic Hooky bass riff and some deceptively tricky guitar playing. Though it sounds straightforward, *All The Way* was always difficult to get right live. The oboe bit after the chorus gives me the shivers every time – it's really lovely. Is litracite even a proper word? Anybody know? Best look it up. We were going to get Brian Eno to produce Technique – but he was too busy.

## 3. LOVE LESS

**@StephenPDMorris**

No keys at all on Love Less just two guitars, bass and drums. Really simple. One of the two songs that were actually finished when we got to Ibiza. The rest were all written in the studio. Love Less got its live debut in front of royalty – well Randy Andy and Fergie at any rate, but don't let that put you off. We first played Love Less at a fashion do at the LA stock exchange attended by the bemused Royal couple who despite sitting next to a large PA speaker – clapped politely. I seem to remember we were handsomely rewarded with hair products for our trouble.

## 4. ROUND & ROUND

**@StephenPDMorris**

Round and Round and Fine Time were heavily influenced by nights at Amnesia, Ku and various places whose names I can no longer remember. If I even knew what they were in the first place. Round and Round's working title was "The Funky One". Think we only had a couple of drum Patterns and few synth bassline ideas in Upbeat when we went in the studio. Love Hooky's bass on this one.

**@Gillian_Gilbert**

"Can you come up with anything for this section, I've just got to pop out for a bit" was the usual prelude to being left to work with Mike on keyboard parts on much of Technique. I made the most of it on the break of Round And Round.

### 5. GUILTY PARTNER

**@Gillian_Gilbert**

Lovely bit of Spanish Guitar playing on Guilty Partner, A nighttime song. I'd completely forgotten about that end string section on Guilty Partner.

**@StephenPDMorris**

Guilty Partner was one of the first songs we did in Ibiza. With everything set up in the studio. One of two ideas we had from Cheetham Hill. The other was All The Way. We did a few takes playing live. Then built it up with overdubs and drum editing. I listened to Forever Changes by Love a lot while we were making Technique. I'd always loved the odd summery atmosphere on that album perhaps some of it rubbed off? Like a lot of Love's tunes – Guilty Partner's got something darkly psychedelic about. Fantastic Basslines from Hooky on Guilty Partner. The bass creates the tension that drives the whole song. "I'm not some kind of foolish lover" – very menacing lyrics. Brilliant.

### 6. RUN

**@StephenPDMorris**

For some reason the single version of this got renamed Run 2. I blame [sleeve designer] Peter Saville for this. The sleeve was an homage to Bold 2 soap powder. We never asked for the number to be added. I think they call it artistic licence. After eight weeks in Ibiza – enough was enough and we returned to the sleepy duckponds of Real World studios just outside Bath. I remember that guitar solo was recorded at around 5am at Real World, we'd been up all night. Bernard had stuck his amp out on the fire escape and cranked it up – The good people of Box village got roused from their slumber quite early. We got in trouble with John Denver over Run, he reckoned he'd heard it before. I got in trouble with John Denver's lawyer for mentioning it in the NME. Oops I did it again.

Dream Attack. Gillian Gilbert, Stephen Morris, Bernard Sumner and Peter Hook.

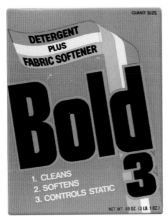

@StephenPDMorris:
For some reason the single version of Run got renamed Run 2. I blame [the band's long-term designer] Peter Saville for this. The sleeve was an homage to Bold soap powder [far right]. We never asked for the number to be added. I think they call it artistic licence.

### 7. MR. DISCO

● @StephenPDMorris
A song on THE PAINS OF THE HOLIDAY ROMANCE, even before we went to Ibiza this one had a holiday vibe – I got a speech synthesiser to recite sun-soaked destinations but then Bernard went orchestra stab crazy and they got lost. I still snuck 'em in at gigs. At one point in Ibiza – the studio became a Club 18-30 coach trip destination. "See a Rock band in their natural habitat." The frisky sunburnt tourists would turn up Thursday evenings and have a barbecue by the pool then throw up all over the studio. We had all the music for Mr Disco more or less completely recorded and ready to go when we got to Bath apart from the vocals. Despite its many distractions and popular belief, we actually did get quite a bit done in Ibiza. We had backing tracks finished for just over half the songs. All the drums were done and I think most of the synths, but Bernard hadn't finished any vocals.

### 8. VANISHING POINT

● @StephenPDMorris
There are at least two versions of Vanishing Point, but there's also an unreleased version with completely different lyrics and vocal line - maybe that's one for the box set? It was very unusual for Bernard to write and record all the vocals then decide to scrap the lot and start again but that's what he did on Vanishing Point. Some of Bernard's best words on Vanishing point – love the Whistle Down the Wind bit [the lyric goes "And they gave him away like in Whistle Down The Wind"] – it's a great film. Vanishing Point is two films [the title comes from the 1971 road movie] referenced in the same song. The end bass solo is ace too.

### 9. DREAM ATTACK

● @Gillian_Gilbert
To me Dream Attack sums up the whole album. It's bright breezy and uplifting – a good song to walk off into the sunset to.

● @StephenPDMorris
Gillian's acoustic one – Dream Attack was the last idea to get completed in Ibiza. Bernard suggested doing an extended outro section that kept building something like Hotel California? He spent a long time doing it. Adding layers of pizzicato strings. Later he forgot all about it and demanded to know whose idea it was to do such a fucking long outro. I think it's great though. Love the words on Dream Attack – it always reminds me of watching the sun come up in Ibiza after a night out. Another great Hooky melody in the break.

# *Heart's Ease*
## Shirley Collins
Domino, 2020

**ARTWORK:**
Alex Merry

⌘ There was almost a sense of completing the circle when folk doyenne Shirley Collins (**@ShirleyECollins**) chose to introduce her latest album, *Heart's Ease*, to the world via a Listening Party on Twitter. Growing up in Sussex, she learnt many ancient English songs from her grandparents, before later in the 1950s visiting America's south to discover and chart its folk music directly from the people who made it. A series of acclaimed records flowed from this musical grounding, but having retired in the late 1970s, Collins – "miraculously" as she describes it – restarted her recording career again in the 21st century to share her music and the traditions behind it to a new generation. Considering how folk music lives through the passing on of songs, stories and ideas, it seemed fitting that the 85-year-old took to her keyboard to illuminate the tracks of *Heart's Ease* just days after its release, in some instances connecting songs that pre-date electricity with an arena made possible by modern technology.

→

Locked In Ice. After retiring from music in 1976 Shirley Collins had a gap of 40 years between albums *Amaranth* (1976) and *Lodestar* (2016). Fortunately, as *Heart's Ease* confirmed, her decision to step away was ultimately premature.

## 1. THE MERRY GOLDEN TREE

✔ @ShirleyECollins

This ballad of treachery, and piracy on the high seas has been sung in the British Isles for generations and travelled those thousands of miles with the early settlers to America, where it was widely sung.

## 2. ROLLING IN THE DEW

✔ @ShirleyECollins

A song I first learned at school in Hastings, East Sussex. To make it suitable for children to sing, the chorus had been changed to Dabbling in the Dew – much more dainty!

## 3. THE CHRISTMAS SONG

✔ @ShirleyECollins

From the singing of Sussex's most famous singing family, The Copper Family. They lived and worked on the land for well over 400 years, pretty much in the same spot until not too long ago.

## 4. LOCKED IN ICE

✔ @ShirleyECollins

This is the true story of The Baychimo, a steam-powered vessel built in 1914. She worked for the Hudson Bay Company, making nine successful voyages round the north coast of Canada. Locked in pack ice at times, she finally floated away from her crew and drifted around the Arctic. She was last sighted in 1969.

## 5. WONDROUS LOVE

✔ @ShirleyECollins

We recorded this Shape-Note or Sacred Harp hymn at what was known as a Big Sing or All-Day Sing in Fyffe, Alabama. People travelled from all over rural Alabama to join in.

## 6. BARBARA ALLEN

✔ @ShirleyECollins

This ballad has been a favourite for centuries. Samuel Pepys, the diarist, wrote in his diary for New Year 1666: "In perfect pleasure I was to hear Mrs Knipps, the actress, singing, and especially her little Scots ballad of Barbary Allen".

## 7. CANADEE-I-O

✔ @ShirleyECollins

Everyone, including me, loves Nic Jones singing Canadee-i-o, but for this album I wanted to sing the original one that had been collected in the mid-1950s from Harry Upton, a shepherd on the South Downs in Sussex.

## 8. SWEET GREENS AND BLUES

✔ @ShirleyECollins

Back in 1964, my then husband Austin John Marshall wrote these four verses, which I set to an American traditional tune.

## 9. TELL ME TRUE

✔ @ShirleyECollins

This tender song was a favourite song widespread among the gypsy communities as well as the settled ones.

## 10. WHITSUN DANCE

✔ @ShirleyECollins

This, too, was written by Austin John Marshall. I set John's words to a Sussex tune from the Copper Family song A Week Before Easter.

## 11. ORANGE IN BLOOM

✔ @ShirleyECollins

I LOVE Morris dancing – when it's done properly, of course. I love the sight of it, and the sound of it. I hear a Morris bell, and my heart leaps!

## 12. CROWLINK

✔ @ShirleyECollins

Crowlink is a favourite place of mine on the South Downs Way, along the great chalk cliffs of East Sussex.

# *Kaleidoscope*
## Siouxsie And The Banshees

Polydor, 1980

Ironically considering the colour with which punk emerged in the late 1970s, some rock bands were becoming a tad identikit by the turn of the decade. The raw sounds remained, but the pageantry was fading. Siouxsie And The Banshees was exactly the sort of group the world needed to break this monotony, and with their third album *Kaleidoscope* they created a record that reflected the band's unique image and creative breadth. "This sort of macho rock bullshit. I've never liked it – and I never will," declared frontwoman Siouxsie Sioux later. "Also for the roles that females are supposed to play within music. I always find it really insulting. It usually has been something that's ornamental, more steered." Backed by bandmates Steven Severin (bass), Budgie (Peter Clarke, drums – **@Tuwhit2Whoo**) and John McGeoch (guitar), Sioux's vocals were the centrepiece of *Kaleidoscope*, providing a compelling focal point for the album's taught post-punk. While revelling in *Kaleidoscope's* musical spectrum for the Listening Party, drummer Budgie proved he is not only one of rock's most influential sticksmen, but also a skilled social media user. Although, with that nickname, what did we expect?

**PHOTOGRAPHY:**
Joe Lyons

**ILLUSTRATION:**
Rose Harrison

Siouxsie Sioux and Budgie in the early '80s.

## 1. HAPPY HOUSE

### ⊘ @Tuwhit2Whoo (Budgie)

Happy House was recorded at Roxy Music's Phil Manzanera's studio. I played [drums] with the floor tom where the snare usually sits. This created the happy accident of stick catching hi-hat returning to the floor tom. Voila, a beat is born!

## 2. TENANT

### ⊘ @Tuwhit2Whoo

Tenant may be the ONLY song with bass NOT played by Severin. Sev played electric guitar, I played Bass and then MXR Flanger. Two knobs to sculpt the flange. The drums enter after 40watt bulb.

## 3. TROPHY

### ⊘ @Tuwhit2Whoo

The Hi-Hat with Ching-ring is prominent in the mix on Trophy. Built around McGeoch's guitar and sax parts. No click tracks so we sped up into choruses and slowed down the endings. When did the click become God?

## 4. HYBRID

### ⊘ @Tuwhit2Whoo

Hybrid is a beat I had from the [previous band] Big In Japan days. Paying homage to [Cream drummer] Ginger Baker in the 'surrogate head' sections.

## 5. CLOCKFACE

### ⊘ @Tuwhit2Whoo

Clockface features Sex Pistols' Steve Jones first of three guitar appearances. A live favourite. Perhaps only I knew the connection to a Northern England brand of potato chips?

### ⊘ @Tim_Burgess

Steve Jones signed my copy of Kaleidoscope.

## 6. LUNAR CAMEL

### ⊘ @Tuwhit2Whoo

Lunar Camel is almost as the original Sioux/Severin demo. Very [Brian] Eno-esque. I love the low flanged bass-line at the end.

## 7. CHRISTINE

### ⊘ @Tuwhit2Whoo

The opening chord that no guitarist after John McGeoch could master. John almost certainly modelled it on The Beatles' opening chord to A Hard Days Night.

## 8. DESERT KISSES

### ⊘ @Tuwhit2Whoo

Desert Kisses features Kevin Godley and Lol Creem's Sitar Guitar. It gives the Captain Pugwash sound. Also introducing the sound of the Sirens (McGeoch, Severin and me) with Siouxsie doing a wonderful version of the incredible Yma Sumac.

## 9. RED LIGHT

### ⊘ @Tuwhit2Whoo

I wanted the drums to fade in over the electronica beat and evoke a smoky club atmosphere. I'm noticing the double tracking of Siouxsie's voice on these recordings. Gives an eeriness to her breath.

## 10. PARADISE PLACE

### ⊘ @Tuwhit2Whoo

Paradise Place is the second of three featuring Sex Pistol Steve Jones on guitar. Siouxsie played her Blue Vox Teardrop guitar. Her tech cut off the strings she didn't use. Who needs six strings anyway? Cheeky blighter:)

## 11. SKIN

### ⊘ @Tuwhit2Whoo

Steve J sounds like he played continuously into this final track. There was a party atmosphere in the control room after we got the guitars recorded. So I asked Nigel [Gray, producer] if I could add a second drum kit. I was playing to myself a 'call and answer' leading into a big disco crush. Disco was a big influence, especially the drummer on Sylvester's Mighty Real! Siouxsie's melodica gives a colourful reference to the reggae sounds that were prominent in 1970s Britain. OMG got totally transfixed listening to Skin.

# Have You In My Wilderness
## Julia Holter
Domino Records, 2015

⚐ Back in 2015, *Have You In My Wilderness* seemed to come out of nowhere, beguiling and impressing all who came across it. But like all "overnight" successes, the singer-songwriter had, of course, been working hard towards that moment for years. Julia Holter (**@Julia_ Holter**) – who comes from Milwaukee, but grew up in LA – had put out several now lauded, but then largely overlooked records before she broke through to a new audience with this album which seemed to bring together a kit of the different elements she had experienced musically. It's a complex, layered and sonically adventurous work, yet *Have You In My Wilderness* never fails to hit emotionally and instinctively.

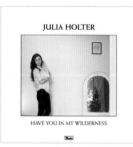

PHOTOGRAPHY:
Rick Bahto

SLEEVE DESIGN:
Matthew Cooper

| 1 | Feel You |
|---|---|
| 2 | Silhouette |
| 3 | How Long? |
| 4 | Lucette Stranded On The Island |
| 5 | Sea Calls Me Home |
| 6 | Night Song |
| 7 | Everytime Boots |
| 8 | Betsy On The Roof |
| 9 | Vasquez |
| 10 | Have You In My Wilderness |

Feel You: Holter's *Wilderness* is inspired by authors Colette and Christopher Isherwood along with real-life bandito Tiburcio Vásquez.

During the Listening Party Julia posted the lyrics for each of her songs before sharing stories about their creation, beginning with the revelation that the record's title track, Have You In My Wildness, actually predated the album it would name by nearly five years. "I wrote it back around 2010," she explained. "It was funny to name the album after a song I had written a while back. But the aspect of "conquering" in romance as well as in life in general was what I was thinking about in making this record. There's this idea classically, especially for women, that we are to be chased or possessed, and that this is romantic," Holter explained of the song's subject matter.

"Sometimes it can be romantic, sometimes it's not, lol! If you think about it, what do these things actually have to do with love? So there is a lot of conquering in love and in life, and manifest destiny, thoughts on this album."

This guiding notion comes through strongly on one of the record's most evocative, exotic and darkest tracks, Lucette Stranded On The Island. "There's a [20th century French author] Colette story called Chance Acquaintances, where a girl named Lucette follows a new lover onto his yacht but he attacks her, steals her stuff and leaves her there," Holter tweeted of the track's inspiration. "She escapes but dies of blood poisoning. So I thought I would make a song about that… lol!"

The doomy, string-laden How Long? is the moment where the album shimmers, and its creator explained how the song was not just inspired by a stay in Berlin in the summer of 2014, but by Julia being "haunted by the ominous atmosphere" of Christopher Isherwood's book *The Berlin Stories*, particularly the character of Sally Bowles who would later become a screen icon in the musical adaptation, *Cabaret*.

Yet while authors might inform her songs, the actual storytelling is all Holter and it is one of the charms of *Have You In My Wilderness*. There's even a song named after Tiburcio Vásquez, a 19th-century "Californio" bandit, and while Holter does not have any first-hand experience of shoot-ups (that we're aware of), the song really places the listener among outlaws. Julia Holter might have set out to create her own wilderness with this album, but artistically she went much further. She breathed new life into a beautiful and thoughtful world of her own.

LISTENING PARTY
1 AUGUST
2020

**@Julia_Holter**
Jose Wolff made a beautiful music video for "Feel You" featuring Tashi Wada's and my dog Francis. I was having trouble being emotionally present for a music video, and thought that having Francis join me in the video would help me channel my feelings and it did haha. He is a deep and special creature who I love very much.

**@Tim_Burgess**
Lucette Stranded On The Island – I must have listened to this album more than any other in recent years. This is where the album just becomes the absolute kaleidoscopic polkadot jewel that it is. Whatever that means typing faster than I can speak.

**@Julia_Holter**
Danny Meyer @xasopheno is the star of this recording [Sea Calls Me Home], he played this incredible sax solo. whenever anyone hears the song, they comment on how much they love the solo. it makes me so happy to hear it always, the warmth and richness of tone and the arc.

**@Julia_Holter**
Betsy [On The Roof] is another song from around 2010 that I played solo for years before recording this. This song feels like "home" to me lol. It's its own creature I never get sick of playing it bc it always makes me feel haha.

**@Tim_Burgess**
[The track] Have You In My Wilderness as a closer! It's the closer of all closers of the best. @Julia Holter just so good.

# Reward
## Cate Le Bon
Mexican Summer, 2019

Artists retreating into isolation to create their works has a noble tradition. However, few songwriters have headed to the wilderness *and* learnt to make furniture as a means to inspire their creative process. But this is exactly what Carmarthenshire singer-songwriter Cate Le Bon (**@CateLeBon**) did, escaping urban life and relocating to the Lake District where she discovered how woodwork inspired her songwriting, in turn helping her create the songs for her fifth album, *Reward*. So intertwined were these two processes that the Mercury Prize-nominated artist later revealed she often had to force herself to sit at the piano just to stop herself "thinking about chairs". Although born of isolation – and while the furniture is solely her own creation – the resulting album was made in a collegiate atmosphere, with other artists helping out during a series of recording sessions that took place in the Californian desert. "So many wonderful people contributed to this album," revealed serial collaborator Le Bon (she has a whole other band called Drinks and was a key vocalist for Neon Neon, the project of Super Furry Animals main man Gruff Rhys) as she began *Reward's* Listening Party. "I am currently listening in Iceland with co-producer and dear friend, Samur Khouja." She did not reveal who made the chairs they were sitting on, but no doubt returning to *Reward* brought to mind not just her favourite songs, but some fine furnishings, too.

**PHOTOGRAPHY:**
Ivana Kličković

**LISTENING PARTY
7 AUGUST 2020**

### 1. MIAMI

✓ @CateLeBon
Miami was the last song recorded but existed in my mind as the opening track for the duration of the recording process.

### 2. DAYLIGHT MATTERS

✓ @CateLeBon
The chorus for Daylight Matters was written on the [train station] platform in Staveley, Cumbria. Much self pity in this song, written about a loss that hadn't occurred.

### 3. HOME TO YOU

✓ @CateLeBon
Written during the making of the last Drinks [Le Bon's side project with songwriter Tim Presley aka White Fence] album, in France. Tim left to find wifi and I drank a bottle of wine and wrote the bones of this song.

### 4. MOTHER'S MOTHER'S MAGAZINES

✓ @CateLeBon
Josh Klinghoffer [former Red Hot Chili Peppers guitarist] holding down the rhythm guitar on Mothers Magazines.

### 5. HERE IT COMES AGAIN

##### ✓ @CateLeBon

The moving guitar parts on HICA were inspired by [US indie artist] Anna Domino. Playing them live and singing is impossible.

### 6. SAD NUDES

##### ✓ @CateLeBon

Sweet Baboo [Welsh solo artist Stephen Black] on the sax and [Welsh singer-songwriter] H Hawkline on the slide guitar. I miss playing these songs live with my beautiful band.

### 7. THE LIGHT

##### ✓ @CateLeBon

This is a white wine induced bass line. I can only play funky bass. Sweet Baboo would want you to know this is not him on bass.

### 8. MAGNIFICENT GESTURES

##### ✓ @CateLeBon

Kurt Vile [US singer-songwriter] sings back up on the chorus of MG.

### 9. YOU DON'T LOVE ME

##### ✓ @CateLeBon

You Dont Love Me is my favourite to play live. Struggled arranging this song for the longest time. H Hawkline played the beautiful guitar in the verses.

### 10. MEET THE MAN

##### ✓ @CateLeBon

*This* is actually my favourite to play live. A love song to a hero.

⊕

Magnificent Gestures: (below) Cate Le Bon onstage in 2019; (bottom left) "recording vox in the desert with Samur Khouja"; and (bottom right) with her "beautiful band".

# *Every Open Eye*
## Chvrches
Virgin EMI, 2015

⚲ Sometimes it is the contradictions that make the best bands. That certainly seems to be the source of the energy behind Glasgow trio Chvrches. The programmed precision of their synths and samples allows the organic beauty of frontwoman Lauren Mayberry's (**@CHVRCHES**) vocals to truly soar. They have enjoyed pop success, yet are not afraid to embrace the darkness with both their lyrics and their music. And they also conducted their Listening Party with the whole band – Mayberry, bassist Iain Cook and multi-instrumentalist Martin Doherty (**@doksan**) – sitting in on a Zoom call together comparing notes before tweeting. Twitter AND Zoom? Surely, that is the yin and yang of 2020 lockdown communication. The result, though, proved a breathless stroll through the trio's second album, a timeless piece of 21st-century pop.

**PHOTOGRAPHY:**
Jez Tozer

**SLEEVE DESIGN:**
Amy Burrows

Afterglow: Chvrches' Lauren Mayberry touring *Every Open Eye* in America in 2015.

## 1. NEVER ENDING CIRCLES

✓ **@CHVRCHES (Lauren Mayberry)**

I think we opened the tour with this for most of the album campaign. These were the first lyrics written for the album. I had writers block for ages but wrote this pretty much start to finish on the train to the studio.

## 2. LEAVE A TRACE

✓ **@CHVRCHES**

Martin Doherty says "Where are the cymbals? These drums are so polite." I think these are some of my favourite lyrics on the album? "I'm as sane as I ever was". Gaslighting before that's what it was called.

## 3. KEEP YOU ON MY SIDE

✓ **@CHVRCHES**

Maaaaan, have not thought about this song in a long time. It's kind of mad Euro trance pop? I remember it being fun at gigs though.

## 4. MAKE THEM GOLD

✓ **@CHVRCHES**

I don't think I did the best job of the lyrics on this because I was so frustrated with writers block. And I think the lyric "we are made of our longest days" gets misheard as "we are made up of our mistakes". Which is probably better.

## 5. CLEAREST BLUE

✓ **@CHVRCHES**

Here we fuckin' go. The breakdown in Clearest Blue. Still into it. We played this one at a festival on our first show back, no one had heard the song before, and everyone lost their shit at the drop. Good memories.

## 6. HIGH ENOUGH TO CARRY YOU OVER

✓ **@doksan (Martin Doherty)**

If anyone is wondering why this is in no particular key, it's because we used varispeed in the master to make it a little faster.

## 7. EMPTY THREAT

✓ **@CHVRCHES**

Definitely trying to channel some John Hughes movies / Electric Dreams energy...

✓ **@doksan**

Lauren just said [on our Zoom] "I like those drum fills at the end, that would be fun to play" forgetting she played it every night on tour.

## 8. DOWN SIDE OF ME

✓ **@CHVRCHES**

We all agreed we still love this one. We never played it properly live because of all the loops. Pop songs about depression…

✓ **@doksan**

That sample sounds like it says "ave it".

## 9. PLAYING DEAD

✓ **@CHVRCHES**

Iain Cook and his bass have entered the chat!

## 10. BURY IT

✓ **@CHVRCHES**

The original version, pre Hayley [Williams, Paramore frontwoman and featured vocalist]. A staple of the live show for sure, even before it was a single, mostly because you guys were so cool about it. Also, this album is really short?! Only one tune left. We all agree that the Bury It and Empty Threat videos are our favourites.

## 11. AFTERGLOW

✓ **@doksan**

This is so short. We should have put Follow You on this record. It's on the special edition.

✓ **@CHVRCHES**

The Sad Closer. Listen out for the radiator clunk that the vocal mic picked up and we didn't edit out…

# *Doolittle*
## Pixies
4AD, 1989

Along with being the drummer in Pixies, David Lovering also has a career as a professional magician. Listening to the band's early records it is not hard to see why he was drawn to conjuring, because together with Frank "Black Francis" Black (vocals/guitar), Kim Deal (bass/vocals) and Joey Santiago (lead guitar) – @**Pixies**, the Boston group truly achieved magic in the studio. With most of their songs barely three minutes long, relying on unadorned drums, bass and guitars that are arranged to leave a clear ambient space between all the elements, Pixies pull off an alchemy that produced hard yet impossibly tuneful songs. Their second record, *Doolittle* – with lyrical inspiration from Salvador Dalí, earthquakes, angelic apes and more – is an exemplar of this forceful yet melodic approach; one which would later inspire Kurt Cobain when writing songs for Nirvana.

**PHOTOGRAPHY:**
Simon Larbalestierr

**SLEEVE DESIGN:**
Vaughan Oliver

Hey: David Lovering, Frank Black, Joey Santiago and Kim Deal at the Pinkpop Festival, Landgraaf, Netherlands in May 1989.

## 1. DEBASER

🎵 **@Pixies (Joey Santiago)**

We all agreed that this should be the first song on the album. It introduces the four of us – one at a time. Kim, then me, then David, then Charles. Hello.

## 2. TAME

🎵 **@Pixies**

A three chord progression wonder. Relentless. I decided to play one chord on the choruses just to be a wise ass. It was based on the Jimi Hendrix chord. First chord on Purple Haze. Tip of the hat.

## 3. WAVE OF MUTILATION

🎵 **@Pixies**

Two words: Great song. A crowd pleaser. That's 5 words now.

## 4. I BLEED

🎵 **@Pixies**

Quite the operatic song. Used one note for the choruses. I am the wise ass.

## 5. HERE COMES YOUR MAN

🎵 **@Pixies**

Charles had the guitar hook kicking around since he was a wee one. Sounds like Here Comes The Night by Them with Van Morrison. Doesn't it?

## 6. DEAD

🎵 **@Pixies**

One word for the choruses, Dead, "sung" three times except for the last one. That was used twice. One note on the guitar for the verses. Had an image of the movie, Psycho, for the word Dead. Wanted the choruses to sound like the shower scene from the movie. Not fake news.

## 7. MONKEY GONE TO HEAVEN

🎵 **@Pixies**

This closes side A of the album. Off to heaven. I love the crowd raising their fingers for the 5, 6, 7 words on this song.

## 8. MR. GRIEVES

🎵 **@Pixies**

Just realised a few years ago the lyrics "Can you swing from a good rope" means hanging on a noose. Dark.

## 9. CRACKITY JONES

🎵 **@Pixies**

This song speeds up live. Some nights it revs up to blinding speeds. Depends on the vibe of the crowd. The title of the album is in this song.

## 10. LA LA LOVE YOU

🎵 **@Pixies**

Doesn't the guitar sound like someone running on the "first base, second base, third base, home run." That was the intention.

## 11. NO. 13 BABY

🎵 **@Pixies**

We can not play this intro long enough live. One night we should play it until the crowd leaves.

## 12. THERE GOES MY GUN

🎵 **@Pixies**

Not much to say about this song. The solo sounds like a Western movie. Two cowboys ready to duel in a one horse town.

## 13. HEY

🎵 **@Pixies**

We recorded this live in the studio. No overdubs. Still the best solo I have done.

## 14. SILVER

🎵 **@Pixies**

Kim on slide guitar singing like an angel.

## 15. GOUGE AWAY

🎵 **@Pixies**

This concludes Doolittle. The ooh sounding bit in between verse and chorus was played with an e-bow. First time I used such a thing. The verses are loud and the choruses are quiet. Just for giggles.

# *Royal Blood*
## Royal Blood
Warner Bros, 2014

🎤 Bass players are often forced to play literal second fiddle to guitarists, not least because "axe"-wielders tend to hog all the limelight. After all, apart from the *Seinfeld* theme, who can name a famous bass part? Of course, there are many, but Royal Blood has gone the extra mile for the bass. In fact, the hard-rocking, big-grooving Brighton duo have really put the rhythm section front and centre, dispensing with guitars, keys and other distractions as Ben Thatcher (drums – **@BenjiTalent**) and singer Mike Kerr (bass – **@RoyalBloodUK**) keep it simple. Despite embracing the instruments that usually get pushed to the back, the pair's self-titled debut album proves to be a heavy yet highly melodious slab of rock. It's drum and bass, but not as you know it… as Thatcher and Kerr explained during a Listening Party for their debut, which hit all the right notes (whatever the instruments they were using).

ARTWORK:
Dan Hillier

LISTENING
PARTY
**25 AUGUST
2020**

### 1. OUT OF THE BLACK

✅ **@BenjiTalent (Ben Thatcher)**
There was no other way to start this record was there?

✅ **@RoyalBloodUK (Mike Kerr)**
Ben played me that opening beat. I picked two notes and mirrored everything he was doing. That moment felt like we tore a hole through spacetime. It was big, dumb and beautiful. I realised alone we are nothing, but together, unstoppable. I'm getting all the gooses bumps.

### 2. COME ON OVER

✅ **@RoyalBloodUK**
I had been playing bass for about 5 mins we wrote this. I think I had just worked out how to 'hammer on' and was stoked that I could play bass with one hand. Lyrically it's basic but beneath it all I can clearly hear what I was getting at. Songs can be like photographs in that way, "that was a great day but who let me wear those trousers?!"

### 3. FIGURE IT OUT

✅ **@BenjiTalent**
To all the karaoke machines out there, the lyric is "trying to cut some teeth" not "cuss and see".

### 4. YOU CAN BE SO CRUEL

✅ **@BenjiTalent**
Mike played me Cruel at our first band practice. We played it later that night at our first show.

✅ **@RoyalBloodUK**
You may not hear this but it's heavily inspired by Alison Goldfrapp. She is one of my heroes!

### 5. BLOOD HANDS

✅ **@RoyalBloodUK**
Lyrics can be mysterious, and subconscious can make its way on to paper. I genuinely worked out what this song was about on stage playing it at Motorpoint Arena, Nottingham. It was rather embarrassing as I nearly cried.

Blood Hands. Kerr and Thatcher onstage in Detroit in 2014.

### 6. LITTLE MONSTER

✅ @RoyalBloodUK (Mike Kerr)

"What if the whole song just stopped for no reason just so you can do a drum fill?"

Ben [plays] *best drum fill of all time* "Yes."

### 7. LOOSE CHANGE

✅ @RoyalBloodUK

The drums in this sound so sick. So much gaffer tape.

### 8. CARELESS

✅ @RoyalBloodUK

Two bass strings, two guitar strings and a tuning not even the tech can remember. Jazzy little number. And that ending is golden.

### 9. TEN TONNE SKELETON

✅ @BenjiTalent (Ben Thatcher)

Nearly missed out on being included on the record. Originally had a double time verse.

✅ @RoyalBloodUK

"Hi this is your record label, you have two weeks but we need two more songs..bye" Bashed this one out mate.

### 10. BETTER STRANGERS

✅ @RoyalBloodUK

Recorded at Rack Studios. Studio 3. The drum sound is mega. I recall finishing the tracking and heading straight to Glastonbury 2013 with our album finished. Boom. We owe our lives to this record! It taught me the most important lesson: never underestimate the power of "wouldn't it be funny if…"

# *Is This It*
## The Strokes
Rough Trade Records, 2001

⚑ Bands are sounding a bit flat. Guitarists are committing the crime of sitting on stools at gigs, and while a guiding light to some great talents, the legacy of the brilliant Jeff Buckley has become a crutch to a series of songwriters not fit to tune the late virtuoso's guitars. That increasingly seemed to be the state of rock'n'roll at the start of the 21st century. Then The Strokes swaggered into view. Taught, vital, melodic yet brutal – with a last-gang-in-town look to match – the simplicity of the songs by New Yorkers Julian Casablancas (frontman/songwriter), guitarists Nick Valensi and Albert Hammond Jr, bassist Nikolai Fraiture and drummer Fabrizio Moretti, proved explosive. A genre was revitalised, bands were formed in their wake, fans' entire wardrobes were changed and indie discos would never be the same again. *Is This It* was recorded in a cramped basement studio off Avenue A on New York's Lower East Side, and one of the most influential records of the century so far was conceived. Having flicked the switches and twiddled the knobs back then, album producer Gordon Raphael (**@GordonRaphael**) was on hand to press the buttons and hit the keyboard to give us a suitably lo-fi Listening Party charting the album's creation.

PHOTOGRAPHY:
Colin Lane

Hard To Explain... the lack of dressing room chairs. Fabrizio Moretti, Albert Hammond Jr, Nick Valensi, Julian Casablancas and Nikolai Fraiture backstage at The Fillmore, San Francisco, in October 2001.

The winning ticket. "Won tix to see @thestrokes off the radio when I was living in Edinburgh back in 2002," fan @fuzzyfuzzylogic told the Listening Party. "Best thing I've ever won."

Trying Your Luck. Albert Hammond Jr (top) and Julian Casablancas playing Cardiff's Clwb Ifor Bach in 2001.

### 1. IS THIS IT

✔ @GordonRaphael

Bassline!! Bassline!!! I'm pretty sure this is the last song we recorded for the album. My memory gets a little fuzzy, hazy, smoky, by this point. Such a sweet song, right?

### 2. THE MODERN AGE

✔ @GordonRaphael

The iconic Strokes song! I think it blasted open the door for everything. What a composition. What a mood. What a vibe!

### 3. SOMA

✔ @GordonRaphael

Soma is from Brave New World by Aldous Huxley who also wrote Doors of Perception.

### 4. BARELY LEGAL

✔ @GordonRaphael

He didn't take no shortcuts! Classic megaphone voice sound. We did an earlier version of this on The Modern Age EP. A super cool sound too.

### 5. SOMEDAY

✔ @GordonRaphael

Oh such a fun and nostalgic feeling in this one, the classic double rhythms of Nick V and Albert! Sweet.

### 6. ALONE, TOGETHER

✔ @GordonRaphael

Classy robotic drums and an impassioned plea from the vocalist, chest down! Who's Lisa? I forgot...

### 7. LAST NITE

✔ @GordonRaphael

The song that lit the US music biz on fire and filled one zillion indie rock clubs with a theme song for 2 decades. Cool.

### 8. HARD TO EXPLAIN

✔ @GordonRaphael

Can you believe that's really Fab playing the drums? They wanted a crazy sound. I had an idea to try 12 different processes to get the sound. All at the same time.

### 9. NEW YORK CITY COPS

✔ @GordonRaphael

Can you imagine, we had to take this song off the US album? Because of 9/11, suddenly the New York cops and firemen were looked upon as heroes in the United States.

### 10. TRYING YOUR LUCK

✔ @GordonRaphael

Most beautiful song, wow! Such incredible rhythms. I love the spirit of this one and I love the rhythm change.

### 11. TAKE IT OR LEAVE IT

✔ @GordonRaphael

Major wow... just wow, and more wow. Major singing... Go JULIAN! Stand back! Power. Albert's SOLO! Star power, bouncing off the walls. One of the MOST insane moments of the whole record watching Albert play this! So few tracks on this album! hahah! crazy! I love The Strokes.

# Song For Our Daughter
## Laura Marling
Chrysalis/Partisan, 2020

⚓ While the rest of the music industry started delaying its releases when the impact of the Covid-19 pandemic became clear, Laura Marling (**@LauraMarlingHQ**) was bringing her album forward. The English folk singer-songwriter decided to release her seventh studio record four months ahead of time, putting out *Song For Our Daughter* in April just as the lockdown began to bite. Arguing that she "saw no reason to hold back on something that, at the very least, might entertain, and at its best, provide some sense of union" the stripped-back record, partly recorded at home, chimed with the circumstances many listeners found themselves in. On one hand taking inspiration from the straightforward, yet warm sound of Paul McCartney's self-made *McCartney* album series, on the other addressing it to an imaginary child, enabling Marling to openly share "all the confidences and affirmations I found so difficult to provide myself". For her Listening Party, rare tweeter Marling logged in and shared a candid, touching commentary which, like her album's early release, proved to be perfectly timed.

PHOTOGRAPHY:
Justin Tyler Close

**LISTENING PARTY
2 SEPTEMBER 2020**

### 1. ALEXANDRA

✔ **@LauraMarlingHQ**
Ok, here we go. Alexandra, vaguely related to Alexandra Leaving by Leonard Cohen...but mostly I say that so I have something to say to journalists.

### 2. HELD DOWN

✔ **@LauraMarlingHQ**
Respectfully stole this spectral backing vocal style from production wizard Mike Lindsay of my other band LUMP. And spent A LOT of time trying to respectfully mimic [American songwriter and occasional co-writer] Blake Mills' tone for the slide guitar parts.

### 3. STRANGE GIRL

✔ **@LauraMarlingHQ**
Wasn't totally convinced this should be on the record but it made it. That's Anna Corcoran on the piano and she is the most wonderful. That's [producer] Ethan Johns on the organ.

### 4. ONLY THE STRONG

✔ **@LauraMarlingHQ**
One of the first songs written for this album. Features a line from [playwriter/director] Robert Icke's version of Mary Stuart, "Love is a sickness cured by time".

### 5. BLOW BY BLOW

✓ @LauraMarlingHQ

Anna Corcoran on the piano, my skills are lacking. Very strange experience to sing without an instrument to hide behind. Sat next to her on the piano for this one. Did I mention she's wonderful?

### 6. SONG FOR OUR DAUGHTER

✓ @LauraMarlingHQ

The closest to my heart, obviously. Rob did the strings with absolutely no direction from me. Said he tried to portray the character of the daughter. Cried a bunch.

### 7. FORTUNE

✓ @LauraMarlingHQ

An absolute bastard to play. Had only finished writing a few days before this recording so there's a few slips and unsuredness (?) Loosely based around my ma's "running away fund" (a small pot of 20p's above the washing machine).

### 8. THE END OF THE AFFAIR

✓ @LauraMarlingHQ

Both my therapist and one of my best friends are named Max... which prompted some awkward questions but actually based on the [Graham Greene] book End of The Affair.

### 9. HOPE WE MEET AGAIN

✓ @LauraMarlingHQ

I wrote this while on tour with Neil Young (back door brag) and remember writing it in a gymnasium style backstage bathroom, which had amazing reverb. Chris Hillman doing his pedal steel joy on here. That's Nick Pini on bowed bass, longest serving Laura Marling band member.

### 10. FOR YOU

✓ @LauraMarlingHQ

Speaks for itself. This is the demo, done at home, mostly on an iPhone. A hopefully charming crap guitar solo from yours truly there. And that's all she wrote.

For You. Laura Marling performing *Song For Our Daughter* at a socially distanced livestream from London's Union Chapel during the 2020 lockdown.

# *Dark Matter*
## Moses Boyd
Exodus, 2020

SLEEVE DESIGN:
Stella Murphy

⚓ At the vanguard of the British jazz rebirth, the influence of producer and drummer Moses Boyd (**@MosesBoyd_**) was keenly felt long before he released his own debut album. With jazz artists taking their musical training into new areas throughout the 2010s, this vibrant scene has not only injected organic inspiration back into the genre, but has seen it develop its delivery through nightclub performances and home studio sessions all around the country. A collaborator with such cutting-edge jazz contemporaries as Sons Of Kemet and Soweto Kinch, Boyd has also contributed his skills and beats to such diverse talents as Floating Points, Four Tet, Little Simz and Beyoncé. Taking its influence from both Miles Davis and Dizzee Rascal, *Dark Matter* is a respectful, informed nod to jazz tradition which also reflects Boyd's own fresh, contemporary vision. Enticing polyrhythmic patterns, echoey guitars and breathy saxes conjure up a true sense of time and place with the record, making *Dark Matter* an album the listener can not only inhabit, but one which they can traverse through, experiencing the vast array of thoughts and feelings that define the band's leader's soundscapes.

Who better than to guide us through this world than Moses himself, who introduced *Dark Matter's* ideas, collaborators and its "infinity groove" (to be found on the vinyl edition) in a Listening Party that took place not long after the drummer learned the record had been named one of the 12 albums of 2020 by the Mercury Prize. Space really is the place.

---

**LISTENING PARTY**
**2 SEPTEMBER 2020**

### 1. STRANGER THAN FICTION

✔ **@MosesBoyd_**
This song was intended to musically blur the line of what is acoustic and electronic. Inspired by the madness of our current world politics. Truth is often stranger than fiction.

### 2. HARD FOOD (INTERLUDE)

✔ **@MosesBoyd_**
So much love and respect for Gary Crosby who features on this track. Without him the UK music scene would look very different. This track is from a 3hr convo we had recorded on my phone at the Southbank Centre.

### 3. B.T.B

✔ **@MosesBoyd_**
The only full live band take on the whole album with very little post production... recorded on a Boat Soup Studios. Arranged by Nathaniel Cross. Also arranged my Rye Lane Shuffle... A true arranging powerhouse.

### 4. Y.O.Y.O.

✔ **@MosesBoyd_**
One of my favourite basslines on this album. Held down by my longtime friend and collaborator [tuba player] Theon Cross. One of the hardest songs to play on tour. Because it's so easy to get excited and speed up on this track.

## 5. SHADES OF YOU

✅ **@MosesBoyd_**

I learned so much about vocal production watching [vocalist] Poppy Judha meticulously do takes, arrange and editing her vocals on this track.

## 6. DANCING IN THE DARK

✅ **@MosesBoyd_**

I was working out of a writing studio not expecting the track to get finished soon. Within a couple hours of hearing the beat Obongjayar [Afrobeat artist] had virtually written and recorded all his parts. We finished it the next day.

## 7. ONLY YOU

✅ **@MosesBoyd_**

I played Theon Cross some of the album. He asked me where's the drum feature? I didn't really have an answer but I've always wanted to hear a drum solo over a techno beat. So I wrote one. Probably won't happen again though.

## 8. 2 FAR GONE

✅ **@MosesBoyd_**

I initially recorded a drum loop demo with one mic. planning later to redo the drums. But to my ears no studio/professional gear beat the sound of my recording with one mic. Sometimes rough and ready is better.

## 9. NOMMOS DESCENT

✅ **@MosesBoyd_**

Probably one of the last songs to finish on the album. My fondest memory of this track is being in the studio with my engineer Wehinm just repeatedly listening to Nonku Phiri's vocals on solo. We were both so mesmerised. She is one of a kind.

## 10. WHAT NOW?

✅ **@MosesBoyd_**

This is like a meditative track for me. If you listen to the vinyl there is an infinite loop at the end. I'm a strong believer in letting music transport you to another place. I wanted to try and induce that atmosphere. Hope y'all liked it.

Shades Of You: Moses Boyd at Rough Trade Bristol on 10 March 2020, shared by Listening Party regular **@Birmingham_81**. "Our penultimate concert before lockdown and a very special experience to cherish. Such an expressive drummer – and a great band too."

# *Kiwanuka*
## Michael Kiwanuka
Polydor, 2019

⚓ If the hundreds of artists volunteering their time and the millions of music fans joining us from thousands of locations around the globe was not enough evidence of the rapid impact of our Listening Parties, then having the Mercury Prize organisers approach us certainly proved its cultural significance. The annual UK album award panel suggested we could do some of the records nominated for the 2020 prize, so we set about getting Parties sorted for as many of the 12-strong shortlist as we could. Brilliantly, the eventual winner, Michael Kiwanuka (**@MichaelKiwanuka**), was among those who joined in.

Michael's blossoming as a singer-songwriter over the last decade has been breathtaking to behold for both fans and musicians. Emerging in 2012 with some sweetly simple, folk-inflected songs, he has subsequently added textures and shades, feelings and thought to his work.

His third album, *Kiwanuka*, the 2020 Mercury Prize album of the year, is a beautiful culmination of this organic growth. Infused with evocative atmospheres and polished production, the album sounds at once like a lost '70s soundtrack and one of the most progressive albums of the last 10 years. Its emotional impact can be experienced universally, its message broad, yet the lyrics of *Kiwanuka* are a deeply personal affair, hence its title.

Always coming across as a truly humble guy in interviews, the songwriter had spoken in the aftermath of releasing *Kiwanuka* in November 2019 that he had actually experienced imposter syndrome while in the studio, and had been forced to resolve his own self-confidence as part of the process of creating this serene masterpiece. Fittingly his Listening Party reflected this approach. Instead of dictating the pace, Michael invited everyone to let the record play while he offered to answer people's questions about the songs. And there were a lot.

Fortunately this Q&A approach allowed Michael to provide fascinating insights into how he made the record while those listening shared their experiences how the album's soulfulness had touched them. Some fans did their own track-by-tracks for *Kiwanuka*'s 14 songs, while others contemplated its artistic impact. The crime author Ian Rankin (**@Beathhigh**) even joined in, responding to a post-out about which track on *Kiwanuka* was their favourite.

Too many records are called "timeless", but it is a fitting description for *Kiwanuka*. The fact that so many people had truly absorbed this album and come to the listening party with so many thoughts and questions to share proves it.

**SLEEVE DESIGN:**
Markeidric

| 1 | You Ain't The Problem |
|---|---|
| 2 | Rolling |
| 3 | I've Been Dazed |
| 4 | Piano Joint (This Kind of Love) (Intro) |
| 5 | Piano Joint (This Kind of Love) |
| 6 | Another Human Being |
| 7 | Living In Denial |
| 8 | Hero (Intro) |
| 9 | Hero |
| 10 | Hard To Say Goodbye |
| 11 | Final Days |
| 12 | Interlude (Loving The People) |
| 13 | Solid Ground |
| 14 | Light |

✅ **@MichaelKiwanuka**

I was just thinking to carry on where I left off but try and go a little bit deeper sonically and conceptually. Almost like the next episode to [previous album] *Love And Hate*.

**QUESTION:** What was the creative process behind choruses on the album?

✅ **@MichaelKiwanuka**

I just love songs building a world of their own. That's what I was trying to do, particularly on songs like Light and I've Been Dazed.

**QUESTION:** What was your inspiration for Piano Joint (This Kind of Love)?

✅ **@MichaelKiwanuka**

I was inspired on that song by singers like Roberta Flack who wrote some beautiful piano ballads that I love the sound of. Almost like jazz and folk music combined.

**QUESTION:** Who were you listening to during the writing process? And what is the inspiration behind the album artwork?

✅ **@MichaelKiwanuka**

I was listening to a lot of more abstract jazz like Miles Davis' Bitches Brew and also bands like the Flaming Lips. Kwame Braithwaite was a big influence on the artwork. A great photographer who took beautiful portraits.

**QUESTION:** How much did Muzzy [Muswell Hill] inspire this LP (if at all)?

✅ **@MichaelKiwanuka**

Muzzy always inspires my music. My love of guitar music from Indie rock to blues to jazz stems from going to school in Muswell Hill and meeting friends that were playing music around me. There were a lot of bands around when I was growing up there.

→

Solid Ground: Michael Kiwanuka onstage at Fabrique Club in Milan, December 2019.

✅ **@Beathhigh**
(Ian Rankin)

It plays like a single piece of music, as if orchestrated, each movement blending into the next.

# RTJ4
## Run The Jewels
Jewel Runners/BMG, 2020

There are very few music outfits that must thank the Cartoon Network for their existence – and non more unlikely than hip-hop duo Run The Jewels. Yet if Brooklyn-based rapper and producer El-P and Atlanta rapper Killer Mike (**@KillerMike**) had not been introduced by someone who worked at the station in 2011, Run The Jewels may never have existed. Appropriately, the pair's blend of dexterous beats, sonics and uncompromising attitude has seen *RTJ4* hailed by the cartoon-makers. Marvel integrated the duo's "pistol and fist" icon (as featured on the cover of this album) into several of its comics, including Dr Strange, Howard The Duck and Deadpool in 2015, while the online faux telethon event they staged in October 2020 further strengthened Run The Jewels' visual impact, as it not only saw them perform *RTJ4* in full, but also ecouraged voting in the in the US presidential elections.

SLEEVE DESIGN:
Timothy Saccenti
& Nicholas Gazin

A blend of entertainment and enlightenment that marries strong beats with rallying cries for social and political reform, *RTJ4* includes guest spots from Mavis Staples, 2 Chainz, Pharrell Williams and Josh Homme among others. Persuasive yet never preachy, Killer Mike provided a suitably pithy Listening Party to chart its creation.

LISTENING
PARTY
**18 SEPTEMBER
2020**

### 1. YANKEE AND THE BRAVE (EP. 4)

✅ @KillerMike

I've been holding that "back at it like a crack addict" line for years... heard the track and knew it was time.

### 2. OOH LA LA

✅ @KillerMike

First 2 beats El played me b4 we started on TTJ4 were Yankee and the Brave and Ooh La La. They were the first 2 songs we finished too.

### 3. OUT OF SIGHT

✅ @KillerMike

I wanted [rapper] 2chainz on [prevous album] *RTJ3* so when we had Out Of Sight, he was first pick! I'll never forget Skateboard P's [Pharrell Williams] face when we played him the beat for Out Of Sight.

### 4. HOLY CALAMAFUCK

✅ @KillerMike

[In response to being asked if the track included a Cutty Ranks sample] That's not a sample... Cutty cut that for us himself.

Family jewels: El-P and
Killer Mike.

### 5. GOONIES VS. E.T.

☑ @KillerMike

@ 9 I knew i wanted to be a rapper. By 12 I was
active in my community elections and advocacy.

### 6. WALKING IN THE SNOW

☑ @KillerMike

I caught the Holy Ghost on walking in the Snow...
El gave me the alley oop.

### 7. JUST

☑ @KillerMike

The first idea for Ju$T (b4 it was ju$t) was to try
to get Missy [Elliott] on it. [It features Pharrell
Williams and Zack de la Rocha]

### 8. NEVER LOOK BACK

☑ @KillerMike

Go further .... WITS into JU$T into Never Look
Back is perfection.

### 9. THE GROUND BELOW

☑ @Tim_Burgess

Not sure anybody in hip hop has the energy, lyrics
and power of Run The Jewels – if anyone does,
please send me a link.

### 10. PULLING THE PIN

☑ @KillerMike

I don't think I've seen el so excited than the day
he went to work Josh Homme for Pulling The Pin.
Really still can't believe we have Mavis [Staples]
on our song.

### 11. A FEW WORDS FOR THE FIRING SQUAD (RADIATION)

☑ @KillerMike

Last words for the firing squad was "fuck you
too!!" That sax thooooooo...

# Strangeways, Here We Come
## The Smiths
Rough Trade, 1987

There is an argument often made that The Smiths represent the "perfect" band. All their songs immediately sound like The Smiths. There are no duff tracks. There are songs left off albums or used as B-sides other groups would kill for. The artwork is both iconic yet immediately recognisable as The Smiths. They are a band of vivid "characters". The name is simple yet brilliant… And whether or not you subscribe to the argument, it is difficult to deny that the Manchester band both defined and inspired guitar music for years to come.

Part of this golden glow around the group emanates from the fact The Smiths never outstayed their welcome. Four studio LPs, then Morrissey (vocals), Johnny Marr (guitar), Andy Rourke (bass) and Mike Joyce (drums – **@MikeJoyceDrums**) were gone. That reputation is also enhanced because they went out on such a high: the immaculate *Strangeways, Here We Come*, produced by Stephen Street (**@StreetStephen**). Though released while the band were splitting up, the evident tensions between Morrissey and Marr never surfaced in the studio. Instead, their creative partnership was spurred on to new highs with songs that placed The Smiths' sound in wonderful new places thanks to a series of brilliant performances and innovative studio work.

PHOTOGRAPHY:
David Loehr

⊕

Arrivederci: The Smiths at the San Remo Music Festival, Italy, in early 1987, one of the band's last public performances.

✔ @StreetStephen

Be in no doubt The Smiths were meaning business and were prepared to surprise people with new instrumentation and ideas.

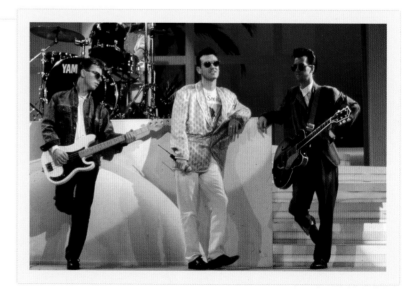

I Won't Share You: Rourke, Joyce, Morrissey and Marr in 1987.

LISTENING PARTY
28 SEPTEMBER 2020

### 1. A RUSH AND A PUSH AND THE LAND IS OURS

**@StreetStephen**

Morrissey's voice trapped into "Infinite reverb" (yes, that old trick again) sweeps you into the song with Mozza's ghostly voice singing the first few lines. I love Johnny's interweaving lines particularly the marimba sample overdub. I remember Johnny Marr telling me he wasn't going to play any guitar on A Rush And A Push. I was surprised but this was Johnny showing his desire to stretch the boundaries and what an incredibly bold statement to place it at the start of an album!

**@MikeJoyceDrums**

A celebrated guitar based band starting an album with a track with….no guitars. Ha! Remember when you used to get a vinyl record and turn the volume right up to the max on the fade to hear every single last note or try and listen to see if there was any talking? Do it with A Rush And A Push… Oh, yeah, here's the guitar!!!

### 2. I STARTED SOMETHING I COULDN'T FINISH

**@StreetStephen**

Definitely a little bit of Glam-rock vibe here with sample saxophones and monstrous claps added to the snare.

**@MikeJoyceDrums**

I love the way the guitar, bass, drums and vocals, "move" on this track. It swings like fuck! Fantastic arrangement too. Another one of those tracks where you just can't put it in a category. What does it sound like? Errr, The Smiths!

### 3. DEATH OF A DISCO DANCER

**@MikeJoyceDrums**

Ok, so if I Started Something… is difficult to categorise. Where does Death Of A Disco Dancer fit in? I'll tell you, nowhere.

**@StreetStephen**

For me, one of the key tracks on the album. Used lots of the natural room sound on Mike's kit on this one. I really like the 'calm menace' at the start with Andy's bass grooving away on top. A masterpiece.

### 4. GIRLFRIEND IN A COMA

**@StreetStephen**

Well, where do you go after that performance? With confidence and swagger, The Smiths deliver a Macca–esque sprightly pop song (nothing wrong with the word 'pop'). A reggae bounce in the rhythm too. I love the juxtaposition between this song and the track before.

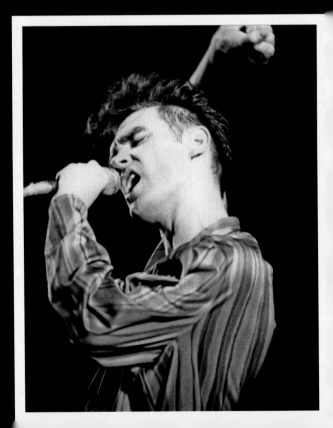

Alone, together. Although the band had split up before *Strangeways, Here We Come's* release, Joyce told the Listening Party: "[This is] the fave album of all four Smiths," revealed. "[It's] One of the few things that I can categorically say we all definitely agree on."

**@MikeJoyceDrums**

The guitar in this is a jaw dropper. I've heard people say you can actually hear the fractious nature that was supposedly being felt by the band during the recording of Strangeways. They're wrong, because there wasn't any. It was the best atmosphere of any recordings we'd ever done… and that's something that we all agree on.

## 5. STOP ME IF YOU THINK YOU'VE HEARD THIS ONE BEFORE

**@MikeJoyceDrums**

Adore the tone in Mozzer's voice in Stop Me… One of his best vocals ever.

**@StreetStephen**

Another masterful powerful performance from the band here. Andy's bass line is incredible and Johnny's chords push and pull you from pillar to post.

## 6. LAST NIGHT I DREAMT THAT SOMEBODY LOVED ME

**@MikeJoyceDrums**

Possibly my fave track off the album and a contender for one of our best tunes. When the album was finished and mixed, we had a playback session of every track in sequence in the studio with all the lights down. As you can imagine, it was pretty incredible listening back to the finished version of, Last Night… and to be honest. It still is now, 33 years later.

**@StreetStephen**

The backbone of the album. Last Night I Dreamt… is a masterpiece. I am so proud of what we achieved here.

## 7. UNHAPPY BIRTHDAY

**@MikeJoyceDrums**

What's this? Another Smiths' track that really swings? Hell yeah!

**@StreetStephen**

One of my personal favourite songs from the album. It was an absolute breeze to record. The band clicked into perfect synchronicity, no notes wasted. Coming after the density of Last Night… it seemed to hang in the air.

## 8. PAINT A VULGAR PICTURE

**@StreetStephen**

A circular song with no real verse or chorus it was hard to know what to make of it until Morrissey put his vocal on and then we knew what we were dealing with! One of the few Smiths songs to contain a guitar solo.

**@MikeJoyceDrums**

Well, one of The Smiths (who'll remain nameless) got the lyric in Paint A Vulgar Picture wrong (much to M's hilarity). Second Verse, "The Sychophantic slags all say…" was misheard as, The Sick Authentic Slags… Moz thought it was the funniest thing he'd ever heard.

## 9. DEATH AT ONE'S ELBOW

**@MikeJoyceDrums**

Lovely bass sound, and of course as always, playing on Death At Ones Elbow. I reckon we pretty much nailed the rockabilly (ish) style from [Meat Is Murder album track] Rusholme Ruffians onwards.

**@StreetStephen**

A bit of a relief after the previous song. You can hear the click track at the start that the band played over. Johnny's mouth harp playing is great on this! Lots of Duanne Eddy guitar twanging on this too. It sounds better than I remember!

## 10. I WON'T SHARE YOU

**@MikeJoyceDrums**

Johnny plays what I think is a type of zither(?) on this that was on the stairs up to the control room. And in true Brian Jones style, got it down and kind of mastered it in about 10 minutes.

**@StreetStephen**

Johnny found an old auto harp on a windowsill in the studio. He managed to tune it up and put together this chord structure that we committed to tape. Morrissey took a cassette copy of it away and came back with a lyric the same afternoon. He recorded the lyric and as elsewhere on the album, his vocal delivery was incredible. Now that we knew what we had, Andy added his bass, Johnny added the beautiful acoustic arpeggio that joins the last verse and last of all, the beautiful melancholic harmonica at the very end.

# When I Was Born For The 7th Time
## Cornershop
Wiiija, 1997

Few records have topped both the late John Peel's iconic Festive 50 and the UK singles chart, but this album is responsible for a "45" that has done both. Fewer albums spawning a British Number 1 have also featured a Beatles song in Punjabi, a collaboration with beat poet Allen Ginsberg, an artistic discourse on the Anglo-Indian community, and sonic melding between the sounds of rock'n'roll and those from the Subcontinent, but then bands like Cornershop (**@CornershopHQ**) are few and far between, and their album When I Was Born For The 7th Time is unique.

Brimful Of Asha is, of course, the song that was Number 1 in Peel's 1997 rundown of his favourite records and – via a Fatboy Slim remix – a UK chart-topper in 1998 having first gone in at Number 60 the year before. Not bad considering the track that celebrates Indian pop (along with references to the likes of Jacques Dutronc, Marc Bolan and Trojan Records) was written in "a bedsit above a chip shop", as singer and guitarist Tjinder Singh explained during their Listening Party. Yet the brilliant Brimful Of Asha just marks the start of the enthralling, head-spinning universe contained within *When I Was Born For The 7th Time's* 15 tracks. After all, as the other half of the band Ben Ayers (**@BenAyres**) warned us as the playback started, this is a record that possesses a unique power. "There is a fair dose of sub bass in the sitar and

PHOTOGRAPHY:
Colin Hawkins

| 1 | Sleep On The Left Side |
|---|---|
| 2 | Brimful Of Asha |
| 3 | Butter The Soul |
| 4 | Chocolat |
| 5 | We're In Yr Corner |
| 6 | Funky Days Are Back Again |
| 7 | What Is Happening? |
| 8 | When The Light Appears Boy |
| 9 | Coming Up |
| 10 | Good Shit |
| 11 | Good To Be On The Road Back Home Again |
| 12 | It's Indian Tobacco My Friend |
| 13 | Candyman |
| 14 | State Troopers |
| 15 | Norwegian Wood (This Bird Has Flown) |

tamboura breakdowns," he explained. "Be careful on Hi-Fi systems of power, it pushes the boundaries of bass possible on a record." It also pushes boundaries artistically, as sharp moments of wry pop gently uncoil into the intricate instrumentals that adorn this album, before heading off somewhere new altogether.

Ginsberg's contribution on the track When The Light Appears Boy was apparently "record in Ginsberg's house onto a cassette," explained Singh. "With Ginsberg being into Eastern philosophy we felt it a fitting marriage. We did not know he was ill, but it was not too long before he passed away and his light appeared in a [William] Blake-like way. I think he had thoughts about this in reciting this particular piece. [The backing] Music was recorded on a mud path in Dhera India, a passing bike with a loudspeaker and a street band."

Further musical paths are also travelled. There's a duet with alt-country singer Paula Frazer on the twangy Good To Be On The Road Back Home Again along with the rolling grooves, addictive riff and all-enveloping beats of the forward-thinking Candyman. Produced by hip-hop innovator Dan The Automator and featuring guest MC Justin Warfield, that track even ended up on advert featuring basketball superstar LeBron James.

Finally, there's the aforementioned Fab Four cover: Norwegian Wood sung in Punjabi. "When we finished this song, we actually knew we had finished the album," recalled Singh. "So there was lots to rejoice." Truly, this is a record to give thanks for.

LISTENING PARTY
3 OCTOBER 2020

What is Happening?: "Here's an unseen photo of me and Tjinder backstage around this time". Cornershop's Ben Ayres shared a few personal photos during the Listening Party.

✓ **@CornershopHQ (Tjinder Singh)**
Ben and Tjinder went to Preston Poly, where they met in the first week of their studies.

✓ **@CornershopHQ**
Butter The Soul taken from our [side project] Clinton laboratory work. The vocals themselves encourage one to go forth and conquer.

✓ **@CornershopHQ**
Chocolat is a motorway driving song. The name came from quite a long time spent in France and record collecting. There were many that wanted it to be longer but we said no.

✓ **@CornershopHQ**
We're In Yr Corner – Punjabi devotional music influenced, especially Dhadi Jatha – ie two small hand drum players singing in tandem, and one main singer with a bow on string instrument, hence the doubled up vocals and stray vocal.

✓ **@CornershopHQ**
[The album was] Demoed on the back of a sleeper bus In America travelling between shows. Vocals are in the hope better times are returning, which at that time they did.

✓ **@BenAyres**
It was a really good time for us. Tjinder's production and song writing really came into it's own at this time…. it blew my mind.

✓ **@CornershopHQ**
Good Shit. This was the first single I think. Debra Norcross at Warner Burbank did the USA artwork incorporating barcodes and numbers as if it was a packet of biscuits.

✓ **@BenAyres**
Indian Tobacco My Friend. This track was recorded at Tjinder's flat above a chip shop on Holloway Road. Memorable for being such an intense, hypnotic session, that at one point we had to run out onto the street for fresh air.

# Róisín Machine
## Róisín Murphy
Skint/BMG, 2020

Whether it is the recent renewed love of brutalist architecture, embracing vintage fashion or collaborating with disco producers, Róisín Murphy (**@RoisinMurphy**) always seems to be one step ahead of everyone else. That was certainly the case with her first band, Sheffield's Moloko, whose mix of synths, beats and slow-burning vocals in the late 1990s and early 2000s created a blueprint for the next generation. Remaining ahead of the curve is Murphy's law, and with her previous solo records exploring exquisite electronics, classic Italian pop hits and daring artpop, her fifth album, *Róisín Machine*, has really marked its place on the dancefloor before anyone else. With some of the tracks initially released as stand-alone singles dating back to 2015, Murphy paved her own way for this out-and-out club assault, and only someone with Róisín Murphy's prescience could get away with releasing a record so designed for dancing in the middle of a lockdown. Yes, no one could actually hit a dancefloor when the album emerged in 2020, but such is the encompassing atmosphere, energy and thought behind *Róisín Machine* that its perpetual hope takes you straight there.

**PHOTOGRAPHY:**
Adrian Samson

**ARTWORK:**
Bráulio Amado

Murphy's Law. Róisín in the studio with her manager Rhianna Kenny and DJ Parrot. "SAFETY FIRST" she declared of the masked-up approach.

We Got Together.
Róisín Murphy
shared this picture
of collaborator DJ
Parrot "in my hanging
chair back in the
day!" during her
Listening Party.

## 1. SIMULATION

✓ @RoisinMurphy

The backing track for Simulation was given to me straight after I finished Overpowered along with a handful more. Most of which have actually found their way on the album, that is to say this record was already a pretty fully-formed entity ten years ago. It was there on paper.

## 2. KINGDOM OF ENDS

✓ @RoisinMurphy

This song is a kind of dedication to Mark Fisher, I've used many of the phrases he uses in his writing in this song and his pre-occupations of the end of desire and the end of capitalism. I'm deliberately trying to channel Bryan Ferry in places here.

## 3. SOMETHING MORE

✓ @RoisinMurphy

This is the only time I've ever asked someone to write for me. To be honest Murphy's Law was such a good song, I wanted to take the pressure off myself by having something to match it, to balance the record. So I asked Amy Douglas to write me a song about exponential need, about wanting more and more and more. This wonderful song was written overnight and couldn't have been more perfect for me.

## 4. SHELLFISH MADEMOISELLE

✓ @RoisinMurphy

What a funky funky funky Sheffield beat! I'd love to hear this on a system with friends. Our icecream's not melted yet kids.

Game Changer. "Who loves the grubby little fanzine?" Murphy shows off the self-published mag that came with copies of the album.

## 5. INCAPABLE

✓ @RoisinMurphy

It's such a characterful track and the music is so perfectly balanced. It has great equilibrium. It took Parrot [long term collaborator Richard Barratt, aka DJ Parrot] a while to finish this cos he couldn't imagine people dancing to a bird singing "I'm incapable" !! But you know I always like to bring little EXTRA.

## 6. WE GOT TOGETHER

✓ @RoisinMurphy

This was a chant I did over the end of Flash of Light live. Parrot heard it and liked it and built this track around the lyric idea. I get so much from that one little bit of lyric, we got together – that's great, we got together in the past – I wish we could get tougher now, we all got together, we got toggery didn't we? Or am I just imagining it? The meaning shifts. It's almost impossible not to do the running man when this one comes on.

## 7. MURPHY'S LAW

✓ @RoisinMurphy

What can I say about Murphy's Law? I reckon it's a stone cold classic, lads. The original version of this we were uncomfortable with, due to the high cheese levels. Nervous I should say. Although we know we were onto something good. Originally it was in a higher key. Wondered if that was the problem so I asked Parrot to transpose the whole

↓

Narcissus. Sharing the artwork for single Incapable with the Listening Party Murphy admitted "she always HAD to have big hair!"

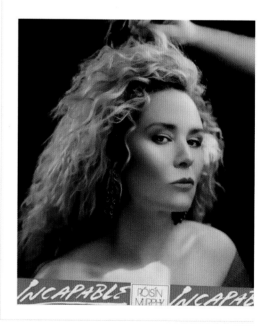

thing down. I copied transposed vocal and replaced it, but we never could quite let go of this gender-bent transposed vocal. What you hear now is a blend of the two. It just needed something a little "off" to make it feel right.

## 8. GAME CHANGER

**@RoisinMurphy**

This is one of my favourites. We're in the funky room, people are jazz dancing doing the splits and spinning on their backs. This album really is like a big building of rooms for having fun.

## 9. NARCISSUS

**@RoisinMurphy**

In the studio, it seemed the track made me think of the word Narcissus which I began to chant over it. I then had to go and look up the myth, it was then just a simple case of inhabiting the characters of Echo. I'm calling out to all those fabulous magnetic men in my life. I'm here,

remember me!? Not saying narcissist, just pronouncing it Narcisciss for some reason.

## 10. JEALOUSY

**@RoisinMurphy**

What a stomper, they don't come around like this too often, lads. This track is literally hysterical. Get your roller-skates on and lets go round and round and round and round and round and round. A lot of art is about an almighty struggle in the very soul of its creator, by the way. You alright Siouxsie Sioux? And though this is an explosive end track, we are still left on the edge of our desire. Teetering on the edge of it. And the build is still going strong. Thank you everyone who joined us to listen to Róisín Machine, I always enjoy these so much and this one was especially celebratory! I can't thank you all enough.

**TIM'S THOUGHTS**

One person who kept appearing on my timeline as the lockdown set in was Róisín Murphy, and I knew she would be able to put the party in *The Listening Party*.

A highlight for me throughout all this has been the opportunity to connect with people that I have admired but where our paths haven't crossed. Everything from music to artwork and an obvious sense of humour got me thinking that we would get on and I have found me a DM-based pen pal. *Róisín Machine* was and is a banger from start to finish and is a dancefloor masterclass. I don't give rules and regulations about how to do a Listening Party – it's more about guidelines – so there is a sense of who the

person is, and Róisín's tweets introduced each track with a list of all the personnel involved, underlining the collaborative effort with her at the helm. I've sometimes said that the listening parties are like hearing an album in 3D and this is never more apparent than when Róisín is captaining the ship, from dance moves to memorabilia. It was like going on a night out without having to move.

# So Tough
## Saint Etienne
Heavenly, 1993

✠ Saint Etienne's debut album, *Foxbase Alpha*, has been rightly described as a "Rolls-Royce gliding through clubland". *So Tough*, their second, scales it up to an ocean-going liner that cruises sublimely between dance music and folk, golden pop and experimental electronics, while it is crewed by a selection of characterful voices and vocal samples that knit its sonic quilt together. "We couldn't believe we'd have the opportunity to record one whole album, let alone two in as many years!" frontwoman Sarah Cracknell told us a few weeks after the Listening Party. "It was an incredibly exciting time for us, every experience seemed so new and full of wonder." In Bob Stanley (**@Rocking_Bob**) – who makes up the group with Pete Wiggs – Saint Etienne have one of Britain's greatest music writers and a consummate compilation compiler amongst their number. Having done some must-read sleevenotes for his collections for Ace Records, Stanley was made for the Listening Party format. Duly he took us through *So Tough* and was joined by friends, including the music writer Simon Price (**@Simon_Price01**).

PHOTOGRAPHY:
Derek Cracknell

⊕
Street toughs. Bob Stanley, Sarah Cracknell and Pete Wiggs at London's Back Street Studios in 1993.

✓ **@Tim_Burgess**
Me and Sarah used to hang out when she was spending a lot of time in Manchester – I think that might've been where we got the idea for our collab.

## 1. MARIO'S CAFE

☑ @Rocking_Bob (Bob Stanley)

We started with dear Dirk Bogarde, reading one of own poems. The next line is "and my train leaves at ten". Pete had a copy of Adam & the Ants' Dirk Wears White Sox. I still enjoy using the phrase "never trust a man with egg on his face".

## 2. RAILWAY JAM

☑ @Rocking_Bob

The title of Railway Jam comes from Pete mishearing a line on Joy Division's version of Sister Ray.

## 3. DATE WITH SPELMAN

☑ @Rocking_Bob

Phil Spelman is a legendary record dealer, if your thing is sixties British 45s.

## 4. CALICO

☑ @Rocking_Bob

That melody was borrowed from Augustus Pablo sample. All sorted out and above board.

## 5. AVENUE

☑ @Rocking_Bob

This is the very first song that me Pete and Sarah co-wrote, with [producer] Ian Catt's invaluable help, too.

## 6. YOU'RE IN A BAD WAY

☑ @Rocking_Bob

You're In A Bad Way was meant to sound like Hermans Hermits with a Moog bassline. Seemed like a good idea at the time…

## 7. MEMO TO PRICEY

☑ @Rocking_Bob

Here we have Simon Price (then at Melody Maker and a heavy Malibu user) and Gareth Sweeney (northern soul fiend and dry wit).

☑ @Simon_Price01

I asked what he wanted me to say, but Bob said there was no script. I should just come to the pub and they'd record me. I filled my head with self-consciously cool, quotable things to say. When the record came out, I was mildly miffed that they ignored all that stuff and instead used an off-guard moment when the dictaphone caught me talking bollocks about how I didn't like harsh-tasting adult drinks like whiskey and lager, and preferred Malibu. In hindsight, though, I thank Saint Etienne from the bottom of my soul, because I know that if I heard the clever-clever, show-off outtakes now, I would cringe myself INSIDE OUT.

## 8. HOBART PAVING

☑ @Rocking_Bob

The album was recorded at RMS Studios, near Selhurst Park. The pavements were being dug up by a company called Hobart Paving.

## 9. LEAFHOUND

☑ @Rocking_Bob

The wants ads in Record Collector always included the one album by a group called Leafhound, one of the rarest albums in the world.

## 10. CLOCK MILK

☑ @Rocking_Bob

[The voice sample is] Marc Almond…

## 11. CONCHITA MARTINEZ

☑ @Rocking_Bob

Conchita Martinez was a clay court tennis player. I think she won Wimbledon the year after the album came out.

## 12. NO RAINBOWS FOR ME

☑ @Rocking_Bob

This was recorded in mono, as a homage to Phil Spector, in particular his Paris Sisters records.

## 13. HERE COME CLOWN FEET

☑ @Rocking_Bob

The title Here Come Clown Feet comes from a page in Dr Seuss's The Foot Book.

## 14. JUNK THE MORGUE

☑ @Rocking_Bob

Detroit techno, with a bit of Space Bass by Slick.

## 15. CHICKEN SOUP

☑ @Rocking_Bob

And here's Jerry Jaffe, our American manager. He had great stories of being on the road with The Osmonds and The Jam.

# *Pornography*
## The Cure
Fiction, 1982

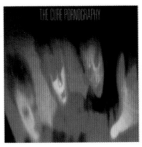

**PHOTOGRAPHY:**
Michael Kostiff

A Short Term Effect.
A 1982 US advert for
the album.

At one point it looked like the mountain of beer cans kept in a corner at London's RAK Studios might have been *Pornography's* only legacy. Having made an arrangement with the off-licence opposite to keep them supplied, The Cure resolved not to throw any of their empties away while making their album and a sizeable collection grew. Possibly influenced by the volume of this inadvertent artwork – and with a few other substances consumed during sessions – the Crawley band's resulting fourth album is a dark, swirling affair of taut energy and deep atmospheres. It was also one that critics at the time could not be more ambivalent about.

However, as the cans were finally binned, the quality of this brutal yet soulful work from Robert Smith (vocals, guitar, keyboards), Lol Tolhurst (drums, keyboards – **@LolTolhurst**) and Simon Gallup (bassist, who left the band after this record), has been gradually appreciated, not only by fans and reviewers but as an invaluable influence for other artists hoping to create albums with similarly dark, claustrophobic elements.

Hosting the Listening Party also gave Tolhurst an opportunity to re-appreciate and revalue his record. "I've been thinking a great deal about this record and time. Trying to put myself back in the state of mind when we made it," he wrote before pressing play. "It's not that simple a process to recall the feelings of the 23-year-old me at 61! I think there's that undeniable nihilism on the surface but underneath it all is the faint glimmer of hope. There had to be. Certainly there's a punk romanticism attached to all the annihilation and despair but I sincerely think with the benefit of many years hindsight we were searching for a way forward. Out of the desperation we felt. In the end, it happened anyway. This is *Pornography*, in all its monolithic grandeur. It's pertinent to remember that when this first came out it wasn't immediately hailed as groundbreaking! Haha!" Its groundbreaking and beer-can-mountain-making qualities will never be underestimated again.

## 1. ONE HUNDRED YEARS

⊘ @LolTolhurst

The first Cure song I ever played keyboards on! We used the Boss DR Rhythm DR-55 drum machine for the drums. We fed it out into two amps (bass/guitar) for the snare and Kick drum respectively then recorded that. Live this song was a little dangerous! I had to leap off the kit, then manically run to the front of the stage whilst avoiding being hit on the head by the descending screen that cut off the kit from the audience's view while I played the keys! For the *Pornography* tour, we took a reel to reel tape machine for the drum track on One Hundred Years and for background sounds on the track Pornography. The first time we hadn't played everything you heard from the stage live. Now it's commonplace.

## 2. A SHORT TERM EFFECT

⊘ @LolTolhurst

The last record we had made before this was Charlotte Sometimes. I loved the drum sound Mike Hedges got for that. So with [producer] Phil Thornalley, we got another great drum sound, massive and giant, it defines the album for me – swirling psychedelia, hallucinatory in its quality. A Short Term Effect spoke to some of what was going on with us at the time. I think with the death of my Mother and Robert's Grandmother we were on a very desperate track. The start of the infamous "Beer sculpture". We kept every can or bottle we drank making Pornography until the end. This looks to be about day 4, we were there for a long time...

## 3. THE HANGING GARDEN

⊘ @LolTolhurst

This song finally came together for me once I sorted out the right beat with floor tom then with Robert and Simon that became a ferocious magic. The only single from the album. The video was filmed at night it was incredibly cold! I was able to get that great pounding drums sound for Hanging Garden in RAK studio one big main room. Phil at the controls! We were young 23 but Phil was even younger (21?) when he recorded us at Rak!

## 4. SIAMESE TWINS

⊘ @LolTolhurst

We paid a visit to the Ray Man store in London. The percussion instruments there were inspirational, we bought some finger cymbals and stuff and I bought an absolutely wonderful Chinese Cymbal. I used it a great deal on this album. As I think I've said before, I admire Sylvia Plath's work. To me, she is among the greatest American writers and poets. My lyrical contributions to Siamese Twins reflects that admiration.

→ Follies of youth. Producer Phil Thornalley at the controls.

↓ But is it art? The start of the infamous beer sculpture Lol Tolhurst shared with the Listening Party.

A Strange Day. "Pensive and deep in thought. It was that kind of recording session," commented Lol Tolhurst as he shared studio pics of Robert Smith (also pictured, opposite, typing out lyrics) and himself with the Listening Party. "I feel we gave our all on this."

## 5. THE FIGUREHEAD

✓ @LolTolhurst

One of the most satisfying songs for me to play live, the manta of the drum pattern would actually be like a meditation. Many people get elevated heart rate going on stage, with me it works the opposite way. I feel much calmer out there. For me, this photo correctly conveys the intangible, almost mystical intensity we felt in the studio making this record. I feel we gave our all on this.

## 6. A STRANGE DAY

✓ @LolTolhurst

Phil used several channels on the desk to play drones we recorded on tape. Then at the start, he mixes them together to create that great droning entrance. Some of my absolute favourite of Robert's guitar playing ever! So emotionally satisfying. Also the closest I ever got to the Dennis Davis (RIP) drum sound on [David Bowie's] Low! Pensive and deep in thought. It was that kind of recording session.

## 7. COLD

✓ @LolTolhurst

My favourite start to any Cure song! Robert's cello intro into my drums always sends a shiver down my spine! The great crashing cymbal was the Chinese cymbal I got from Ray Man. I loved that thing but I think it caused some hearing loss! So loud! Before laptops were a thing... Or even invented! Robert typing out the words (or maybe our drinks order for that night? haha!)

← Smith performing live in Brighton in 1982.

→ Smith, Tolhurst and Simon Gallup in 1982.

## 8. PORNOGRAPHY

✔ **@LolTolhurst**

The voices at the beginning we taped from the TV in the studio and then Phil sonically mangled them. The only words you can make out are "poor joe" which live I used as the cue to start playing the drum pattern. I remember it was a program about sex. Don't recall who was talking. To us what was pornographic was war and destruction of lives by subjugation, power, and greed. The lyrics are both prophetic and appropriate for these times I think. "I must fight this sickness/ find a Cure / I must fight this sickness".

# Live At The Round House
## Nick Mason's Saucer Full Of Secrets
Nick Mason Music/Sony, 2020

ARTWORK:
Chris Peyton

What is left for an artist like Nick Mason? The drummer of one of the world's most famous groups (Pink Floyd), a pioneer who helped define a genre (prog rock), a player on one of the most-heard records ever (*The Dark Side Of The Moon*) and a performer who has transformed how live music works (hello stadium rocker!). The answer, refreshingly enough, is to keep playing music. With Floyd seemingly permanently parked, Nick Mason (@**NickMasonDrums**) formed a new band, Saucer Full Of Secrets, to go out and perform those songs all over again. Of course, when you're part of Pink Floyd getting a band together is a bit more sophisticated than sticking a photocopied ad in a music shop. Hence long-time Floyd musician and bassist Guy Pratt (@**GuyPratt**), Blockheads guitarist Lee Harris, keyboard player Dom Beken (@**DomBeken**) and Spandau Ballet's Gary Kemp (@**GaryJKemp**) all signed up for a series of gigs at The Half Moon pub in Putney, South London, before playing Floyd-inspired shows the world over. Their homecoming show at London's Roundhouse in May 2019 was recorded for a live album that Beken, Pratt, Kemp and Mason offered to take listeners through… just. "No one in the Saucer's know which song we're currently on," tweeted Beken early on, "just like the real show ;-)" Fortunately the cosmic forces soon aligned, presenting Nick Mason with yet another accolade to add to his considerable collection: the honour of being involved in the 500th Listening Party.

@tomsbfc [fan]
I'm being taken back to being 15 again, playing these songs in my bedroom and attending my first Pink Floyd show!

EMPIRE POOL, WEMBLEY

NOVEMBER **17**

HARVEY GOLDSMITH for
JOHN SMITH ENTERTAINMENTS PRESENTS

**PINK FLOYD IN CONCERT**

SUNDAY, 17 NOVEMBER, 1974
at 3 p.m.

Official Souvenirs and Programmes on sale inside the auditorium only.

SOUTH UPPER TIER

**£2.20**

ENTER AT
SOUTH DOOR
ENTRANCE

**58**

ROW
**H**

SEAT
**79**

TO BE RETAINED See conditions on back

LISTENING
PARTY
25 OCTOBER
2020

Fearless. Nick Mason onstage at the Roundhouse in London, May 2019.

### 1. INTERSTELLAR OVERDRIVE

@GaryJKemp

Interstellar is the best punk riff never written, surely? We wanted to start the show with this cos it set out our stall straight away with this improved psychedelic madness. If you didn't get this you may as well leave...

### 2. ASTRONOMY DOMINE

@GaryJKemp

Here comes another mega Sad riff. Lee [Harris, Blockheads guitarist] and I swapping solos through this.

@GuyPratt

1 of only 3 songs we do that I've ever played before...

### 3. LUCIFER SAM

@GaryJKemp

Another great Syd Riff. Lee's solo is strident! Dr Feelgood style. All praise to Syd. Look out for the Lady and the Tramp reference from Guy on lead Vox.

### 4. FEARLESS

@NickMasonDrums

People are often confused as to why we [Pink Floyd] didn't use an Arsenal chant for Fearless when we were Arsenal fans...

### 5. OBSCURED BY CLOUDS

@GuyPratt

Obscured is such a highlight. I love doing the bass pads with the swells, and Dom is seriously channelling Rick [Wright, Pink Floyd].

### 6. WHEN YOU'RE IN

● @GaryJKemp

When You're In is proper 70s rock. Reminds me of seeing Man at this very venue [Roundhouse].

### 7. REMEMBER A DAY

● @DomBeken

I nearly destroyed my upright piano bashing it to make the samples I trigger in the drum break here.

● @GuyPratt

Always poignant for me singing a song about childhood written and sung by my son's grandfather. [Pratt was married to Richard Wright's daughter Gala]

### 8. ARNOLD LAYNE

● @GaryJKemp

One of my all time favourite songs of the sixties. What a lyric... and way before Lola! Spot the riff Guy plays in the solo... What Other song is it from?

● @GuyPratt

The first Who reference coming up in the solo section.. There it is..5.15!

### 9. VEGETABLE MAN

● @GaryJKemp

Here's the weirdest cheese song ever but I love singing this one. Syd's songs are always so odd timing wise here and there but we always tried to stay faithful to the original and not posh them up.

### 10. IF

● @GaryJKemp

The idea to do this melody of If into an abbreviated Atom Heart Mother was something that really allowed us to claim the show as not just straight up "tribute". You can only do this sort of thing if you have an original member in the band.

### 11. ATOM HEART MOTHER

● @GaryJKemp

It was really exiting when we discovered turning the horn part into my guitar and then to take the cello part and reinvent it as a classical guitar part. Making this piece our own but staying faithful to the essence sums up the band's entire approach.

⊕

Interstella Overdrive. Gary Kemp – something of a Listening Party regular having staged playbacks with his other groups – onstage at the Roundhouse with Nick Mason's band.

## @NickMasonDrums

[The drums here] should have been tubular bells but we could only afford one! It required its own roadbox which was the longest roadbox of the lot…

### 12. THE NILE SONG

## @GaryJKemp

Guy and I never seemed to have a problem choosing who sang what, it all seemed natural when making those decisions. The Nile Song had to be Guy though, SO HIGH!

## @GuyPratt

Absolutely no prizes for spotting the Sex Pistols and Clash references.

### 13. GREEN IS THE COLOUR

## @GuyPratt

Pink Floyd goes Yacht Rock.

## @GaryJKemp

We really changed this quite a lot. There were quite a few different versions which we looked out so we figured that if Floyd had various ideas for it then we could go our own way. Great song to play… Enjoy my solo into Guys. Yes, Yacht Rock!

### 14. LET THERE BE MORE LIGHT

## @NickMasonDrums

Mildenhall was an American Air Force base. At the time, it was quite famous, then they moved to Greenham Common.

## @GaryJKemp

Bought it when I was a teenager from music shop in Camden Passage, Islington.

### 15. CHILDHOOD'S END

## @GuyPratt

We originally did this based on an old live version with awhile other section, but it was very long. Very, very, very, long.

### 16. SET THE CONTROLS FOR THE HEART OF THE SUN

## @GuyPratt

When Roger Waters joined us for this in NY I realised I'd been singing a wrong word every night up to then. No I'm not telling you which one. The build up here is so on. Massive drama, and I get to play the gong!

### 17. SEE EMILY PLAY

## @GaryJKemp

EMILY! I actually first heard this song as Bowie's version on Pinups and so through in one of Ronson's riff's in the solo passage.

### 18. BIKE

## @NickMasonDrums

I wonder if we ever played this live? I do remember when we played Long Tall Texan, but that was in 1966.

### 19. ONE OF THESE DAYS

## @NickMasonDrums

It's been said so many times, but basically my vocal was recorded at regular speed, but with me talking as high as I could, then slowed down…

### 20. A SAUCERFUL OF SECRETS

## @NickMasonDrums

I always remember playing it at the Royal Albert Hall, with Norman Smith conducting on the rostrum. Happy days! Still one of the best tour moments was playing at Den Atelier in Luxembourg… The audience sang along with the vocal part. Truly memorable!

### 21. POINT ME AT THE SKY

## @GaryJKemp

This song is so Roger to one voice being the "I" character and the other the narrator… Firebell from Nick and it's goodbye from me and it's goodbye from him.

# Another Music In A Different Kitchen
## Buzzcocks
United Artists, 1978

⚲ "What Do I Get? – simple, straight to the point and so catchy," declared Buzzcocks guitarist Steve Diggle (**@Stephen_Diggle**) of his band's undeniable classic as he hosted a Listening Party for album *Another Music In A Different Kitchen*. What is perhaps even more remarkable is the single did not feature on the Manchester band's 1978 debut album and was only added with later reissues. Yet despite omitting that classic, and equally iconic first single Orgasm Addict, *Another Music In A Different Kitchen* still proved to be a deeply imaginative and influential record that brought bold tunes and musical innovation to the punk blueprint. The album is made all the more remarkable by the fact that as they entered the studio, guitarist Pete Shelley had just taken over main vocals after the departure of singer and songwriter Howard Devoto. Yet he, Diggle, Steve Garvey (bass) and John Maher (drums) were undeterred, creating a record that covered a dazzling amount of ground in just over half an hour. Equally "straight to the point", Diggle hosted a Listening Party that illuminated *Another Music In A Different Kitchen* in a fashion in keeping with Buzzcocks' penchant for breadth and brevity.

**PHOTOGRAPHY:**
Jill Furmanovsky

Kitchen cabinet. Steve Garvey, Pete Shelley, John Maher, Steve Diggle getting some refreshments in 1978.

## 1. FAST CARS

### ⊘ @Stephen_Diggle

I wrote Fast Cars before I met the others and at an early rehearsal. I had the music and chorus but left my verses at home, Howard and Pete had some words that's how it was born.

## 2. NO REPLY

### ⊘ @Stephen_Diggle

Another Music had attitude and that was so important to this record made you rethink your whole consciousness about what music should be and what it was doing to you. Making you feel alive!

## 3. YOU TEAR ME UP

### ⊘ @Stephen_Diggle

It's hard to see when you make an album but *Another Music* did seem to be quite influential in its insight and gravity.

## 4. GET ON OUR OWN

### ⊘ @Stephen_Diggle

I saw a film of the Rolling Stones doing Sympathy For The Devil with all these colour screens we used the same ones. We had cheap h n h combo amps in a really big room I think that's what gave the album the sound and texture.

## 5. LOVE BATTERY

### ⊘ @Stephen_Diggle

The album never lets up it puts Electric in your veins, everything was quick fast furious and exciting at the time this album was made – Love Battery, You Tear Me Up, No Reply – they went straight for the throat an assault on your senses.

## 6. SIXTEEN

### ⊘ @Stephen_Diggle

This album covers so much ground from the fast and furious to the heavy chord of Sixteen. I think this album was quite futuristic at the time as the other bands first albums were all quite linear we had experimental stuff like Autonomy, Fiction Romance and Pulsebeat.

## 7. I DON'T MIND

### ⊘ @Stephen_Diggle

Buzzcocks had a very distinctive style. From avant garden stuff to great pop songs like I Don't Mind. And of course Pete had a very unique voice. The chemistry was amazing. John Mather was an amazing drummer, Steve Garvey a great bass – Buzzcocks were a powerhouse.

## 8. FICTION ROMANCE

### ⊘ @Stephen_Diggle

Pete had chug cord for Fiction Romance. I looked at him and put that one note in dadada da da. Just shows one note can make all the difference.

## 9. AUTONOMY

### ⊘ @Stephen_Diggle

I was listening to the German band Can and thought it was weird Germans singing English so I imagined being an Englishman being a German singing English. A weird way to get to a song, but the music was Krautrock inspired.

## 10. I NEED

### ⊘ @Stephen_Diggle

We were rehearsing and went to the pub for a break, when we came back I just started playing all the chords to I Need and Pete started singing the words, that was very spontaneous magic. Maybe going to the pub helped with that song!

## 11. MOVING AWAY FROM THE PULSEBEAT

### ⊘ @Stephen_Diggle

This was so ahead of its time. From a chord rhythm, everybody out there thing in John the drums. I did the riffs. Mick Jones from The Clash said at our Hammersmith Apollo gig only Buzzcocks could end with this.

# Songs From Northern Britain
## Teenage Fanclub
Columbia Records, 1997

⚓ From the album artwork – Donald Milne's poignant photograph of a parked-up, packed-up funfair – to the vocal harmonies and chiming guitars, there is a special light that enthuses Teenage Fanclub's *Songs From Northern Britain*. Enamoured by America's West Coast folk-rock sound from their very beginnings, the Scottish band's sixth studio album takes that golden hue and – through their own personality and dexterous guitar playing – truly makes it their own. Brightly lit by hazy summer sunshine and brilliant autumn blue skies, it is perhaps less celebratory than its American influences, but the group's then line-up of Norman Blake (vocals/guitar – **@MrNormanBlake1**), Gerard Love (bass/vocals), Raymond McGinley (guitar/vocals) and Paul Quinn (drums), offer a sharper focus. "The album title *Songs From Northern Britain* should not be construed in any way as us making a political statement," explained Blake. "I think Raymond came up with the name. We thought that it sounded funny. We figured that no one would ever refer to Scotland as Northern Britain, but technically it is the northern part of the island that is called Britain. I'm pretty sure that at least one of the songs was written in the South, but *Songs From Britain* doesn't sound as snappy. Oh how we laughed."

PHOTOGRAPHY:
David Milne

LISTENING
PARTY
1 NOVEMBER
2020

### 1. START AGAIN

✓ @MrNormanBlake1
I was struggling to come up with a guitar break for the middle section and decided to just kick on a pedal and dig in to the guitar a bit more. I think I just about got away with it. Raymond does the "real" solo on the end section.

### 2. AIN'T THAT ENOUGH

✓ @MrNormanBlake1
We made our one and only appearance on a Thursday night Top Of The Pops when this entered the chart at something like number nineteen. Alas, we didn't get any higher than that and so never made it back on the show, but it was a real thrill to do it. Every young musician dreamed about being on that show back in the day.

### 3. CAN'T FEEL MY SOUL

✓ @MrNormanBlake1
This is a Raymond McGinley song. I really like this one. We still play it live. I played Vox Jaguar organ on this. Right hand only. When we do it live I hold my left hand in the general vicinity of the keyboard so that it looks like I'm playing with two hands.

### 4. I DON'T WANT CONTROL OF YOU

✓ @MrNormanBlake1
This is a song that expresses paternal love. I wrote it for my daughter Rowan. She was just a baby when we recorded it. The voice you hear saying "hey" at the start of the song is that of the one and only [singer-songwriter/sometime Teenage Fanclub guitar tech] George Borowski. He also played the little acoustic guitar figure that introduces the song. The birdsong is from a field recording that was made somewhere in Surrey.

The band (Norman Blake, Raymond McGinley, Gerard Love) making sweet sounds in 1997.

## 5. PLANETS

### ☑ @MrNormanBlake1

I was living near Perth when I wrote this tune. Bloke in Perth, with beard. That was me :-) I had the verse part worked out for this but wasn't sure what to do with the chorus. Francis [Macdonald, Teenage Fanclub drummer] very kindly came up with a great chord sequence for that. We got to record the strings at Abbey Road. In the famous studio two no less.

## 6. IT'S A BAD WORLD

### ☑ @MrNormanBlake1

Raymond's guitar playing is awesome! He has used the same amp on all of our albums apart from the first one. It's a 1958 Fender Deluxe. We have tried many others, but we always come back to this one. It's an incredible amp.

## 7. TAKE THE LONG WAY ROUND

### ☑ @MrNormanBlake1

A bit of a staple of our love set over the years and a song that always goes down well with the audience. Great fun to play too. Gerry came up with that nice little vocal exchange thing in the breakdown. I was once more on the high harmony. Potentially a bit of a throat shredder if you're not careful.

## 8. WINTER

### ☑ @MrNormanBlake1

I, with my family, was moving around a lot when we made this album. I think this song is about looking for somewhere to call home. We started off in a basement in the Southside of Glasgow before moving to a place called Path Of Condie in the Ochil Hills near Perth. We lived in an old schoolhouse that belonged to the singer Sam Brown. Sam very kindly let us house sit while she was off on tour with Pink Floyd.

## 9. I DON'T CARE

### ☑ @MrNormanBlake1

I remember us recording those big thick piano chords on the intro at Ridge Farm. For me, this is like a sister song to Gene Clark. I mean in terms of the groove. Not the tune. We were getting pretty good at the harmonies by this point. There's Raymond and that Fender Deluxe again.

## 10. MOUNT EVEREST

### ☑ @MrNormanBlake1

A huge sounding song and a great Gerry tune. We should have played it more than we did. Ach well! That's either a hammer dulcimer on the outro or plucked piano strings. I would suggest that this is one of our most popular live songs. It always gets a good reaction when Raymond opens up with that vocal and the acoustic guitar.

## 11. YOUR LOVE IS THE PLACE WHERE I COME FROM

### ☑ @MrNormanBlake1

This definitely has plucked piano. As that is difficult to do live, I now cover that part on the glockenspiel. All five notes.

## 12. SPEED OF LIGHT

### ☑ @MrNormanBlake1

A great album closer. The ring on the drums on the intro is amazing. I reckon there's a fair amount of compression on there. The synth sounds are coming from Gerry's Novation Bass Station. Pretty sure he still has that. We toured it for a while and it got pretty beat up. I think you call that patina.

# Cupid & Psyche 85
## Scritti Politti
Virgin, 1985

⚓ If ever a band has been able to straddle the apparent divide between indie authenticity and major label success, it is Scritti Politti. Formed as a Marxist musical collective releasing records on independent labels, frontman and songwriter Green Gartside (**@ScrittiPolitti**) was able to transform the group to deliver his polished yet heartfelt musical vision. Unusual during the 1980s, Scritti Politti were one of the few bands able to create chart-friendly albums while retaining their artistic credibility.

*Cupid & Psyche 85* is a breathtaking expression of this approach. An amazing, kaleidoscopic meld of different sounds and worlds, it blends '80s synths with wiry guitars and philosophy-quoting lyrics. The album's fresh approach caught the ear of jazz legend Miles Davis, who would go on to cover Perfect Way from this LP before later recording with Gartside. With this ever-evolving spirit still at the heart of his music, the Scritti Politti frontman's Listening Party was a neat snapshot of the album's genesis and an illustration of how the singer continues to drive forward creatively. Joined by American keyboard player and engineer David Gamson, plus Rhodri Marsden (**@Rhodri**), Rob Grovesnor and Dicky Moore (**@DickyMoo**) from the current Scritti Politti live band, Gartside and friends brought the album back to life after over two decades since its release.

"In 2006 when the band regrouped, we were all hired from Green's local pub," explained keyboardist Rhodri Marsden of how the modern-day Scritti Politti came into being. "If he liked us, we were in the band. Pure serendipity." Pour yourself a drink: you're in, too.

**SLEEVE DESIGN:**
Keith Breeden

⊕

Don't Work That Hard. The 1985 line-up for Scritti Politti (opposite). In a career that has spanned Marxist squats to sessions with Miles Davis and Mos Def, frontman Green Gartside (below) has been the band's ever present guiding light.

## 1. THE WORD GIRL

### ✓ @ScrittiPolitti (Green Gartside)

Green Gartside: Although much of the work on this album was done behind massive gleaming SSL consoles in huge New York studios (with trouser-wateringly exorbitant hourly rates) we did the vocals for this at a residential studio in the English countryside. It was winter, and from the vocal booth I could look out of the window across the snow laden fields. I remember seeing a handful of particularly forlorn looking sheep standing, staring vacantly, in the drifts as the flakes fell. One in particular was eyeing me purposefully. I think my vocal performance somehow captured or embodied something of the plight of that disconsolate ruminant.

### ✓ @ScrittiPolitti

David Gamson: Those melodies! Green really knocked it out of the park on this song. Still love it. When it became clear that it was sounding like a single, we did a bunch of edits trying to figure out how to get a 3rd chorus in there. Never did figure it out.

## 2. SMALL TALK

### ✓ @ScrittiPolitti

David: The first song that Green Gartside and i collaborated on after Geoff Travis suggested we get together. There was an earlier version started in the summer of '82, remixed by Nile Rodgers (never released). But we ended up re-recording it.

### ✓ @Rhodri (Rhodri Marsden)

Small Talk is unbelievable. What a piece of work. We've never played it live, but I've spent hours picking it apart with the eventual aim of doing so. It was like panning for gold. All these tiny jewels waiting to be discovered. Informally, the album is known within the band as Stupid & Crikey. I'm not sure of the genesis of this – I heard it might have been taken from a review of the record back in 1985. Made me laugh, anyway.

## 3. ABSOLUTE

### ✓ @ScrittiPolitti

Green: The mighty Paul Jackson Jnr on guitar. He worked with The Jacksons and Michael on "Destiny", "Triumph", "Thriller" and "Bad", so... you know... GODDAM! I remember his slight discomfiture at my earrings and Marxism. Will Lee played bass. He was in the David Letterman band at the time. So yes, I DID feel beyond terrifyingly inadequate in that company.

### ✓ @Rhodri

This synth solo is apparently a sample of Green singing the word "Girl". I never realised this until he started singing "Girl" during that bit in rehearsals. Seems obvious now.

## 4. A LITTLE KNOWLEDGE

### ✓ @ScrittiPolitti

Green: Aaah! Lovely stuff. Makes me feel sad, in a good way. Makes me want to be back in the studio with David. Lump in the throat time certainly. David was precociously masterful at creating the most wonderful synth sounds or patches. He still is, of course.

## 5. DON'T WORK THAT HARD

### ✓ @ScrittiPolitti

Green: This reminds me of sunny days driving in David's little orange open top MG from his family home in Westchester into Manhattan... I remember kinda striving for a lyrical balance

Green Gartside at the Montreux Rock Festival in Switzerland, January 1988.

between the pointedly banal and trashy, and the artlessly philosophical. That sweet spot between pop gibberish and thought provoking. Man, did I get that wrong a heap of the time!

## 6. PERFECT WAY

##### ✔ @Rhodri

In 2017 we did a series of concerts in Tokyo. The promoters asked we play Perfect Way almost as a condition of the engagement. We had to learn the thing, which wasn't *too* difficult – except the bridge into the chorus, which is preposterous. Perfect Way was a hit in the USA, making @scrittipolitti a one-hit-wonder over there, bracketing them with, I dunno, Harold Faltermeyer or something. How unfair.

## 7. LOVER TO FALL

##### ✔ @ScrittiPolitti

David Gamson: My first Yamaha DX7!! Beautiful melodies, but geez the verses are long. Really coulda used a little editing. I think we recorded a guitar solo by Andy Gill (Gang Of Four) for this one, but we didn't use it.

##### ✔ @Rhodri

This song is probably best known for the extraordinary lyric "I found a new hermeneutic / I found a new paradigm / I found a plan just to make you mine". Green, there. Once described as the second brainiest man in pop. (after Brian Eno)

## 8. WOOD BEEZ (PRAY LIKE ARETHA FRANKLIN)

##### ✔ @ScrittiPolitti

Green Gartside: As The Funky Four Plus One said ... "That's The Joint!" Wood Beez started with an idea based on part of a lyric in Dave and Ansell Collins' record "Double Barrel". I love playing this live nowadays.

##### ✔ @DickyMoo (Dicky Moore)

This was the first of the Cupid & Psyche 85 tracks we learnt to play live ahead of the first US tour in 2006. We rehearsed and rehearsed until it was really tight, and then on the first night of the tour couldn't play it. It was the last track of the set list and all the keyboards broke just as we started. So we ended up doing our only ever acoustic version of it, without the stunning stabs or bassline.

## 9. HYPNOTIZE

##### ✔ @ScrittiPolitti

David: Man, I just remember this one took forever. We mixed this for like two weeks at Sarm West with Gary Langan while inhaling fumes from the mannequin factory next door. (I mighta made that up? I think it was a mannequin factory.)

##### ✔ @ScrittiPolitti

Green: I spent much of the time making this album with a stomach churning sense of inadequacy and lack of self-worth. The rest of the time I felt extraordinarily fortunate to be playing the part of someone whose idle fancies had become a reality.

##### ✔ @Rhodri (Rhodri Marsden)

Informally, the album is known within the band as Stupid & Crikey. I'm not sure of the genesis of this – I heard it might have been taken from a review of the record back in 1985. Made me laugh, anyway.

# *Disco*
## Kylie Minogue
BMG, 2020

PHOTOGRAPHY:
Simon Emmett

Listening Parties are not called parties for nothing. There is always a great atmosphere and a communal celebration when an artist and a host of music fans get together to listen to a record at the same time. However, when the album in question is by none other than Kylie Minogue (**@KylieMinogue**) and it is called *Disco*, you know the *party* factor is going to be turned right up to 11. Showing a remarkable ability to both tweet and dance at the same time, Kylie hit the dancefloor and the keyboard to glide us through her then just released, mirror-ball-lit new album. Like all the other Listening Parties, there were studio stories and artistic revelations, but there but there was also that little bit more neon and a load of dancing GIFs, too.

→

Especially for you. Kylie took to the keyboard to introduce her 15th studio album, *Disco*.

---

**LISTENING PARTY
11 NOVEMBER 2020**

### 1. MAGIC

 **@KylieMinogue**

Magic was always going to be the first song on Disco. For me it's the perfect intro to the album "I feel like anything could happen…" Magic was produced by an amazing Danish team, Pete Wall and Daniel Davidsen!

### 2. MISS A THING

 **@KylieMinogue**

DANCE! It's time for Miss A Thing. When I first heard the demo for this song I knew it had to be on Disco. It's a heady mix of nostalgic and futuristic disco. Dance dance dance … The writing for Miss A Thing was finished in lockdown and all of the vocals were recorded from home.

### 3. REAL GROOVE

 **@KylieMinogue**

"I saw you dancing with somebody, looking like me and you!" REAL GROOVE! So much love to [songwriters] Teemu Brunila and Nico Stadi for this Real Groove!! When we were recording this song we experimented with taking it down a semi-tone or a tone lower, but this key was the sweet spot.

### 4. MONDAY BLUES

 **@KylieMinogue**

Monday Blues is the first change of pace on the album! The original version had a completely different chorus, but it wasn't a PROPER chorus. We kept going until it ended up like this! This song finally clicked with me when I listened to it on a (rare) lockdown walk. It's just so positive and uplifting!

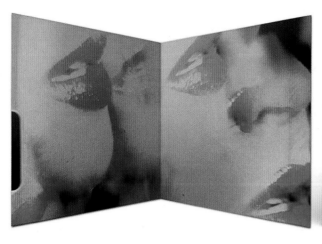

I was driving to Rockfield Studios with some new songs going round my head and a few days set aside for recording them. At the start of the journey I received a text that said, "looks like Kylie is up for a Listening Party". This was seven months after we'd started the listening parties and we'd established an underground network of well-connected fans. As its reputation grew, Channel 4 news, Radio 4, Later... With Jools Holland and Rolling Stone magazine all ran features and helped spread the word. For the first few months it was mostly my phone book and email contacts, but that river would always run dry.

There are lots of seachange moments and this was a major one. I had briefly met Kylie a couple of times at an awards do and on the ramp up to the main stage at T In The Park in Scotland. My drive to Rockfield should have been five hours but this journey took an extra exciting 90 minutes as I would stop at each services to catch up where we were at with Ms Minogue. Add into the equation that each stop would involve a coffee and by Monmouth I was a crazed wreck of caffeine and excitement.

Do the bright thing: the glow-in-the-dark deluxe edition.

Unstoppable. An invite for *Disco*'s Listening Party.

## 5. SUPERNOVA

🔵 @KylieMinogue

Another lockdown baby. If you weren't awake already, you would be after this! Written with the awesome Maegan Cottone and Sky Adams, we had so much fun with this one! The "space voice" is me on vocoder!

## 6. SAY SOMETHING

🔵 @KylieMinogue

Where it all began! Disco's first single. Say Something was recorded in the first ever session for the album. I didn't have the album title at that stage, but I knew I wanted to head back to the dance floor. I wrote this with my longtime collaborators, Richard "Biff" Stannard, Jon Green and Ash Howes. Biff and Jon hadn't worked together before so I arranged a writing session. We all loved Say Something and were overwhelmed with joy that it's a song that made it out into the world!

## 7. LAST CHANCE

🔵 @KylieMinogue

So when I was younger I was obsessed with ABBA. (Still am) Can you tell? Ironically, this was one of the last songs that made the cut for Disco. Last Chance!

## 8. I LOVE IT

🔵 @KylieMinogue

I Love It is a song that I started with Richard "Biff" Stannard and Duck Blackwell just before lockdown. We then finished it remotely. We would say to each other, we need Lionel Richie to leap into this song in the musical breakdown.

## 9. WHERE DOES THE DJ GO?

🔵 @KylieMinogue

Where DOES the DJ go? Yes there is also a little nod to I Will Survive in these lyrics. Love you Gloria Gaynor!

## 10. DANCE FLOOR DARLING

🔵 @KylieMinogue

I love Dance Floor Darling SO MUCH! There are some amazing [dancing] fan vids for this. So what you waiting for? This song reminds me of wedding discos specifically… when the tempo picks up towards the end there will be no one left sitting down. I can't get enough of the old school talkbox by [bassist/co-writer] Linslee Campbell.

## 11. UNSTOPPABLE

🔵 @KylieMinogue

Unstoppable is my Diana Ross moment! (In my dreams!!) Produced by Troy Miller who is actually working with the great lady herself!

## 12. CELEBRATE YOU

🔵 @KylieMinogue

Celebrate You is the first song I've EVER written in the third person. I have already been asked a lot, Who is Mary? Well, Mary is you, me, anyone who needs a reminder of how much they're worth.

Kylie DISCO
TIM BURGESS LISTENING PARTY
TWITTER 11TH NOVEMBER
9PM GMT/8AM AEDT

# Songs From The Big Chair
## Tears For Fears
Phonogram Records, 1985

Having made their debut with the insular – by their own admission – *The Hunting*, for their second album Tears For Fears hoped to be more "outgoing". Truly, they achieved that with *Songs From The Big Chair*. Not only is the album a bright wave of warm synths, sprightly guitars and soaring high-octave vocals, but the Bath-based band wrote a series of songs that immediately joined the "timeless pop" category – not a bad follow-up to the melancholic hit Mad Word from a few years before. The home of Shout and Everybody Wants To Rule The World to name just two, Roland Orzabal (vocals/guitar), Curt Smith (bass/vocals – **@CurtSmith**), Ian Stanley (keyboards) and Manny Elias' (drums) second record helped define '80s pop, yet was not trapped by it like some of their contemporaries thanks to the quality of their songwriting and a desire to embrace and push the technology on offer. Settling back into the *Big Chair*, Smith – together with producer Chris Hughes (**@C_M_Hughes**) and engineer David Bascombe (**@D_N_Bascombe**) – offered us an insider's guide on how Tears For Fears really did end up ruling the pop world.

**PHOTOGRAPHY:**
Tim O'Sullivan

LISTENING PARTY
**4 DECEMBER 2020**

### 1. SHOUT

**@CurtSmith**
And off we go – turn up the triangle & cowbells please! It's so weird to hear that break down on synth bass after playing it live for so many years. 80s sax. What's not to love? Let's just open with a chorus & end with endless choruses - works for me! We should film Roland playing that big guitar solo on top of a cliff!! [That's exactly what the band did]

**@C_M_Hughes (Chris Hughes)**
That Cliff idea will never catch on... Ahh that triangle and shaker, those milk bottles Roland playing the "You take the high road". Fab solo.

### 2. THE WORKING HOUR

**@CurtSmith**
I love this intro – you can tell it is a track we did live before recording it. Would like to do it live more often but it's just not the same without a sax player. Probably our most requested live song that we rarely do. Tears For Fears still being paid by those who learn from our mistakes.

### 3. EVERYBODY WANTS TO RULE THE WORLD

**@CurtSmith**
A lesson in how four bars of guitar riff can make you happy. Everybody... was the last track recorded on the album and the simplest to do. A lesson in less is more (sometimes). Brings back memories of Union Studios in Munich. I remember the studio manager was called Herbert Koehler – so he was Herr Koehler. Cue Neil Taylor's guitar solo!

### @C_M_Hughes
Those four bars make me happy. But Neil's Gtr at the end makes me go mental. Union Studios was a fun place, it's true...

### @D_N_Bascombe (David Bascombe)
Oompah band next door!

## 4. MOTHERS TALK

### @CurtSmith
Still not convinced by this version of Mothers Talk (yes even after all these years). We went through so many versions. It just doesn't sound as big as the rest of the album, a little too intricate for its own good. Although the guitar at the end is cool (before the bass sequence nonsense). What were we thinking at the end?

### @C_M_Hughes
WE weren't thinking, we were doing x Love the playout of Mothers Talk.

So nuts.

## 5. I BELIEVE

### @CurtSmith
Ah – Roland doing his best Robert Wyatt impersonation. Great song though. Of course, since then Roland has discovered that he's actually a Leo. [the lyrics go "I can't deny that I'm a Virgo too"] Just got a flashback of Roland shouting "William!" [Gregory, saxophonist who played with the band, later went on to become one half of Goldfrapp] which he did before that sax break live every night.

## 6. BROKEN

### @CurtSmith
I have a big soft spot for Broken — originally the b-side of Pale Shelter and then became this and Head Over Heels...

## 7. HEAD OVER HEELS/BROKEN (LIVE)

### @CurtSmith
Much like the beginning of Everybody Wants To Rule The World, this time on piano. A lesson in how a few bars of just music can change one's mood completely. Head Over Heels is another track that was played live before recording it, for whatever reason those songs seem to feel effortless on record. Let's all sing along shall we!

### @C_M_Hughes
I remember Roland and I went for a walk while Ian [Stanley, keyboards] had a look at the melody at the end. WE came back and Ian said it's great how it was. What a guy, love you mate. Hang on back to Broken...

### @CurtSmith
And now the actual live recording of Broken. Head Over Heels and Broken are still fun as hell to play live! Although I feel like saying "thank you and goodnight" at the end.

## 8. LISTEN

### @CurtSmith
For the record, I adore Listen. Sends me every time. This is such a great way to finish an album. We used to play this as an intro tape before our live shows, it set the mood perfectly on huge speakers in a venue.

### @C_M_Hughes
This too brings back so many memories. Roland's guitaring, Ian's fantastic synth work, Bascombe's balance, sensitive Curt vocal. All great. Roland's ultra high vocal is God sent. It is truly a very final piece of music.

### @CurtSmith
And here we come to the "wrap me up a chicken tikka takeaway" part (as it was affectionately known). [The backing vocals feature "Kenyan words" most of the band didn't understand, but that Smiths says sounds like "Wrap me up a chicken tikka takeway"].

Desk job. Roland Orzabal and Curt Smith fashioning their *Songs* in a London studio in 1985.

# To Drink The Rainbow *(An Anthology 1988–2019)*
## Tanita Tikaram
Needle Mythology, 2019

⚓ Sometimes it is not about the prizes and accolades, it is just about writing a good song. Having conquered the pop charts in the late 1980s with tracks like Twist In My Sobriety and Good Tradition, Tanita Tikaram (**@Tanita_Tikaram**) has let her songwriting lead her forward rather than attempting to recapture any past glories. Since her chart glories, the Germany-born, Basingstoke-raised singer-songwriter has quietly amassed a canon of perfect pop, marrying her breathy vocals with smouldering emotions while touching on an impressive spectrum of influences from Leonard Cohen to Italian torch songs and beyond.

Among her legion of fans is music writer Pete Paphides whose Needle Mythology label seemed the perfect place to showcase Tikaram's impressive catalogue, resulting in the pair curating the *To Drink the Rainbow* collection.

"So, a bit of background to Needle Mythology releasing this album," wrote the *Broken Greek* author who co-hosted the Listening Party with Tanita. "Like many people, I realised that I'd lost track of Tanita Tikaram's movements in the preceding years. And this seemed a bit baffling to me, given how much I loved her voice. No-one in the world has a voice like Tanita. You'd spot it anywhere. The depth, the richness, the sensuality, the grain of it. In some ways, she's like Tom Waits, Paolo Conté or Randy Newman. It's a voice whose owner grows into over time. When her last album *Closer To The People* came out, I just thought it was so cool that she clearly wasn't interested in emulating the sound that had propelled her onto Top Of The Pops with Twist In My Sobriety. You could tell that in the intervening years, Tanita had really lived and learned, and fed her curiosity in all sorts of ways. Tanita had clearly listened to a lot of jazz and blues; surrounded herself by musicians who valued spontaneity. The ensuing deep dive into her back catalogue confirmed that hunch. She's amassed an incredible body of work almost by stealth. I made a playlist of my favourites and then I approached Tanita about the idea of perhaps using that playlist as the basis of a new compilation. A primer for people who, like me, had lost track of what she'd been up to. The ensuing conversations were hugely enjoyable."

Equally enjoyable are Tikaram's own thoughts on the songs that found their way on to *To Drink the Rainbow.*

**@Tanita_Tikaram**
What I like about this recording, is that it has something which you probably don't associate with me. Energy! It's such good fun to play live with a band & it has enough twists & turns to keep a band on it's toes.

LISTENING
PARTY
**6 DECEMBER
2020**

### 1. MY LOVE (ACOUSTIC)

✓ **@Tanita_Tikaram**
My Love is an early piano song. The piano helped me fall in love with music again, and taught me to listen. A simple melancholy melody that expresses romantic disappointment and distrust but who can resist it?

### 2. PLAY ME AGAIN

✓ **@Tanita_Tikaram**
I like to think this song is still driving recklessly around 1920s Paris in her green Bugatti looking for her lover! When younger I didn't realise you COULD change keys, so a lot of earlier recordings are unnaturally low like this.

### 3. COOL WATERS

✓ **@Tanita_Tikaram**
This reflects my love of singers like Helen Reddy and her infectious 70s country pop sound.

### 4. ONLY THE ONES WE LOVE

✓ **@Tanita_Tikaram**
Jennifer Warnes' Famous Blue Raincoat introduced me to Leonard Cohen and Warnes' incredible voices [Warnes was a regular backing singer for the Canadian poet/crooner]. FBR's sound influenced my first album – thrills me to hear her voice on this song making my voice shine but she's doing the hard work.

### 5. TROUBLE

✓ **@Tanita_Tikaram**
What I like about this recording, is that it has something which you probably don't associate with me. Energy! It's such good fun to play live with a band and it has enough twists and turns to keep a band on its toes.

### 6. I THINK OF YOU - E PENSO A TE

✓ **@Tanita_Tikaram**
E Penso A Te is the original Italian song by legendary Lucio Battisti and Mogol. I fell in love with the song and decided to do an English version.

### 7. THE WAY YOU MOVE

✓ **@Tanita_Tikaram**
I co-wrote this with Bryan Day. It's built around two guitars riffs that I had come up with — the opening riff and one that became the sax part. "If I could only change my ways" is Bryan's, I can't take credit for that! This record is also special because it features all the musicians I was touring with at the time: Matt Radford, Bobby Irwin and Martin Winning. When I began touring again we were often an acoustic trio without drums – it's scary but wonderful!

### 8. LOVE IS JUST A WORD

✓ **@Tanita_Tikaram**
Bobby Irwin is the drummer on this track, he

played famously with Van Morrison and Nick Lowe, we met working on Sentimental. Sadly, Bobby died of cancer in 2015, he influenced me a lot. And really cared about the whole song.

## 9. AMORE SI

🔘 **@Tanita_Tikaram**

I wrote with Marco Sabiu who produced [album] The Cappuccino Songs. I suppose this is my "poppiest" album. If I'm honest my ambivalence about some of the songs on The Cappuccino Songs stems from the feeling that some of the songs are "well-written" as opposed to written from the heart. Perhaps, a lack of identity is a risk you take in a collaboration.

## 10. TO DRINK THE RAINBOW (ACOUSTIC)

🔘 **@Tanita_Tikaram**

I saw the 1940 Disney film Fantasia with [author] Gillie Bell. She loved the scene where the cherubs drink the rainbow and suggested I write a song with that idea. A song about not having the confidence to fully assume your identity.

## 11. CAN'T GO BACK

🔘 **@Tanita_Tikaram**

The first bars of this! What a rhythm section Paul Bryan, who produced the album, on bass and Jay Bellerose drums. My happiest experience of recording was with PB. He is so inspiring and groovy!

## 12. EVERY DAY IS NEW

🔘 **@Tanita_Tikaram**

When I wrote this I was fixated with The Carpenters' song "We've Only Just Begun". Paul Williams and Roger Nichols originally wrote it for a bank advert! It's an optimistic and forward looking song. I wanted to express a similar sentiment with Everyday is New – I was also listening to Carole King. Her song You've Got A Friend influenced the song too. So Every Day Is New ends up being about friendship and how a good friend can lift you out of the darkest times.

Can't Go Back. The boss of the Needle Mythology label and Listening Party regular Pete Paphides wanted *To Drink The Rainbow* to capture the evolving dynamics of Tanita Tikaram's life in music.

# I Grow Tired But Dare Not Fall Asleep
## Ghostpoet
PIAS, 2020

✝ Making the most of the time during the lockdowns of 2020 has inspired some truly creative activities. For Ghostpoet (**@Ghostpoet**), AKA London musician Obaro Ejimiwe, it seems a lot of his downtime was spent watching swords-and-dragons drama *Game Of Thrones*, as there's definitely a "medieval" influence apparent on his fifth album, *I Grow Tired But Dare Not Fall Asleep*. Released at the start of May during the first Covid-19 lockdown, the themes and lyrics of Obaro Ejimiwe's fifth album actually considered, highlighted and protested against many of the issues that would then come into sharp focus following the murder of George Floyd by an American police officer later the same month. Accompanying Ghostpoet's words on the record is an equally powerful musical atmosphere of synths, guitars and those aforementioned "medieval" elements that lend the album a brooding, angry edge, while Ejimiwe's soulful raps switch effortlessly from righteous rage to warm, uplifting hope.

Staging his playback of *I Grow Tired But Dare Not Fall Asleep* half a year after its release, Ghostpoet guided us through an album that has seen the world dramatically shift not just since its creation, but even since its release. "Welcome to my Listening Party for *I Grow Tired But Dare Not Fall Asleep*," he quipped, "one of the best and cursed albums of 2020!"

**PHOTOGRAPHY:**
Emma Dudlyke

---

**LISTENING PARTY**
**11 DECEMBER 2020**

### 1. BREAKING COVER

✓ **@Ghostpoet**
It was all about making an opening statement, basically "fuck everyone else I'm here, listen up".

### 2. CONCRETE PONY

✓ **@Ghostpoet**
This was my little Krautrock wonder, a song to make babies to... or demons, depends on your preference really.

### 3. HUMANA SECOND HAND

✓ **@Ghostpoet**
I wanted to create a theatrical journey exploring the mundane life of a single man in the times that we're living in. I was watching too much Game Of Thrones which I feel was an influence on this I would say. This features Sarasara, a brilliant singer-songwriter signed to Björk's Little Indian [label].

Nowhere To Hide Now.
Ghostpoet, AKA Obaro
Ejimiwe, in 2020.

### 4. BLACK DOG GOT SILVER EYES

☑ **@Ghostpoet**

It's me writing about the last moments of my father, such a strong man but illness took his strength away by the end.

### 5. RATS IN A SACK

☑ **@Ghostpoet**

Next up is a song about Brexit and the disgusting ongoing Windrush Scandal. Another song weirdly influenced musically by medieval times. Also a song where I wanted to flex my guitar muscles. I LOVE GUITARS. In case you didn't know. This song features the delightful [Skinny Girl Diet's] Delilah Holliday on vocals, I love her and her music so much.

### 6. THIS TRAIN WRECK OF A LIFE

☑ **@Ghostpoet**

This features once again the delightful Sarasara reciting a poem I wrote that she translated into French. Influenced by Portishead on the strings, Geoff Barrow I LOVE YOU. I'm drunk, forgive me. Also this was homage to Serge Gainsbourg, love his strings.

### 7. NOWHERE TO HIDE NOW

☑ **@Ghostpoet**

This song is about my love/hate relationship with Artificial Intelligence. The incessant piano here was influenced by Iggy Pop's early work.

### 8. WHEN MOUTHS COLLIDE

☑ **@Ghostpoet**

It's a tragic love song, you keeping holding on even though deep down you know it's over. This features the wonderful guest vocal of Art School Girlfriend [singer-songwriter Polly Mackey]. Basically I'm obsessed with Brazilian music from the '70's so the record is covered in Brazilian percussion.

### 9. I GROW TIRED BUT DARE NOT FALL ASLEEP

☑ **@Ghostpoet**

Pretty self explanatory, I'm writing about being fucking tired of the status quo and wanting to head off to Ecuador (nod to Iggy Pop's Paraguay).

### 10. SOCIAL LACERATIONS

☑ **@Ghostpoet**

This one's about the draining nature of social media – calm before the storm. This guitar outro is everything. This is the best record of my career thus far. Don't worry I can do better… well I hope so…

# Paul McCartney
## McCartney III
Capitol, 2020

Everyone loves a sequel, but there is something more impressive about a trilogy. After The Beatles disbanded, Paul McCartney (**@PaulMcCartney**) made his solo debut with the near self-titled *McCartney* in 1970. In contrast to the Fab Four, the songwriter secretly recorded the album himself, playing all the instruments, leaving his efforts a little less polished than perhaps his old band would have allowed. Ten years later – this time after his next group, Wings, had ended – Macca did it again, recording *McCartney II* in much the same way and then… nothing. Well, nothing until the Covid-19 pandemic left Paul McCartney stuck at home like everyone else. However, while the majority of lockdown tasks, hobbies and resolutions might have petered out uncompleted, the ex Beatle went the other way and inadvertently made a whole album's worth of songs, mainly in his home studio. Solo? Home self-recorded? There really was only one title that fitted… hello *McCartney III*!

ARTWORK:
Ed Ruscha

**@PaulMcCartney:**
(Below left) I used my Mustel Harmonium which was from Abbey Road on Long Tailed Winter Bird; (below) We used our Studer J37 Tape Machine on Slidin'. The drums were recorded at double speed.

## 1. LONG TAILED WINTER BIRD

✓ @PaulMcCartney

Here we go! The great thing for me about this album is that I didn't know I was actually making an album and it all started with this track really as I was making a bit of music for a film project. The title came about when it was extended into a full-length song so we called it Long Tailed Winter Bird. And a little fact for you, in my bird book I saw a long tailed duck!

## 2. FIND MY WAY

✓ @PaulMcCartney

I started Find My Way on the piano, it was based on an idea that I'd had in the car when I was listening to music and there was a beat on the radio I liked so I just started singing along with it making up my own words and tune. I actually had a whole different idea for the verses which I decided I didn't like and eventually put in a new idea which is now the middle!

## 3. PRETTY BOYS

✓ @PaulMcCartney

Pretty Boys came from a newspaper article about some male models who'd got annoyed at a photographer who'd been too aggressive and a bit abusive. I was walking along the street in New York, I saw a big line of bicycles and I thought ok well that's a nice idea, "a line of bicycles for hire…" So the idea is about male models being for hire.

## 4. WOMEN AND WIVES

✓ @PaulMcCartney

Women And Wives I wrote when I had just been reading a book on the Blues artist Lead Belly, so I was trying to get in this bluesy mood so I played simple chords and started singing in what I imagined was like a bluesy style. If anyone asked me to sing one of the songs off this album it would be this one!

## 5. LAVATORY LIL'

✓ @PaulMcCartney

Lavatory Lil' is about anybody that you don't like and that you didn't get on with and I think in our lives we have a lot of people like that. It's not about anyone in particular but it is a fictitious character.

## 6. DEEP DEEP FEELING

✓ @PaulMcCartney

Deep Deep Feeling was from a kind of jam that I had done, I'd wanted to get in a particular mood, a very sort of empty spacey mood, so I just made up stuff so it was just a combination of ideas that became an eight minute song. I was thinking of editing it down to a shorter more reasonable length but when I listened through to it I liked it so much (he said modestly…) that I kept it eight minutes.

## 7. SLIDIN'

✓ @PaulMcCartney

Slidin' came from a soundcheck jam when we were playing in Dusseldorf in Germany. During soundchecks when I'm checking my guitar, I like to try and make something up and the band will join in. I started jamming and this riff came out that I liked, it stayed in my brain, so we recorded it for [previous album] Egypt Station with my band but it didn't work out. I had it half finished and I changed some things here and there, and it became Slidin'.

## 8. THE KISS OF VENUS

✓ @PaulMcCartney

A friend of mine gave me a little hippy book which was fascinating because it's all about the movements of the planets and Earth and Venus and Mars and the moon. In the book it shows you that if you look at all the orbits over time, they actually trace out really fascinating patterns and some of them look like a lotus flower which is kind of wow, kind of magical! I was looking for ideas and the book said the phrase "the kiss of Venus" meaning when Earth comes closest to Venus, and I thought well that's a great idea for a song.

## 9. SEIZE THE DAY

✓ @PaulMcCartney

I started this on the piano, at home on the farm and was letting the words spill out so I didn't know what the song was going to be about. I got to this line "Yankee toes and Eskimos can turn to frozen ice" and thought what is this about? I think it's best not to question lyrics too deeply, so instead of it making an amazing amount of sense it becomes a little bit surrealistic which I like.

Once, twice, three times the charm. The 2020 lockdown finally teased a self-produced solo album out of Paul McCartney to join 1970's *McCartney* and 1980's *McCartney II*.

## 10. DEEP DOWN

⊘ @PaulMcCartney

I didn't quite know what I meant by "deep down" except "I want to have a deep relationship with you" or whatever, so I just really kept going on it. Some songs you know you don't quite know where you're going, you've just got half an idea and it's really just that you're enjoying the groove and that one was one of those, I just thought of ideas as I went along and it ended up as this.

## 11. WINTER BIRD/WHEN WINTER COMES

⊘ @PaulMcCartney

This song is kind of an idealistic thing, a hippy existence on a farm, planting trees, mending fences and living the good life which is something I like. I love nature and I love that idea of getting down and getting your hands dirty.

## 12. LISTENING PARTY BONUS TRACK WONDERFUL CHRISTMASTIME

⊘ @PaulMcCartney

I recorded this during sessions for my McCartney II album, it was actually the summer time too! We filmed the video at a pub in Sussex which was a lot of fun.

TIM'S THOUGHTS

When we started The Listening Parties we drew up a wish list as if there were no limits as to who would take part. Paul McCartney was the first on that list. Out of nowhere during lockdown the great man announced the third in the series of his self-titled albums – it was now or never.

⊘ @Tim_Burgess

Hey @PaulMcCartney - just wondering if you fancy doing a @LISTENING_PARTY for McCartney III. Give us a shout if you do ;)

36 days 1hr and 22 minutes later Paul McCartney tweeted back:

⊘ **Paul McCartney**

# You've Come A Long Way, Baby
## Fatboy Slim
Skint, 1998

As man who achieved music success playing bass in indie band The Housemartins and in dance groups Beats International and Freak Power long before striking out alone, there is something fitting that Norman Cook's iconic musical statement as Fatboy Slim (**@FatboySlim**) builds on so many different musical foundations. A sonic cross-stitch of vintage samples, co-opted beats and some considerably hefty studio work of his own – particularly considering the severely limited computer powers of the late 1990s – *You've Come A Long Way, Baby* is possibly the hardest-worked-on good time you'll ever hear. Channelling his sources into the big beat sound he helped to create, there is a real character and atmosphere that flows through the heart of Fatboy Slim's second album. While *...Baby*'s brilliant use of obscure samples dazzles and intrigues, it's the album's touch-the-sky, head-rush moments – all Cook's own, selected from a lifetime's experience onstage and behind the decks – which makes this record such euphoric, dancefloor magic.

**SLEEVE DESIGN:**
Red Design

**@Tim_Burgess:** Hey Norm, We've come a long way, baby ; )

⊕

Cream of the crop.
Fatboy Slim, AKA
Norman Cook, ahead
of performing *You've
Come A Long Way Baby*
at a very muddy
Creamfields festival
in 1998.

## 1. RIGHT HERE, RIGHT NOW

✓ @FatboySlim (Norman Cook)

After Unfinished Sympathy by Massive Attack got voted best dance song of all time in a poll I thought, "What makes it so special?" it was the strings that lifted it above the others so I decided to make a tune featuring strings.

## 2. THE ROCKAFELLER SKANK

✓ @FatboySlim

Inspired by Natural Born Chillers' Rock The Funky Beat, a big hit at the Big Beat Boutique club where I was resident. Chop up the syllables to create a different rhythm. Big up Aphrodite.

## 3. FUCKING IN HEAVEN

✓ @FatboySlim

[DJ] Freddy Fresh sent me some stems on a DAT tape and stupidly recorded his voice saying, "If I could have a Fatboy Slim remix I would be fucking in heaven... By the way, please don't use my vocal." Red rag to a bull...

## 4. GANGSTER TRIPPING

✓ @FatboySlim

Inspiration was these AV8 records hip hop sample tracks that we used to play at 45, particularly DJ Rags Yes Yes Y'all it was through sampling on this him off DJ Shadow's Entropy. Roman Coppola directed [the video for this track] and we went down to the 007 backlot at Pinewood studios and blew a lot of shit up! Here are some of the floppy discs that the tunes were stored on.

## 5. BUILD IT UP – TEAR IT DOWN

✓ @FatboySlim

Northern Soul meets Jimi Hendrix. Why not? I loved this on the opening credits for Human Traffic. Sounds a bit like Moulin Rouge, huh?

## 6. KALIFORNIA

✓ @FatboySlim

Nobody ever twigged where the vocal came from. My tribute to the 90s west coast breakbeat rave scene, particularly the Crystal Method. The album title came unwittingly from a cigarette advert campaign, via these pair of shorts that I bought my girlfriend in Seattle...

## 7. SOUL SURFING

✓ @FatboySlim

I met a guy when we were shooting the video for Rockafella Skank in Ventura Beach who told me about these dudes who were going back to old skool long boards, less tricks, longer waves, they called it Soul Surfing. The working title of the album was Viva la Underacheiver...

## 8. YOU'RE NOT FROM BRIGHTON

✓ @FatboySlim

Had to give my home town a namecheck. Me on vocals! Working title Funk UK. I'd just been working with Bootsy [Collins] and he taught me that true funk has to be on the one. No offbeats. The idea came from Groovy Thing by Minimal Funk. We thought it sounded like "you're from Brighton" so I re-recorded it with a vocoder.

Right Here, Right Now. "So many luscious memories, wonderful times and people," recalled Norman Cook of his experiences making and touring this album.

### 9. PRAISE YOU

⊘ @FatboySlim

I recently bumped into the guy who sold me the copy of Take Yo Praise [by Camille Yarbrough and the tracks' main sample] in Camden market back in the day. Best £7.99 I ever spent.

### 10. LOVE ISLAND

⊘ @FatboySlim

I made this for Mike and Claire Manumission's film soundtrack. Working title Song For Manumission. The only club in Ibiza that would book me in those days, the only Club in Ibiza I wanted to be at in those heady days.

### 11. ACID 8000

⊘ @FatboySlim

My attempt at an acid opus... Higher State of Consciousness meets Champagne Supernova... "If this don't make your booty move your booty must be dead..."

---

⊘ @FatboySlim

We couldn't find the fat kid in the photo and under US law we couldn't use his photo without his express permission.

⊘ @pkwilkins [fan]

Where was the photo from?

⊘ @FatboySlim

It was from a beer festival in the 80s. I saw the photo in a newspaper and licensed it from the photographer.

⊘ @LillivickBaker [fan]

Did you ever actually meet the kid on the cover, or know him after you used his photo for the album cover?

⊘ @FatboySlim

To this day we have not found him!

(Above) The North American cover design.
(Below) The UK cover design.

# Index

# MVT
## Music Venue Trust

Music Venue Trust is a UK registered charity which acts to protect, secure and improve Grassroots Music Venues (GMVs). These venues have played a crucial role in the development of British music over the last 50 years, nurturing local talent, providing a platform for artists to build their careers and develop their music and their performance skills. As well as being a vital part of the UK's cultural infrastructure, GMVs are social hubs, providing important meeting places for communities and contributing to the local night-time economy.

MVT represents over 900 venues across the UK, members of its Music Venues Alliance. Prior to the creation of MVT in 2014 these venues were overlooked and under-represented, failing to be credited for their valuable work by governments or the wider music industry. Happily, this has changed in recent years and we are building a powerful movement, assisted in no small measure by artists who champion the venues which helped them build their career and fanbase.

Since Covid-19 closed venues across the land in March 2020, MVT's work has been practical: gathering data to lobby for support, helping venues apply for funding, supporting people deal with crisis situations and providing advice and solidarity. It has also been about profile-raising and campaigning: the #SaveOurVenues campaign was launched in April 2020 and has so far raised over £4million for Grassroots Music Venues. Key to this success has been artists such as Tim Burgess, KT Tunstall, Frank Turner, Arctic Monkeys, IDLES, and Billy Bragg explaining how important GMVs are to them. When an artist with a loyal following stands up for a cause it makes a huge difference. Tim is loved and trusted by many, so every mention of MVT, grassroots venues or #SaveOurVenues is priceless.

Donations to #SaveOurVenues enable us to run our Crisis Service, giving bespoke support to any venue in danger of imminent closure. It helps pay for our team of Coordinators across the country who work with venues to access funding. When other avenues of support are exhausted, MVT gives out small grants to pay for essential venue costs that enable a venue to sustain until it can reopen. Behind all of this we are working on guidance and tools to Reopen Every Venue Safely as soon as Public Health guidance allows. 2020/21 has shown how powerful our music community can be when musicians, fans and venues come together.

If you would like to help please visit: **saveourvenues.co.uk** where you can watch streams, buy merch and donate.

For further information about MVT see: **musicvenuetrust.com**